FREEDO

A long walk

ANGELA MICHEL & NICK WARLOW

A CIP catalogue record for this book is available from the British Library.

ISBN 978-1-86720358-6

Book layout and cover design by Clare Brayshaw

Prepared and printed by:

York Publishing Services Ltd
64 Hallfield Road
Layerthorpe
York YO31 7ZQ

Tel: 01904 431213

Website: www.yps-publishing.co.uk

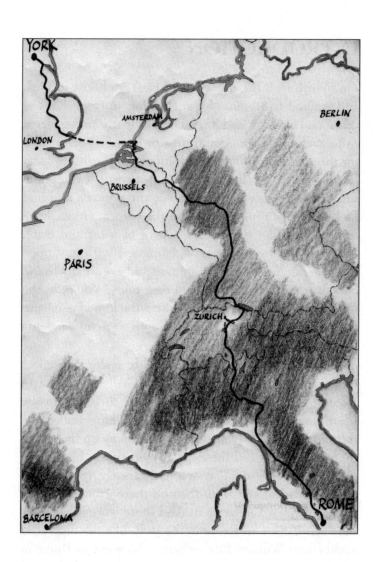

INTRODUCTION

On March 1st, 2012, my wife and I left our house in York and walked to Rome. Not such a big story perhaps in this YouTube day and age, when so many people seem to be walking across Antarctica or standing on a pillar for three weeks. What made it more significant for us at least is that Angela had not been able to walk further than across the room without pain for three years, and had had both hips replaced 18 months before. (Mine were original but had sixty years' worth of wear and tear). After having been wrongly diagnosed with a slipped disc she pursued a second opinion and eventually found herself in a specialist's office being told: "You're in the wrong place. You're walking like a duck; a classic case for a hip replacement: I could show you to my students as a typical presentation!"

After the operations we wanted to make up for lost time and go for a good long walk. "All roads lead to Rome? OK, Alcuin went from York to Rome to see Charlemagne in about 800 AD. He must have walked…" Actually, Alcuin travelled most of the way up the Rhine by boat and crossed the Alps on horseback, but by the time we discovered that we had already told friends about our idea, and from then on there was no turning back – we just had to do it. And there were other links between York and Rome in the past, like the disgraced archbishop William Fitzherbert, who went to Rome in 1154 to get his reputation back after being dethroned and came back to a hero's welcome, exaggerated by the Ouse Bridge collapsing under the weight of all his supporters, after which he was declared a saint because none of them drowned; and Mary Ward, from York, who walked to Rome from her convent in Belgium in 1631 to plead with the Pope to be able to set up an order of nuns which could work in the community (the Pope, who was the same one who imprisoned Galileo for suggesting that the Earth orbited around the Sun, turned her down).

We researched European long-distance footpaths (there are currently ten or eleven of them criss-crossing the continent, including the E1 from Sweden to Sicily). If we could only make our way through Eastern England and the Low Countries to Aachen and then cross the Eifel region of Germany to just past Koblenz, we could pick up the E1 at Nassau and walk south as far as Perugia. We decided to set up an online sponsorship account to raise money for Médecins Sans Frontières, and the ball was rolling!

We did wonder how we would fare being together 24 hours a day for so long, but not as much as some others did. Before we left many acquaintances (particularly those who did not know Angela at all), were astonished when I told them I was going to make this journey with my wife. "I could never do that", said more than one: "We'd be arguing the whole way", or: "Won't you run out of things to talk about?" Well, we did argue once or twice, and we did have long periods of silence together, but it was a kind of meditative silence, one in which you become attuned to each other's senses. It helped that we had been together for thirty years already, and it helped that we both felt we were at a perfect juncture in our lives to be able to set aside this time to be alone together away from the hurly-burly of daily life. We were able to support each other through this new single-minded routine and strengthen our relationship in the process: indeed there were times when we became able to tune into each other's thoughts and feelings to a remarkable degree.

Looking back on what we have written, it may seem that not much happened during the first phase (England & the Low Countries) compared to the latter stages of the walk. This probably comes from the fact that it took a month or so to get the knack of keeping a journal. We both faithfully sat down with book and pen at the end of each day after having had a shower and washed our clothes, and a certain quality and quantity emerged, but this was necessarily patchy as there were evenings when we were so tired that we fell asleep halfway through or forgot to mention the kind of details which enlivened the day. Reviewing and editing all our notes, along with the photos we took (over a thousand) and the maps we had with us has reminded us of all the time we spent just plodding. It's an unusual feeling to know when you start walking early in the morning that you will be doing it all day, for a seemingly endless number of days. The brain constantly wants to count the days and miles, to compute and order and quantify, while the body wants to have regularity: regular sleep, food and drink; and the soul wants to dawdle and soak up sensations and feel the spirit of each place.

Sometimes we felt uninspired, sometimes too tired to feel; but there were many, many times when we were no longer walking to somewhere: we were just happy to be walking, and then G.M. Trevelyan's words rang true:

"I have two doctors, my left leg and my right. When my body and mind are out of gear (and those twin parts of me live at such close quarters that one always catches melancholy from the other) I know that I have only to call in my doctors and I shall be well again."[1]

In many ways we were extraordinarily naïve long-distance walkers. For a start we had no extensive training or experience: we had once in about 5BC (Before Children) walked from the south coast of Spain to the highest peak in the Sierra Nevada, about ten thousand feet up, in three days, and five years ago went up Helvellyn one day at the end of January, and that was about it. We practised for this trip by walking out of York for 15 miles and getting the bus home on several weekends through the winter. Furthermore we had no specialist hiking gear. We went to an outdoor gear shop and bought lightweight rucksacks, sleeping bags, trousers and a T-shirt or two, but didn't take a tent, along with all the accessories needed for bivouacking out on mountainsides like cooking-pots, gas stoves, etc. We didn't buy new specialist anoraks, relying on our old showerproof jackets, and we didn't buy those special hiking sticks like ski-sticks. We did need to buy a couple of regional maps in Germany but once we hit the E1 we only needed Arthur Krause's excellent guide (Kompass, Innsbruck) until we got to Italy, where we had to purchase one local map to make the connection back to the E1, and then from Pavia had the invaluable collection of maps of the Via Francigena with directions in Italian and English (Terre di Mezzo, Milan).

The trip was planned with meticulous foresight in the certain knowledge that:

a) we didn't want to book every night's accommodation before we left;

---

1 "Clio, a muse, and other essays literary and pedestrian", Longman, Green, London & New York, 1913.

b)   we wanted to be able to change each day's route or destination at the drop of a hat depending on the weather, tiredness, hunger, etc.;

c)   nothing would go according to plan anyway, but

d)   we would cover at least the minimum number of miles needed to walk from York to Rome, which we calculated to be about 1,750 and turned out to be more.

We created a long-distance footpath of our own to cover the first section, based roughly on a part of the E8 (which in total goes from the west of Ireland to Istanbul!), taking us from York to Harwich initially via such paths as the Viking Way, the Wolds Way and the Stour Valley Path. It unavoidably crossed a large swathe of fenland between Boston and Newmarket, trying to keep to the smallest possible tracks and lanes while still finding the necessary – and rare – bridges over rivers, canals and ditches. After that we would have to find and follow the Deltapad in Holland, the GR5 in Belgium and then make up a way of our own across Germany to somewhere near Koblenz.

The question which loomed over the whole adventure was "Where will we stay overnight?" We could let our house for six months so would have some income, but by no means enough to stay in hotels every night. For some years we had been members of an online accommodation exchange group called Hospitality Club. You just register, say what you're prepared to offer, e.g. a spare room for 3 nights/a sofa for a night/a guided tour around your town; and wait for people to call. Then when you're going travelling you get in touch with people on your route and see if you can stay with them. We had had quite a few visitors to our house from various countries and were hoping to be able to meet some friendly and hospitable people who would do the same for us. In addition we joined two other such organisations: Couchsurfing and Servas. Servas was set up as a means of reconciliation after World War II, and is particularly popular in Germany and Italy, although it too has members worldwide. To join you have to go through an interview process with a regional co-ordinator and are encouraged to stay at least two nights with your host to get to know them: the emphasis is definitely on mutual acquaintance and understanding.

Armed with our various registration documents, addresses to contact, letters of introduction and passwords, we put out a general notice on the Hospitality Club (HC) website about three months before setting out, announcing our intention and approximate route, and had a reply almost immediately from 'Bluebells' in Northern Italy, which was encouraging.

Since Angela grew up in Germany, we were offered places to stay in advance by various friends and relations both there and in Holland and Switzerland, so could look forward to staying in someone's house more often than not. Beyond that we had no idea where we'd stay. We thought we'd find mountain refuges further south, and if we were stuck we'd catch a bus to somewhere bigger then return to the spot we'd left, or maybe we'd knock on a vicarage door…

We were perhaps different from many long-distance walkers in that we didn't work out our route in fine detail beforehand. Just enough not to be constantly getting lost. Equally, we hadn't spent days and weeks poring over guidebooks and manuals about the history and geography of the places we would be passing through, along with exactly which sights we should see. We had maps, but we didn't know what we might find on the way. We didn't know where we were going although we knew how to get there…and we liked it like that. Looking back now and trying to make a list of "Our 10 Favourite Places", a large number are places we'd never heard of before: little towns or villages or unexpected swathes of forest, or shrines or chapels, in unexpected corners. stumbling across a village like Ponzano Superiore in the hills north of La Spezia, for instance, or Clare in Suffolk – a gem on our own doorstep, but we were ignorant of it beforehand – was such a treat because they suddenly appeared, unbidden and unanticipated.

The other thing was that as soon as we decided to raise money for a reputable and deserving charity we became convinced by our well-wishers that we were doing something terribly important, and although we did want the walk to have some meaning, we didn't want it to be a self-important philanthropic gesture. But then neither did we want it to be just a holiday. It needed to represent or mirror an inner journey for each of us as well as giving us the chance to spend some quality time together after spending almost 30 years being busy with children, work, etc. The middle way seemed to be a way of trust: to travel lightly with eyes wide open and trust that all would be well. We had prepared for just such an eventuality without knowing what it would be by living frugally for years and saving some money, and we did have the luxury of being able to let our house, but that in turn meant we wouldn't be able to give up walking halfway there and go home.

Many thanks are due to all those good people who wished us well, both before we started and along the way. Without their encouragement we would not have had the wind behind us, nor the heart to satisfy all the conflicting demands of head and body, nor the perseverance which led to great joys:

Thanks to Thomas A. Clark, who graciously granted us permission to reproduce lines from his poem "In Praise of Walking"[2] as chapter headings (unattributed), and to Louis Gibb, who sent us a line of the poem by text soon after we left home and continued every few days a line at a time until it was finished and we were almost in Switzerland. Each line seemed appropriate to the moment, and lifted our spirits;

respect to Jean Bono and dear Jannah, who accompanied us through the most gruelling part of the whole trip without complaint and couldn't have encouraged us more;

thanks to Michael and Eva, who offered their house for several days' stay and his company for several days' walking;

to Harald and Willeke who gave us a much-needed break in Holland and showed us how to paint a picture, throw a party and organise a singing workshop;

to Anch, who got out his walking boots twice (and enjoyed doing it!) and did a massive job on the proof-reading;

to Elke Elli for teaching Nick a lesson; to Chris for joining us for the last week and being our witness;

and to Annemarie for arranging our ambassadorial reception in Rome; Soundsphere for singing for us and with us; Chechelele for letting us take time out and welcoming us back; Judith and Ian, Nigel and Vivienne, Johannes, Jens, Anne and J-C for organising

---

2 Published by Cairn Gallery, 1988.

workshops and/or gigs for us/MSF; to all at York Publishing Services;

and all the other people too numerous to mention one by one who contributed by their hospitality, their company or their messages to keep us going...

NB. This is an account of *our* walk. It is not intended to be a comprehensive guide for a pedestrian journey from York to Rome, but rather the story of what we experienced on our particular trip. Of course anyone else who undertook the same journey, even by the same route, would experience something completely different, but readers might be encouraged to dig out their walking boots and try a similar adventure themselves. If so we wish them "Buen camino!" as pilgrims bid each other, and may they have the wind behind them; and if not we hope they will share our joys and hardships from the comfort of their armchairs!

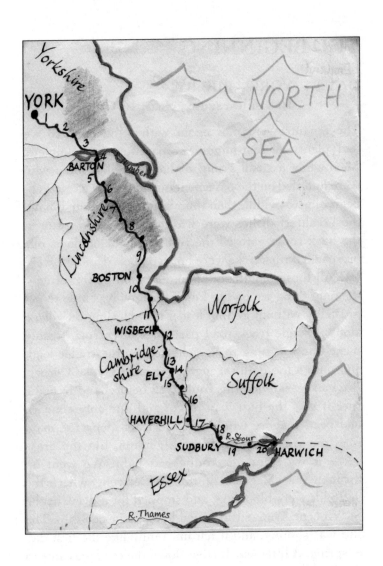

THE BEGINNING

DAY 1   YORK – BIELBY
16.8 miles; sunny, clear; 16°C

The tenants were moving in within the hour so we had plenty of last-minute preparations to complete. Meanwhile a small group of hardy well-wishers who were huddled on the pavement outside to see us off were beginning to twiddle their thumbs in anticipation. Finally the breakfast dishes were washed and stored away in the back room with all the rest of our belongings, our pre-packed rucksacks were hoisted aboard and we were off! All those months of planning could be forgotten – the only thing we had to know for now was how to get to Bielby without getting lost. From Heslington village along a single track road past piles of carrots, freshly picked and waiting to be collected by the trailer-load, and onto a footpath through a wood to Gypsy Corner. We had researched this route well beforehand to make sure it was the best way to go, and our only concern had been that we would have to walk along the main road out past the airfield to Elvington, but the grass verge is wide and the traffic was light. We went on through the village to Sutton-on-Derwent, where the daffodils were blooming, and stopped for a drink at the St. Vincent Arms, sitting outside with our pack-up. The sun was shining, and it felt uncannily like the first day of spring. A little way further down the road we came to the Pocklington Canal, which is no longer used by the barges which plied up and down laden with timber and paper and charcoal, but has abundant wildlife nearby and a good footpath along the left-hand bank. A pair of swans made sure we kept our distance from their nest, and a heron flew low overhead. The path led us past eight footbridges, many ducks and rabbits, and the sound of woodpeckers across the field. By the time we got to Bielby we were starting to flag, but we'd always known it would be a long first day, and we arrived at Ian & Judith's house to a warm welcome. After being spoilt with cups of tea, a siesta and offers of foot baths, we adjourned to the conservatory where a crowd of people were gathering for a charity concert featuring several of our friends and musical companions and an audience of about 50 others, including some supportive colleagues from the British Library who contributed a goodly sum towards our running total for Médecins Sans Frontières (MSF). We retired to bed tired and elated at the success of the concert and the generosity of everyone involved.

DAY 2   BIELBY – NORTH NEWBALD
11 miles; fresh, cloudy; 13°C

Our daughter Jannah, rehearsing for a production of 'Moby Dick' in Bristol, texted us this quote from it today: "They say that men who have travelled the world become quite at ease in manner, quite self-possessed in company."

We woke up to a cup of tea in bed, and after having breakfast Judith packed a picnic and we strolled off down the village street and along country lanes through Everingham and Harswell to a transport caff on the main road near Holme-upon-Spalding Moor. It's exceedingly flat country here, and marshy. When Henry VIII travelled between York and Hull with his Congress to the North in 1519 the whole mighty shebang allegedly stopped at this very spot, taking up acres of camping space around Howlme Manor for a night. At least the campsite was flat.

We turned off the main road at North Cliffe and went over the hill through some fields scattered with sheep, where a red kite delighted us with its aerobatics, and into a little patch of forest, where we stopped for our picnic before continuing to North Newbald to meet Ian at the Tiger Inn. There are two pubs in the village, the Tiger and the Gnu. I know where my money would be if it ever came down to a fight for survival between them. Ian had parked their camper-van at the eerily quiet Bungalow Farm which had a corrugated iron shack/wash-house out the back with a static caravan next to it and no hot water. After a convivial evening at the pub we bade a fond farewell to our friends and walked up the hill for a mile in the light of a half-moon. We shivered in the middle of the night and were mortified to find that our new sleeping-bags were both leaking feathers, but were buoyed by the sense that the adventure had begun!

DAY 3 NORTH NEWBALD – BARTON-ON-HUMBER
18 miles; cloudy; showery; 9°C

We awoke to a chill bleakness and a mist so thick we could barely see the wash-house (*Fig. 1), and quickly packed up and set off to get our limbs moving. Up the hill where we joined the Wolds Way we were greeted by a couple of people drinking mugs of steaming tea at a refreshment stand placed there for the participants in a sponsored walk, and as we walked along the edge of the Wolds briefly then dipped down through a beautiful wooded glade we were overtaken by groups of sweaty runners and mountain bikers all out for their Saturday morning exercise. At South Cave we paused for a late breakfast and bought some rolls for lunch from an Italian bakery - run by a Roman! From there we found ourselves on the Roman Road to Brough, which was once a substantial Roman settlement on the banks of the Humber Estuary. It began to drizzle. The road would not have been picturesque even on a sunny day as it goes past several factories with rubbish-strewn verges, but Brough was pleasant enough. Brough Haven gave us our first view of the sea, or at least the estuary, and we stopped to nibble on our rolls. The rain had stopped but there was a bracing wind coming up from Denmark. We walked along the waterfront, sometimes right next to the water as it was high tide and sometimes along the edge of fields, with kittiwakes swooping around us. At one point we crossed a toads' migration path to their breeding-ground, and near North Ferriby we came across a notice-board commemorating the discovery of three Bronze Age boats between 1937 and 1963 by Ted and Willy Wright, two local lads. They were subsequently dated at about 2000 BC, which gave a new twist to contemporary ideas about the history of ocean-going vessels.

As we arrived at the woods on the edge of North Ferriby it started to rain again, more heavily, so we made a dash for the nearest café, which had newly opened. The women who had started it heard our story and gave us a pen, which lasted us all the way to Rome. When we took our leave of them the sun had come out and we climbed up through the nature reserve onto the Humber Bridge, which we crossed as the sun was setting and we gazed down to Hull in one direction and up to the confluence of the Trent and Ouse in the other.

It is such a long walk across that it feels as though you are gradually approaching a foreign land. Arriving in North Lincolnshire we stumbled through the dark to Nigel & Vivienne's house, where we received an excited welcome.

4/3/12

Dear All,

Wasn't Thursday just the most glorious day to set off on? We wandered out of Fulford, being calmed by the beauty the day after frantic beginnings. Mary and Martin, our tenants, started moving in three-quarters of an hour after we left! But the place was ready for them, and of this we feel very proud.

We walked through Heslington and beyond, had a couple of drinks in Sutton upon Derwent, and then toddled up to the Pocklington Canal, which we followed all the way to Bielby and Judith and Ian's house, where a warm welcome awaited us, and cups of tea, and baths and rest. We had done our first 17 miles!

At about 7.30 people started arriving for the concert which Ian & Judith had organised, and a most warm-hearted, glorious evening commenced! Ian started it off with a lovely song then Tim Phebey shared a couple of his songs, warming everyone to sing along, followed by Paula Ryan, who dedicated songs to us, which was very moving, and Sarah Dean too, who played her harp and sang a specially adapted version of 'These boots are made for walking'. Maggi Stratford sang a couple of songs very beautifully, in English, which is unusual for her as she sings in French like a Frenchwoman! Rory Motion delighted everyone by making them laugh out loud as well as giving them some real bits of 'grit' to ponder. Then it was my great pleasure to have one more really good sing with Soundsphere. I won't see them again until June when they will meet us in Vevey at the side of Lake Geneva. And we will have a gig and a weekend together – the longest break we will have had since we began (12 years ago?!). Nick and I sang a couple of songs too, and people were very generous to us, since we don't even know all the words off by heart! Nick finished the evening off with a lovely bedtime folksong called John o'Dreams, which in a sweet way signalled the end of proceedings, which in all raised £400 for Medecins Sans Frontieres!! Hurray for Judith and Ian, who then continued to host us until the next day. Judith even walked with us all the way to North Newbald through another very clement day, full of skylarks and English villages at their crocus-flowering best.

We met Ian in the pub, spent a lovely evening with them both, and then they caught a taxi back home having left us their camper at a little campsite where we slept soundly until waking up to day three, still able to breakfast on the provision Judith had supplied us with. What wonderful friends they are!

Day 3 began in the mist without much horizon, and as we walked through the stillness of it onto the Wolds Way, we experienced the greatest variety of landscape changes: bleak rolling hilltops in misty shrouds, a sudden flinging aside of the clouds as we dipped down into a coomb-like woodland valley, a cavernous vividness of mossy greens and orangey browns of ash, beech and oak. We emerged onto the ancient rolling vistas above South Cave, had a cup of tea, found an Italian Bakery with a cheerful well-travelled baker from Rome (!), and then followed a Roman Road to Brough, and ultimately onto the Transpennine Way along the River Humber – a different world! The rain which was forecast gave us a wide berth mostly – a couple of showers met our spot just as we were under shelter! The rest of the time we walked in glorious sunshine again. After another café, run by a couple of lovely chatty ladies since last Monday (!) in North Ferriby, we trudged the last four or so miles across the elegant, imposing and altogether stunning Humber Bridge – what an experience! I have always wanted to walk across it, but it really exceeded all expectations, a bit like flying without an aeroplane. All in all it was another 17 miles or more, we both had quite sore feet and were very ready to arrive at the most welcoming house of Vivienne and Nigel in Barton-on-Humber. We were greeted with scones made by Rafi, their daughter – delicious! Then, again after baths and rest, we were fed with the most delicious curry produced by Nigel and spent a lovely evening talking about things we shared until my eyes rolled away from me and dictated that I begin my – fantastic – night's sleep!

Dear friends, let me thank you all once more for all the good wishes (they are working extremely well!) and support and encouragement. The last few weeks have been like no other I have ever experienced in my life!

I'll write again when I get a chance, and if I go on too much, you can always stop reading it, can't you?

Much love to all,

Angela and Nick

DAY 4   BARTON-ON-HUMBER
0 miles; rain all day; 5°C

After a sound night's sleep we had a slow Sunday morning as the rain fell in torrents and we took the opportunity to relax after the exertions of the previous day. Angela was developing some mighty blisters despite the fact that we had bought our new boots at the same time the previous September in Cornwall and walked them in together. In the afternoon we had scheduled a singing workshop in a church hall, and there was a good turnout – everyone enjoyed themselves and also contributed more towards our MSF funds. In the evening we had a convivial neighbourhood meal, shared with Godfrey and his family who brought food and conversation from down the road.

DAY 5   BARTON-ON-HUMBER – GRASBY
19 miles; cloudy; 7°C

We left our friends behind with some trepidation: we might not see a familiar face for weeks and now we were well and truly on our own. We had our OS map to refer to, but just to be sure we were on the right track going out of town we stopped a tall man without a dog collar on a street corner. He confirmed that we were going the right way and asked us where we were making for, and became very animated when we told him. He introduced himself as the parish priest and was pleased to bless our journey. Feeling suitably blessed we continued up the narrow lane which led straight, up hill and down, past large fields of turnips and beet and, bizarrely, a TV set perched in a tree, to Barnetby-le-Wold, which calls itself the gateway to the Lincolnshire Wolds. After stopping for a bite and a sup at the Flute and Whistle we had an encounter with a black dog. It had been disobediently refusing to come to its owner, a young woman, but came meekly to Angela and allowed her to hold its collar for the lead to be put on.

The road then leads along the low-lying eastern flank of the Wolds through Bigby and Somerby, Searby,

Owmby and Grasby, and we took a path parallel to the road which dipped in and out of the villages and crossed fields and pastures, each village standing at the head of a great swathe of rich arable land stretching down to the plain below. We met no-one all day out in the country, apart from a couple of dog-walkers and a man who cycled past us when the trodden mud path was at its narrowest crossing a cabbage-field and stopped to chat about the badger sett he was going to look at, and the weather, and walking. He was the first to mention, after finding out our destination, the mythical Road to Santiago, as he had heard of people walking there. When we got to Grasby it felt as if we had done enough walking for the day and we stopped at the Cross Keys, but they had no rooms and the B&B next door was empty. We were sitting dejectedly outside wondering what to do next as we had been assured that there was a B&B in the village and the next place was miles away, when a car drew up and a woman of about forty got out and opened the gate to the B&B. When we approached her she said she wasn't ready to open for the season yet, but upon reflection she could get a bed ready and she had enough food for breakfast, so we could come in and take our boots off and have a cup of tea and eat supper later at the pub. Sorted!

We found out later that she worked at Humberside Airport, just up the hill, which featured quite a lot over the next day or two as we walked beneath the flight path. There was a great view from the window of our bedroom, and an even better one from the pub restaurant, looking down towards Lincoln. The pub landlady was very interested in our plans and helped us with connecting to the Internet. We also spoke to an old gent in the bar — a Conservative councillor – who gave us £10 for MSF.

DAY 6   GRASBY – TEALBY
19 miles; clear and breezy, cool; 9°C

A chilly start saw us taking a footpath uphill to Caistor, an ancient Roman settlement, where various paths and bridleways criss-crossing the Wolds converge. We visited the library to see if we could get a decent local map, and were offered a copy of a portion of OS map which was missing from the small number we were carrying then set off along the scarp and into wooded dales. Outside Nettleton the path climbs up to a great viewpoint where we stopped for a picnic then followed the ridgeway to Walesby. Although the Wolds are only about 300 or 400 feet high at most, walking along this ridge on the western edge felt like being on top of the world. On a clear day like this we could see for 50 miles, and we strode out relishing the fresh air and sunshine despite the chill breeze. Later as we climbed a curved swing of grassland, nibbled so short by sheep that it could have been the fairway on a golf course, we met a father and grown-up daughter out for a couple of days' walk. We admired the views and the birdlife together and confirmed that we were actually all going in the right direction. We somehow missed the 'Ramblers' Church' nearby, as we followed the signs to Tealby along a country lane (1¼ miles) and started chatting to a man mending a fencepost who told us about it, but by that time we were almost at our destination for the night. The wind had veered round to blow from the north, but that was fine as it pushed us along on the last mile to our B&B, which was in a converted garage in the front garden. The lady who ran it and looked after her disabled husband was very interested in our endeavour and knocked £10 off the cost of staying the night, which we put into our MSF collection. We went out to look for something to eat and found ourselves in rather a posh version of a village pub, which did very good food and surprisingly turned out to be owned by the same consortium as our local, the Saddle in Fulford, just round the corner from our house.

6/3/2012

Dear friends,

A moment ago my next epistle to you all was swallowed by the tightly-timed processes in a public library here in Caistor in the West Lincolnshire Wolds. Never mind, I will however be working against the clock again, and have to give myself a little more margin, so less story and more of a 'hello', and all is going really well! Our time with Nigel and Vivienne was delightful, and of the highest order of hospitality! In Barton we had the first workshop, a lovely mixture of ages in a group of about 15, and all were very involved and sang beautifully – to their own surprise, it felt like! Enjoyed by us all.

As we left Barton in the morning yesterday, the wind was at our back indeed, so thank you for continuing your excellent wishes! Thank you also for all the lovely emails you've sent, but forgive me when I cannot answer them all individually. I don't get to use the tablet, as Nick is turning into Gollum (only joking!) with his precioussss…

Rolling hills, sunny days, cold invigorating wind, lots of lovely friendliness along the way, and random giving of total strangers just about sums it up!

We are now heading to Tealby, and Horncastle tomorrow.

Speak to you soon, and thank you for thinking of us so much.

Lots of love from

Nick and AngelaXX

DAY 7   TEALBY – SCAMBLESBY
20 miles; cloudy, blustery showers; 8°C

We had been invited to stay the night near Horncastle by
some friends of the niece of a friend (Maggie) who comes
from this part of the country. We had been in touch with
them by phone and they had told us that we could stay,
and if we liked we could join them in their regular yoga
group session at the house, but it became a bit of a slog in
the morning after Ludford, which was without charm or
amenity despite being billed as another ancient Roman
town. From there we went over the top by footpath
rather than taking the quaintly-named Bluestone Heath
Road, which goes East-West across the Wolds, and
came out at Burgh-le-Bain, undoubtedly an early Saxon
settlement, whence we could follow the river Bain as it
meandered gently through fields to Donington, where
we stopped at the Black Horse for a break and met the
father and daughter again. They helpfully researched
some accommodation possibilities for us on an iPhone
and we looked again at our options. It was going to be
a long walk to get to the other side of Horncastle, so we
decided to press on as far as Scamblesby and see what
was there. Up the hill we went, past a sheep farm where
we chatted to the farmer about his flock – there was a
hint of snow in the air but some lambs were already out
at pasture in a paddock with the mother ewes while the
pregnant ewes were in a separate enclosure which we
had to pass through. When we got to the Green Man
at Scamblesby they had no beds left and sent us to a
riding stables which had holiday cottages to let. Luckily

we were welcome to stay the night in one, which was comfortable and warm. It had been a long day's walk, but through beautiful country: the Wolds – both here and in Yorkshire – are such a contrasting mixture of smoothly curved hills and valleys with hidden woods and sheltered corners, and there is so much sky to see. On days like this, clear but with great banks of cloud billowing over the Peak District and across the flatlands, it is a perfect location for cloudspotters.

DAY 8   SCAMBLESBY – SPILSBY
17.5 miles; fresh and clear, becoming cloudy; 10°C

We found ourselves in a Black Spot. It was another of those times where we were in between two maps for a large portion of the day. We were trying to get to Hagworthingham (although when we got there we wondered why) but none of the road- or footpath-signs we passed mentioned it. It was increasingly as though its name had been deleted during the War to confuse enemy paratroopers, or maybe its name was just too long to fit on standard sign-posts. All the villages we passed through were either deserted or only contained people who didn't know how to get anywhere without going by car. We were diverted to Tetford after going up to the top of a hill to a place with a radio mast which we continued to see for hours afterwards from different angles, which became confusing. Looking for a bite to eat in Tetford we found the café closed so went to a pub for a bar snack. The landlord gave us directions to 'Hag', which were promptly questioned by a group of hikers we met outside as we left. The old footpath we chose hit a small road and we had to guess which way to go. After a while a 4x4 came along driven by a park ranger, who told us to carry on and turn right at the big dead tree. We did that and somehow ended up in Ashby Puerorum, where we saw him again. He said we must have picked the wrong tree. Ashby Puerorum, or Ashby of the Boys, was so named after an estate in the parish was bequeathed to the choristers of Lincoln Cathedral in the late 13th century. We went across a farmyard and round the church to take another path across some pasture-land, and finally found a muddy track leading across some beet-fields to Hagworthingham, which was a huge disappointment after so much anticipation, being a small gathering of houses on the main road with no B&B or pub. There was a greasy spoon run by an Elvis fan with a quiff. He was just closing up as we arrived but let us in for a cup of tea and advised us to get a bus to Spilsby, the nearest town, about 5 miles away. Since the alternative seemed to be to walk along the busy road to Spilsby and get there in the dark, this seemed like a good plan. We put up at the White Hart coaching inn, an old-fashioned small-town main-square hotel which had staff in smart waistcoats but had been refurbished – probably in the 1970s – with flock wallpaper, ill-fitting doors, etc. We found the key didn't actually work in the door and no-one could find another key so they gave us another much bigger and more pleasant room instead. The TV didn't work and we couldn't get a WiFi connection but they did a good breakfast, and as we were leaving we were accosted by a staff member who was cleaning the ceiling, who was the first of many to ask us to "Give my regards to the Pope!"

DAY 9   SPILSBY – BOSTON
22½ miles; cloudy, sunny intervals, breezy; 12°C

"We can walk between two places and in so doing establish a link between them, bring them into a warmth of contact, like introducing two friends."

In a bakery/delicatessen in the town square the owner seemed to already know our story as soon as we walked in. As it happened she was a friend of the people we didn't stay the night with near Horncastle, and had heard about us from them. We bought some provisions for a picnic and decided that rather than walk back along the road to Hagworthingham we could go directly to Stickney: we would have ended up walking the same distance anyway. So we took a road straight down the southern flank of the wolds and with a huge panorama ahead of us stretching as far as the coast at Mablethorpe and the Stump at Boston we dropped down to the chequer-board flatlands below. Suddenly we were in a different world where everything is rectangular: there are no bends or curves any more; all the roads, lanes, paths, drains, channels and dykes are straight; the isolated farm-houses are square, and the landscape is punctuated by telegraph poles and electricity pylons rather than trees. At Stickney we found two pubs – one was closed for repainting and the other was just closed during the day. This was a recurring theme: we would head for a reasonably large blob on the map with PH printed next to it and then find the PH was only open in the evening, which was not surprising in little villages but seemed unfair in larger places like this. Anyway we sat on the church steps like a couple of tramps and ate our pack-up with some juice from the supermarket over the road. The sun was shining and we could take off our boots and lie down – who needed a pub?

From Stickney it was supposed to be another seven or eight miles to Boston, but it turned out to be at least ten along the drain, which is actually a river which has been channelled to run straight across the fenland. Since both the road and the drain went directly to Boston it was hard to see where the extra miles came from. At any rate it was a long walk and by the time we got to Boston we had sore heels and more blisters. On the way across the plain we had seen old fighter planes wheeling above us, which added to the feeling of vulnerability you get from crawling slowly across such a vast expanse of open flat land, and as we approached Boston passed close by our first old-style windmill (*Fig. 2). All around here were many skylarks, which seem to feel at home in large ploughed fields, but the farms are mostly big monoculture agribusinesses. As we got into the outskirts of Boston and were looking for a place to stay the night, we stopped a man pushing a bike who gave us directions to a street full of B&Bs, then wanted to hear our story and gave us £5 for our collection. Just then his mate came cycling along, stopped, and gave us another fiver! We found a bed in an elderly house belonging to an elderly couple with an elderly but longed-for bathtub. Ah, bliss!

N.B. I find a note in my diary saying "Pity about the algae". I'm sure it had nothing to do with the bath so it must have referred to the drain we walked along.

March 12th 2012

Hello everyone,

Today we are in Boston in Lincolnshire, though you might be forgiven in imagining yourself in Holland, as the canals are flanked with windmills and the roads dotted with smiling chaps on bicycles. The sun has been shining most of the week although we have had a bit of rain one morning up on the – beautiful!

– Lincolnshire Wolds, and part of our 140+ miles (!) has been clocked up meandering round the stunning countryside. Yesterday, after many friendly chats with passers-by, pub landlords and B&B hosts (there is a dearth of Youth Hostels in Lincolnshire, and no personal contacts until further south except one, and that one we had to let go as it was just a bit too far on the day), anyway yesterday we dropped down from the lofty heights of the Wolds to the Fens, and goodness me what a difference! We walked for many miles along totally empty roads in completely straight lines, meeting maybe one car every four miles. By and by we came across a few dire sites: animal concentration camps earning someone a deathlihood. And then there are skylarks (I am a skylark anorak, counting them, and we're up to 85 since we left York), and deer and March hares, even a barn owl yesterday. It was the longest day's walk so far, and both of us had sore feet. In the evening we managed to learn some song lyrics, go for a very cheap Indian meal, mend my socks (again!) and then fall over and sleep like logs.

I have no difficulty going to sleep and getting a good night's rest regardless of the many beds I sleep in. We are pretty much walking a nine to five day on the whole!

A few nights ago I had already written to you all, and wondered whether you would be so kind as to search your minds for contacts in certain areas (I will list them again in a moment) but it does not work from the tablet to address you all, and my gmail site does not show me the group contacts away from our home computer, so I have to be inventive, and also intermittent. Here in Boston Library I wonder: do you know anyone in or near these places to whom you might recommend our acquaintance and whom you feel alright to ask if they'd have us for a night, us supplying our own sleeping-bags and mats, but appreciating running water and toilets, and the warmth of a roof over our heads? Nick's list is this: Holbeach, Wisbech, Thurlow, Sudbury, Bures, Manningtree, Harwich; then on the continent: Antwerp, Maastricht, Aachen, Koblenz, Frankfurt, Stuttgart, Zurich, Andermatt, Milan, Florence, Perugia, Rome?

Dear friends, I am always really glad to hear from you; forgive me if I cannot answer every individual email on account of opportunity, but it is a great joy to get messages from you! York already feels very far away. I know it's only a couple of hours by car but it took us nine days to walk here...

Outside this library is a market place with the most fantastic display of wares, and every European language seems to be spoken! It seems to be like an old fashioned harbour town, and it was in the middle ages, but it's very different to anything I've ever come across in England – hard to believe it IS England!

For now I will stop and go on the road again, but come the next library I'll write to you again.

With lots of love and thanks for your good thoughts in our direction,

Angela and Nick XX

DAY 10   BOSTON – HOLBEACH
18.3 miles; dry, cloudy; 13°C

We pottered about all morning after a hearty breakfast, visiting the library and having our first experience of the missing Tourist Information Office, which overall is almost as common as the closed Tourist Information

Office. Arriving at the large market square near the old docks we found a signpost advertising it pointing across the square towards a large Georgian building. Leaving Angela in a café, I set off to visit the Office, trusting that I would find ample information about places to stay on the way to Wisbech. Halfway there I spotted a sign pointing back the way I'd come. Undeterred I continued to the Georgian house to find a notice saying the T.I.O. was no longer there but omitting to inform the reader where it might be. After retracing my steps I asked a number of residents standing next to a large trench in the road for directions but they all denied any knowledge of a tourist information office and eyed me curiously, furrowing their brows, as if to say: "Why would any tourists come here anyway?" I eventually found a priest who pointed me in a third direction, which proved to be correct.

We left Boston to get to Holbeach St Mark's, which sounded delightfully rural and probably had a stout Saxon church and a selection of village pubs with bedrooms and excellent beer. It looked like a substantial place on the map, a large black patch on the landscape of the marshland, but you do have to make a detour from the sea bank near the coastline of The Wash to go inland in order to cross the River Welland at Fosdyke, and then turn northwards again for a little way off the main road. (This would present problems over the next few days, the fact that there are surprisingly few road bridges across the major rivers flowing into The Wash.) Crossing the bridge, we made our way through the late afternoon past huge fields of daffodils (*Fig. 3) along a dead straight road which would suddenly turn at a right angle or two. After negotiating the road for a good five miles with increasing numbers of cars speeding towards and past us as the light gradually dwindled, we eventually arrived at Holbeach St Mark's at about 7 o'clock to find a large council estate with a rather boring redbrick 19th century church and a dimly lit pub at the far end of the sprawl. It had no rooms, and no-one in the village did B&B. There were no buses running to anywhere. It was Saturday night but the pub was almost empty. As the barmaid said: "They're all at home taking drugs". It transpired that there had been a big food processing plant here which closed ten years ago, laying 850 people off, and there's not been enough work around these parts to give even half of them another job. We ended up having to get a taxi to Holbeach itself – a market town with at least half a dozen pubs or hotels which were all either closed down, closed on Saturdays, or empty ("everyone goes to Boston on a Saturday"). We found one pub which had a room, but the light didn't work in the corridor, the room was too cold then later much too hot, the water in the shower was a barely luke-warm trickle, and there was nothing to eat. Apart from that it was OK.

We went out and found a takeaway pizza which was like eating a car-tyre. Not the best day so far…

DAY 11   HOLBEACH – WISBECH
17.6 miles; very warm, clear and still; 18°C

"A dull walk is not without value…"

We were set onto the right road by an old fellow pushing a bike who walked with us out through a council estate and across the middle of a ploughed field. "This is definitely a public footpath. Definitely. And if it isn't, it should be!" He chattered away about the decline of Holbeach from being a thriving market town and the influx of foreign workers from Poland and Latvia and how they had taken all the jobs. "But would local people do those jobs, like picking flowers or potatoes?" Angela asked. "No, most wouldn't. Most would rather sit at home and complain. They'd say they wouldn't want to do gypsy work!" We waved him goodbye as he set off to cycle unsteadily home, after saying: "I'm a useful sort of fellow, really." We walked through a couple of villages and out into empty country; along a drain to a lock and alongside some very long fields full of flowers and new potatoes then more country roads, with their very uneven camber testing our foot muscles. We stopped for a lovely picnic beside the road at a quiet spot and indulged in a rest: stretching out in the sunshine with the sound of the skylarks all around and our boots and socks off, it felt more like May than March, and there was something about that particular lane which, perhaps because of the almost complete lack of traffic, was timeless to the extent that it could have been the 1950s. Moving on, we came across a kingfisher, and a barn-owl, sadly drowned in a ditch, on the way to Gorefield (the site of a long-forgotten battle by the looks of its name) and stopped for a cup of tea at The Woodman's Cottage, a village pub which *was* open in the daytime. Mind you, it was Sunday. A group of locals became very animated after hearing our story, and one man was in tears as he shook us by the hand and wished us a safe passage. Going into Wisbech by an old wooded path then onto a road beside the docks on the river, we met two old gents who stopped separately to tell us their experiences of long-distance walking in the forces, which made me think about the number of soldiers in whose footsteps we were treading the length of our journey, from Roman times or even before. On the way we spoke to one of the present-day armies of flower-pickers, who said they were picking 300 bunches of daffodils an hour, which seems an incredible rate. He was English, but most of the workers are from the Baltic states. We saw trailer-loads of workers being ferried about from farm to field, and when we arrived at Wisbech town found many shops dedicated to Baltic delicacies and home comforts. We stayed at the first B&B we came to, as we were dog-tired, and found an ancient statue sitting in the car-park behind the house. (*Fig. 4) We forgot to ask which was there first, the statue or the car-park?

Day 12   WISBECH – WELNEY
21.9 miles; dry, misty; 11°C

"A traveller on foot in this country seems to be regarded as a sort of wild man or an out-of-the-way being who is stared at, pitied, suspected and shunned by everybody that meets him."[3]

The day started misty and it never properly lifted all day, which was frustrating as we had the feeling that above the mist was a sunny blue sky and a day like yesterday was just around the corner. We didn't get out of Wisbech until nearly noon after we'd been to every chemist's shop in town looking for blister plasters and to the library to look at more maps, which involved long queues to become members of Cambridgeshire Libraries... When we did set off we spent about an hour walking out of and round the outskirts of Wisbech before finally getting out into the country. At Friday Bridge we stopped to eat our pack-up and got talking to a sad

---

3   Karl Philipp Moritz, German author and essayist, upon a journey from London to the Peak District in 1782.

boy of 17 who had walked out of his class at the Tech that morning and couldn't think of a reason to go back. "It's shit," he said. "There's no jobs round here anyway. What's the point of training for anything? Whatever jobs there are are shit jobs, and they've already been taken by Poles. I'm stuck out here now. Hope it doesn't rain. Can't go home, me dad kicked me out. I'll have to wait for him to go down the pub. It's all shit."

It did look like rain at that point. The mist had risen as far as it was going to and solidified into a sort of damp grey blanket. We trudged along for endless miles of extreme flatness, feeling tired, with nothing to see except the dark brown of the soil on either side and the grey of the road losing itself ahead of us, but at moments like this we could always play word games or compose haikus for fun, like these:

Lark is twittering
above the open ploughed land.
White the spring sunshine.

Flat fields all around
growing needs for hungry folk.
Skylark's song rising.

Eventually we found a footpath marked Hereward Way, but it soon turned into a grass verge on the side of the main road to Welney, and by the time we got there it was 7 o'clock. We were tired and fed up after stumbling along in the dark avoiding traffic for the last hour. Luckily Angela insisted on phoning the B&B we had booked to say we would be arriving late, as the wife was out singing and the husband was just about to go out to a function. We checked in then went to the village pub, which is a favourite haunt for fishermen and bird-watchers, for an excellent meal, then slept like babies.

Day 13   WELNEY – ELY
15.3 miles; grey, warmer; 13°C

We had been setting such a cracking pace since we left Barton-on-Humber that we were undaunted at the prospect of a day of 15 miles, but beginning to long for the opportunity to have a day off, which we were planning to do in Ely. After breakfast in the conservatory with our hostess, who told us about her involvement with the Worldwide Compassionate Farming movement and her singing with the choral society in Ely, we packed our bags – this was becoming an automatic manoeuvre by now – and set off to see what we could see of the migrating birds that her husband had mentioned the previous evening. As a warden at the Nature Reserve he knew all about the phenomenon which sees thousands of swans, ducks and other wildfowl arriving to winter in the water meadows around the Ouse Washes. As we crossed over the Hundred Foot Drain and walked alongside it for several miles on an elevated path looking out over the flood-plain we could see vast numbers of birds, including various waders we weren't able to name as we're not knowledgeable twitchers. Anyway we didn't have any binoculars, having left them at home in the interest of lightening our loads (along with guidebooks, Wellington boots, radios and umbrellas among countless other items which may have been useful on the odd occasion). Leaving the waterfowl behind we took a path off at right angles to our left near the railway bridge and walked across farmland for a few miles, past a field dotted with wild geese, all standing in pairs like courting couples at a country dance. Hereabouts we climbed the first slope we had seen for days as we found an old drovers' path leading to Little Downham. Probably only about twenty feet up, but we'd forgotten what it felt like! Walking into the village we were accosted by a youth who was sitting on the pavement at a crossroads. "Hello! Are you New Age Travellers?" We didn't really know the answer to that. We stopped on a bench outside a village pub which had obviously undergone many changes over the years and was now run by a Yorkshireman with his Thai wife, who offered curries and massages, then found ourselves doing the last lap on the Bishop's Way, the old cart-track to Ely. Part of it felt like an authentic hollow way, a tiny remnant of an ancient landscape where one could imagine the tread of merchants and monks, shepherds and shoemakers, in former times.

The Tourist Information Office in Oliver Cromwell's house in Ely had a marvellously helpful Dutchwoman working there, who was even more helpful when she found out we were on our way to Holland. Having initially said that regrettably everywhere was full, she phoned round all the cheap B&Bs to check and came back to say that unfortunately there was not a bed to be had in the town. Unless... "Well, there is a place just around the corner but I don't think they do B&B any more. Let me just try them.... Yes, they'll let you stay – and for a good price!" (this last with a smile and a wink). The house was indeed just around the corner, the furnishings were exquisite – the result of years of collecting antiques – and the hosts extremely pleasant and interesting people who engaged us in long conversations and were kind enough to knock something off the stated price <u>and</u> let us stay for a second night. We could finally have a day off to rest our bruised heels and heal our best blisters after ten days and 170 miles since the last day of rest. The suite we stayed in included a proper Victorian bathroom and a little sitting room. Luxury or what?!

Dear friends,

Another library, another missive. This time I had to join Ely Library which gives me a daily hour on the computer, but it will only be this day, and the remaining portion of the hour which I began by finding some of your incredibly useful replies. They will be responded to shortly and individually, and most probably from the tablet, which seems to cope with individual emails but not with the whole list of email recipients here! We are having our first day's break in this cathedral city on the Isle of Ely, surrounded by vast expanses of very very flat land, in which much of our country's wheat, potatoes, cabbage and daffodils are being grown. Endless stretches of so-called drains draw straight lines through empty terrain, and a couple of days ago it began to feel quite sad, as a very grey day followed on from the gloriously sunny mid-summer feel of Sunday, and we did not meet a single person to talk to or find a footpath which would take us across the waterways. Trudging along the sides of roads is OK when they are not busy, but no fun when you're trying to beat the descending darkness and still have a couple of miles to go to an unknown B&B address!

But strengthened by a good night's sleep and a change of view we approached Ely yesterday afternoon, singing our little yet increasing repertoire as we walked along the top of a dyke for several miles with the 'usual' flat vast fields vista on our left-hand side, but the most amazing wetlands teeming with waterfowl to our right, where the last of the swans were brightening dark patches, some of which rose in clusters periodically, swooping some distance only to set down on a watery carpet a bit further to one side or the other. A fantastic spectacle, especially as we had learned that these swans travel annually to Siberia for the summer!

I am learning more and more in very practical ways how much difference the care of a single person can make in any given moment. Yesterday, as we arrived in this – rather stunning – town, which after all is still a tourist destination just as York is, we enquired at the tourist office about accommodation, only to be told there was hardly anything available, especially in our price bracket. Then this very helpful woman rang around a bit and found us a place where she forewent the commission and which turned out to be almost like staying in a palace! Such an unusual and beautiful house, and very interested and interesting people, who sat down with us at breakfast time and began to put the world to rights! This morning we met the first person connected to Servas, who reassured us with tales of travelling in other countries where the hosting contacts worked beautifully. I look forward to meeting many new people on the continent. But I pledge once more to try my utmost to be wakeful to any person with a need or a question, knowing how much difference it can make to someone's day!

Well, dear friends, expect a little gap now, and some of you may receive individual answers in the meantime. We think of you all with fondness and gratitude, and know that you will keep recognisable life going in the best way possible while we walk along an unknown path of which we tell you as much as we learn as soon as we can express it.

Yours,

Angela and Nick xx

DAY 14 ELY
0 miles; grey, misty, chilly; 10°C

So we made the most of our rest day, sleeping and strolling, lounging and pottering.

A long slow breakfast, another look at the Cathedral and the stained glass museum, a cup of coffee, an unhurried visit to the library... Last time (the only other time) we were at the Cathedral we bumped into a couple of friends who live on the Suffolk coast. Quite by chance our paths had happened to coincide in that place at that time, which seemed extraordinary. This time we met a new person at a pre-planned meeting-place, who told us much about the local Servas group. It was instructive that of all the Servas members in England not one of them lived on our route through East Yorkshire, the East Midlands and East Anglia apart from a handful who were all based in or near Cambridge, and it was a similar story with Hospitality Club.

DAY 15 ELY – EXNING
17.5 miles; clear and warm; 17°C

Looking back from the riverside at the octagonal tower of the Cathedral looming up from the top of its low hill shrouded by mist, with a blanket of mist settled upon the horizon and scraps of mist rising from the river, it was hard to imagine it ever being otherwise, and easy to see why it has often been described as the big ship of the Fens. By 11 o'clock the sun had burnt the mist away and it soon became warm enough to strip off a couple of layers. We walked along a cycle path beside the river with a military-style operation going on to our left: huge machinery taking turns to plough, harrow and sow the enormous fields of black earth. Meanwhile to our right was a tranquil water-world of river, reeds, dykes and waterfowl. Every so often a narrow-boat would putter slowly by. At a field full of long-horned cattle we turned off to the left and dipped down past a wetland nature reserve where we stopped for a while to appreciate the soundscape – the honking and hooting, squawking and squeaking, peeping and trilling and croaking of thousands of birds in a reedy lake hidden behind a stand of poplars – and have a picnic.

Following an old carters' track between villages across fields which were becoming gradually chalkier, by the time we got to Exning, a couple of miles short of Newmarket, the landscape had turned and become slightly hilly with more trees, and we walked into Exning down a lane lined with flowering hawthorn, feeling glad to be back on the road again after our relaxing day off. To think that in the original planning stages of the trip I had wanted to leave on April 1st, thinking that in March we would be beset by the cold winds of late winter, that we might be bogged down on the Wolds and then have to struggle across the Fens into a Siberian gale. How differently it had turned out so far! We were past the open flatlands now, going into a different country. Soon we would be in Suffolk, aiming for the Stour Valley, which would lead us all the way to Harwich.

We arrived in Exning and asked around for a B&B. We were directed down a side road to a pub called the Wheatsheaf, which was also known as the Ring of Fire. It turned out to be owned by a horse trainer and frequented by many jockeys from nearby stables. The landlord had clippings from newspapers up on the wall detailing his prosecution and acquittal for assaulting another trainer, and we had a drink to the strains of Johnny Cash. The clientele were friendly enough, although there was an undercurrent of adrenaline and hormonal overload, and the accommodation was comfortable but rather expensive: we were beginning to count our pennies, with the thought that if we had to stay in places like this all the way to Rome we'd spend more than we we'd be able to collect for MSF.

DAY 16   EXNING – THURLOW/HAVERHILL
19.3 miles; cloudy, dull, chilly; 11°C

We set off at a cracking pace to Newmarket and stopped there for a library break to get onto their computer and search for places to stay the night, as we had again been stymied in our attempts to get onto the Internet. Out of Newmarket the road is straight but uphill for a fair way as far as Wooditton, passing several enormous stud farms/racehorse stables; then a smaller lane goes off to Kirtling, which was, unusually, a small village with an open pub. The terrain hereabouts was now of long saddles of pasture or winter wheat and oats, green-edged by hedges beginning to bud and leaf, with more flowering thorn trees in clumps. There were more thatched cottages about now, and some houses with elaborate stucco relief work on their facades. From Kirtling we could drop down the hillside and pick up the Stour Valley Path, which had bypassed Newmarket. So we tramped across a couple of muddy fields then took the path, which zigzagged its way across country, more or less following the course of the Stour – still a tiny stream. Everything seemed to be young and new: the stream, the lambs, the budding leaves and blossoms. The chill in the air kept us moving, however, and we passed through Great Bradley and on to Little Thurlow, by which time we had done almost 20 miles and were feeling ready to stop. Angela's blisters were resurfacing and I was starting to get sore heels and bouts of cramp from all the road walking we had been doing, while this day's field-path hiking up and down hill again had stretched our calf muscles. There was only one pub open in Thurlow, and it had recently changed hands so was not yet ready for guests, and no-one could tell us where we could find a bed. "Oh, you'd have to go to Haverhill" was the general opinion, but that was another 5 miles away, and there weren't any buses. Hmm. Then the chef spoke up and said his dad was coming in a minute to pick up a bed and take it to Haverhill. He'd give us a lift. So we thought well we could come back to Thurlow in the morning or maybe, as at Spilsby, we could walk two other sides of a triangle and get back to the path further on, so when his dad Tony came we bought him a pint and got a lift to his house on the edge of Haverhill where we met his South African wife and helped to move an old bed out of the house then unload the bed from the van and take it upstairs. Tony showed us the full-size kit car he had built himself and the underground TV channel he watches which shows alternative news and political views along with various conspiracy theory programmes. Patsy found us a room at the Rose & Crown and they took us down there. We slept in a 4-poster bed, had a bath and went to the local Wetherspoon's for a cheap meal. Haverhill is a surprisingly big town which I'd never heard of, largely made up of housing estates clustered around an old market square with a few medieval buildings and a general air of tedium and neglect, as in so many English town centres on a weekday evening.

DAY 17   HAVERHILL – CAVENDISH
17.2 miles; grey, light rain; 14°C

We left Haverhill on the old railway track past Wixoe through a large country estate to Stoke-by-Clare and then beside the river to Clare on a small country road, which was a lovely walk despite the drizzle. Through a farmyard and onto another lane we came across a troll. (*Fig. 5) Angela was delighted and overwhelmed by this genial example of the English folk-spirit, and we wondered aloud how people had celebrated its existence over the years or centuries – maybe as a meeting-place for the jurymen of the hundred, or the site of the local Maypole? Stopping at Stoke's village shop just before it closed for lunch, we bought some provisions and went for a cuppa in the pub. We had arranged to go to a B&B in a village called Pentlow after searching online for local guest-houses, but it was quite a bit further on down the road to Sudbury, although there was some confusion as there were two places called Pentlow about two miles apart on our map, which was odd. Also when we got to Clare we were so taken with the town that we wanted to stay the night there. Unfortunately a lot of other people had obviously had the same idea and booked in for the weekend. When I finally knocked at the door of the poshest B&B in town the lady was very sweet and helpful. She saw me standing on her doorstep, cap in hand with my boots all muddy, and invited me in while she phoned a couple in Cavendish who she thought may still be running a guest house, "although they are getting on a bit." While Angela had cups of tea in a café and did her handwork while sharing philosophical musings with a young couple from London who were in the country antique-hunting, I had been traipsing around town for some time, but having reached a satisfactory conclusion my search came to an end at The Swan, where I was pleased to watch Wales claim the Grand Slam by beating France 13-6 in the final match of the Six Nations Tournament. (That is to say that Wales beat England, Scotland, Ireland, Italy and France, for anyone who doesn't speak Rugby). I met Dave, a social worker, who said: "Put me down on your email list! If I'd known you were coming you could have stayed at my place!"

Before leaving Clare we spent some more time looking around and imagining what it must have been like as a border fortress between the kingdoms of the Angles and the Saxons in the Dark Ages, or as the seat of the Lords of Clare when the castle was built in Norman times and the town became an important centre for the Suffolk wool trade. There are some remarkable remnants of this medieval wealth to be seen in some of the houses still standing near the market place, notably the Ancient House, part of which dates from the 13th century. Another wing of the same house has the most impressive display we'd yet seen of pargetting (plaster relief work), which set us thinking of Angela's daughter Katharina and her studies in the restoration of old plaster work some years ago.

We left Clare on a path leading up through fields which were probably vineyards at the time of the Domesday Book, which notes that at the time there were sixty vineyards in the parish. We walked on a path along the hillside in the gloaming looking down over the valley of the Stour across chalky grazing land and wheat fields, past an old hall which used to have a moat around it according to the OS map, and down into Cavendish, passing a present-day vineyard on the way. We found our B&B in the middle of the village – a lovely old

Edwardian house run by a mature couple – I think he said he was 92 and she 88 – who were full of vigour and stories about their lives. In the 1940s she was working at the first Waldorf School (run along lines indicated by Rudolf Steiner) in England, while he was working in the theatre in London. The house was stuffed with books, folios and copies of Opera magazine, and Angela came across a copy of a little book made up of dictations to a visionary from the elemental forces which weave our existence.

Interestingly, after we had finished the walk and were on the verge of sending our collected total so far to MSF, we were given a large sum towards it from a charitable trust administered from an address in Cavendish. If we'd known beforehand we'd have called in to thank them!

DAY 18   CAVENDISH – BURES/SUDBURY
20 miles; grey, some drizzle; 13°C

As we set off briskly along a country lane for a few miles, under overhanging trees, a footpath soon branched off to the left through a gate and led along the riverside for a while before climbing uphill onto a very muddy cart-track. Many fields later as we squelched through the effects of last night's rain it began to feel like a major cross-country yomp rather than a shortish easy Sunday stroll. The Stour Valley Path turned out to be an elusive beast which strayed far from the river and took us through a farmyard past the village of Foxearth and alongside a series of ploughed fields. As we were tramping up a hill we heard a voice calling out a greeting from the other side of the thick overgrown beech and holly hedge beside us. Peering through, we spotted a middle-aged couple striding along who paused to chat.

The man introduced himself as the gamekeeper for that estate, and on hearing where we were walking towards he immediately wanted to give us some money for MSF. Unfortunately he had on the wrong trousers, but took our details and promised to send something via our online JustGiving account (and we later found that he had!). We continued as far as Sudbury, where we paused for a picnic, sitting on an old wartime bunker on the water-meadow across the river from the town, then went on towards Bures, where it seemed we would be able to find a place to stay the night. This involved taking a long detour up a steep hill for no apparent reason other than to avoid walking on the road and when we got to Bures, a small town on the river, we were tired. The pub was full of a rough crowd who had obviously gone for a Sunday lunchtime session several hours before. They told us there was actually nowhere to stay there and we'd have to go back to Sudbury or on to Colchester, just across the border in Essex. We did find a B&B in the village but it was closed until April 1st, so we were a fortnight too early. We decided to catch a train back to Sudbury and ask for a bed at the Black Boy, which someone in the pub had advised, then come back on the train in the morning. We found the Black Boy in the main street, but it was closed and didn't look like opening soon, although we waited until the clock struck six and there was nothing on the door to indicate that it would be closed. Several other pubs were either closed or had no vacancies, and just as it looked as if we had exhausted every possibility we met a crumpled fellow in a side street who took us to ask at another pub, although he wouldn't come in as he said he was banned. A buxom young barmaid with brightly coloured hair peered through the window at our guide, who seemed quite mild and well-mannered, and said they were full, but after chatting a bit she said there was another place down the road and her boyfriend put down his pool-cue and volunteered to take us there. It was a Fifties-style motel with a room in a little house in the car park overlooking the river, and gave us all we needed – a shower, a place to wash and hang our clothes, and a bed….

DAY 19   SUDBURY – DEDHAM
20.1 miles; warm and sunny; 15°C

After a cold and frosty night we left the motel after breakfast to catch a train back to Bures. We were expecting to get to Dedham to meet a couple from Colchester, who had kindly offered to put us up for the night. Since Dedham was on the river Stour we had been thinking we'd have a pleasant ramble along the valley, but on closer inspection of the OS map we realised that for much of the way the path goes along parallel to but about a mile away from the river. However, it was a lovely warm day, the countryside was peaceful and wooded and the villages picturesque. In addition we found that we were already in Essex, the last English county we would be passing through, which was encouraging. Yorkshire, Lincolnshire, Cambridgeshire, Suffolk and Essex: surprisingly few counties for a walk of about 300 miles. The last few miles from Stratton St Mary did take us along the riverbank through open land managed by the National Trust: the landscape painted by Constable two centuries ago with some of the same landmarks still standing, such as the old watermill a little way further down the valley. At Dedham we were joined by Chris and Annie, who drove us to their home in Colchester. Both are writers and former teachers who spend half their time in Annie's homeland of Bulgaria. We sang together, ate richly, drank ouzo, and Skyped with our offspring, which was a great pleasure!

DAY 20   DEDHAM – HARWICH
22.9 miles; warm, clear; 17°C

Annie and Chris gave us a lift back to Dedham and came for a walk with us past the old mill on a beautiful still fresh morning. (*Fig. 6) Chris is tall and the years of sitting at a desk writing have taken their toll on his back so he had to pull out after a few miles, but it made a good start to the day, rambling in a companionable way through such countryside. We bade them a fond farewell and followed the river on to Manningtree, where it becomes an estuary, suddenly widening out to be even more of a haven for wildlife, with cormorants and gulls and waders joining the woodpeckers and pigeons, the blackbirds, robins and jays of the woodlands and fields. Shortly after Manningtree the road took a wide detour which we had to follow until we could cross the railway line and get down onto a coastal path. After that we could walk along the high tide line until Harwich Docks began to look quite close. It was becoming warm and the sea and sky were both sparkling clear blue as we picked out the path among reeds, pebbles and seaweed. The Essex Way fizzled out at some point around here, and we could no longer continue along the coast so cut in to Ramsey, which is where it became difficult. The only way of getting to the ferry port apart from wading through a flooded tunnel under the main road was on the massive busy dangerous road itself, so we had to add several miles to the journey, which is never fun at the end of the day. Still, we arrived at the terminal with hours to spare and boarded the ferry in good time to find our cabin and have something to eat without having to pay an arm and a leg for it. The cold Bulgarian vegetable stew tasted much better then than it sounds now.

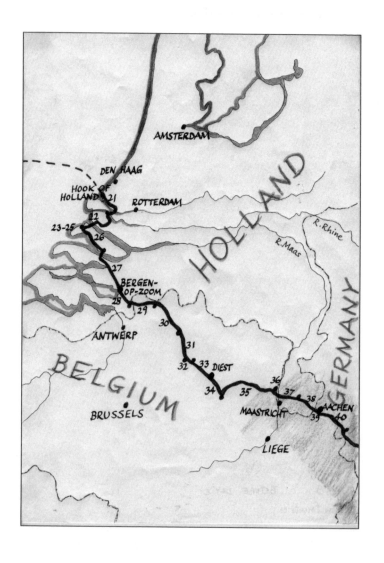

AMSTERDAM

DEN HAAG

HOOK OF
HOLLAND 21

ROTTERDAM

23-25 22

26

27

BERGEN-
OP-ZOOM

28

29

30

ANTWERP

31

32 33 DIEST

34 35 36 37 38 AACHEN

BRUSSELS

MAASTRICHT 39 40

LIEGE

HOLLAND

R.Rhine

R.Maas

BELGIUM

GERMANY

THE LOW COUNTRIES

DAY 21   HOEK VAN HOLLAND – BRIELLE
18.5 miles; very warm, clear; 18°C

I've never understood why people queue up for ages to disembark from a ferry. I mean, everyone doesn't stand in the aisle of a train with all their baggage for half an hour before it pulls into the station, stops and opens its doors. Some nervous people do get up well before their stop just in case they don't get out before the train shoots off to its next destination, but the ferry isn't going anywhere else, is it? Not for hours.

So everyone queued for half an hour or more, blocking all the corridors and staircases to create a major safety hazard in case of fire or flood, and ignored any announcements they could hear/understand – they were in at least four languages but you had to be listening quite hard to get the gist – and the motorists got muddled up with the non-motorists and the coach passengers didn't know which they were anyway. Meanwhile we waited for everyone to get off first then shouldered our packs and began a determined trudge along the cycle path beside the River Maas – and miles of oil and gas storage tanks – which eventually leads to Maassluis. We immediately encountered some generous Dutch people who stopped and asked if we needed help with directions, one on a racing bike who got out his iPad to show us how to avoid walking on the flyover and one on a moped who screeched to a halt next to us when he saw us scratching our heads at a crossroads wondering how to get on to a bridge. "Can I help you?" he asked (in English).

We had done the same trip a couple of years before but on the other side of the river when we had come in to Rotterdam and were travelling by bike to Delft so had to cross over to go north at Rozenburg, where a little ferry-boat goes to and from Maassluis every twenty minutes or so. Going south from Rozenburg looked difficult and built-up on the map, but was very pleasant in real life. However when we arrived at Brielle, the first town of any size, we were surprised to find it devoid of any guest-houses or hostels. We were tired by then, having been thrown off the boat at some ungodly hour, and had no desire to keep on walking hopefully for another ten miles, so reluctantly parted with €100 to stay in the only hotel in town and prayed that it would not be the same story everywhere in Holland. And Belgium, and Germany.... we were going to run out of money before we even got to Italy at this rate! However we did have a counterbalance to this overspending when we called in at a print-shop where the man in charge printed twenty copies of our leaflet describing the details of our sponsorship agreement and giving people the information about how to contribute. He was not apparently paying much attention to what he was photocopying but refused to accept any payment and wished us well on our walk as we left.

DAY 22   BRIELLE – GOEDEREEDE
17.7 miles; very warm and clear; 18°C

Another warm sunny day. On the way out of town I persuaded Angela to visit a cobbler who mended her boot for nothing, which was a great relief as it was too tight and was contributing to her blisters. He did a proper job with a special tool which resembled a medieval torture instrument. I could see Angela looked horrified at the time, but after this point her feet became increasingly healthy while my feet (and ankles and shins) were only just beginning to hurt. We went out on a cycle-path past Hellevoetsluis to the Haringvliet dam which connects the mainland to the island of Goeree-Flakkee. Down to our left as we approached the dam was a big field dotted with people, some doing a version of trotting which involved sitting on a tiny carriage being pulled along by a pony, while others were flying kites in the perfect late spring weather with a light breeze fluffing the seawater. We walked across the dam, which is two or three kilometres long, and is used as a means of regulating the height of the water in the Haringvliet, or Herring Fleet. This great expanse of water, now effectively a freshwater lake, was speckled with fishing boats and the sails of small yachts, while to our right was the North Sea. Looking down from the path, the water was only half as far down as it had been at the Humber Bridge, but it felt equally awe-inspiring to be on such a massive structure. Beneath our feet were the sluices which allow enough salt water in to prevent freezing of the lake, which is actually a part of the delta of the rivers Maas and Rhine, and enough fresh water out to prevent flooding. The idea of the Deltaplan, which was originally planned after the great North Sea Flood of 1953, was to shorten the coastline and create storm-surge barriers: it consists of a series of thirteen massive dams, some of which were modified to include sluice-gates. The Delta Works also comprise locks, dikes and levees and have been declared one of the Seven Wonders of the Modern World by the American Society of Civil Engineering. The Dutch, of course, have a long history of flooding which came to a head on the night of January 31st to February 1st 1953, when as much as 9% of the total Dutch farmland was flooded and some 2,500 people lost their lives, mostly in the Netherlands but up to 300 in East Anglia. Just as a catastrophic series of floods in 1421, 1530 and 1570 had initiated an earlier prevention programme of dike-building to keep the sea out, the Dutch unhesitatingly did something to try and ensure it could never happen again.

Arriving at the other side of the dam we were met by an extravagant system of roundabouts and traffic lights, with an industrial estate off to our left. We took a right turn to find ourselves going past a row of fish-canning factories (to satisfy the Dutch appetite for herring), and then a high dike flanked by sand-dunes. Setting our sights on the church tower at Goedereede we arrived at the little old fishing village by following the canal which runs through the middle (*Fig. 7). On the right-hand side are the cobbled village square, the row of artists' studios and galleries, the church and, in Kerkstraat, Harald's house. Harald and Willeke were waiting for us to arrive, eager for news, and proved to be welcoming and generous hosts, looking after us for three days as we had our first proper break, three weeks after setting off. Harald first moved to the village almost forty years ago after having been a pupil of Angela's father Oswald at the Art College in Wiesbaden, and since his arrival Goedereede has developed a reputation throughout Holland for his studio and gallery which is a centre for artists.

While we were at Goedereede we went one evening to the 'capital' of the island, Middelharnis, where Harald was due to put on a performance art exhibition which involved him creating a painting on stage to the accompaniment of a pianist and a drummer. With his long white hair flailing as he hurled paint at the canvas it was an arresting sight, and can surely never have been seen before in this small-town college. Another day we sat outside basking in the sunshine with the local cats beside the canal. Since it was still some weeks short of Easter the streets were empty of the tourists and art-lovers who flock here in the summer and at weekends to stroll about the village and admire the gallery offerings. On the Saturday afternoon a public singing workshop had been advertised to raise money for MSF. A select group gathered in a neighbour's house full of objets d'art and beautiful flowers and were surprised to find themselves learning to sing several songs in different languages in four-part harmony. The same evening Willeke had invited a few dozen friends and acquaintances to her significant birthday party at the studio and had asked us to bring a musical contribution, so we sang several songs we had been learning as we tramped the lonely roads and paths of England. Afterwards we met many interesting folk, who all spoke excellent English, including a woman from Surinam who had been sailing the world for seven years with her husband. On Sunday we had a lazy breakfast and a lazy stroll along the canal before a more sedate gathering in the afternoon of older acquaintances who were meeting at the studio for coffee and cakes. The Dutch are so civilised!

24th March 2012

Dear Friends,

After many days of bemoaning the absence of communication means we are now indulging in a feast of free computer use at the house of our friends Harald and Willeke in Goedereede on the Goeree

Island in Holland. We are here for the second day, another scorcher which would do any June day proud! Spring has leapt in with such unrelenting impatience that there are balmy nights and every kind of flower out in bloom already. I don't suppose I had the chance to tell you of the garlands of blossom, delicate white and pink, lacing the streets as we trundled into Newmarket? After the flat Fens and their peculiar kind of bleakness, which was saved by the nearby detail in hedgerow and soundscape, we arrived with unexpected suddenness in a landscape of rolling hills and soft spring green lushness dominated by everything to do with horses. They are such graceful creatures as they canter around huge paddocks full of seasonal surges, or follow us passers-by with ear-twitching attention full of a kind of intelligence that is at least capable of curiosity. We won't mention the vast estates of their owners, stretching over miles of guarded fenced land, stud farms worth billions, which rendered some of the walking experience (even just the discreet place in the bushes one needs every so often) rather a stand-offish experience!

We have met many delightful people who really wanted to talk to us, wanted to tell us what they had done in their time, who were moved to tears or exclamations of enthusiasm, who directed us, gave us good advice, even leapt into the hedge to hand us money, and then when they discovered they had none, sent the money later on the JustGiving site!

We were picked up by a wonderful couple one evening from the beautiful village of Dedham near to Constable's birthplace, who took us to their house in Colchester, fed us the most wonderful meal, sang with us, broadened our historical knowledge especially of Eastern Europe, offered us a comfortable room to sleep in, and then, after furnishing us with a nourishing pack-up, walked with us, again from Dedham, for the first few miles through Constable's paintings along the river Stour before turning round and leaving us to continue the rest of that day's journey by ourselves. This was our last day in England. We reached Harwich that night, having wandered along the river, which broadened into a most bird-rich estuary near Manningtree, through various marine nature reserves, to the sounds of waterfowl as well as woodpeckers, the plaintive little warble of robins as well as the croaking of crows and rooks, the squeaking of jackdaws, the screeching of the odd jay, and of course the inevitable trill of skylarks.

The previous day we counted the 200th lark since York at the very moment as Nick looked at his pedometer to find it registering exactly 300 miles! Well, I warned you we were closet geeks all along...

The ironic thing is that after the huge sense of elation at reaching the outskirts of Harwich it ended up being impossible to walk the last mile along the road, simply too dangerous! So we had to make a detour of about three or four extra miles to approach the harbour. There we entered into a world which had already begun to slip away from us: the cold clinical world of officialdom, laced with suspicion and mistrust, inhospitable and inflexible. We contemplated also the view which will meet any of the many visitors to our shores who choose to come into Harwich as they drive out of the port authority area along those streets leading to the beautiful and excitingly varied land that is England. What they will see is shabby industrial bleakness, grubby unkempt roads lined with the flotsam and jetsam that document our love for cheap excess to any needs. The ferry was fun though, and we had a good chance to behold the latest position in the dance performed in the clear night skies at the moment by Venus and Jupiter on the one side and Mars on the other. This visible performance has delighted us all along the way, ever since the first night in Bielby.

When we arrived in Holland we had to keep pinching ourselves that we really had walked here! Now we were walking again through a straightened landscape made by man, with huge fields, orderly arrangements of trees framing the horizons, and occasionally the chuckle's worth of a delightful windmill appearing in the picture. The larks have been completely supplanted by chiffchaffs, whose assertive tones punctuate the soundscape much more rhythmically.

We have already stayed in Brielle before arriving here in Goedereede, and were surprised by the beauty of an historic Dutch town, with gables of every imaginable shape and wonderful shopping opportunities (if that's your bag), and even a proper cobbler, who finally did some miracle thing to my walking boots "and for you it's from the house!" – so that they at last don't hurt me any more. And as we walk through Holland at this late end of March we do already have to watch out that we don't burn in the sun!

I will now have to go and get ready for another workshop, after this morning I gave an interview on the local radio about the walk and the workshop, so I will sign off, again thanking you for all your good wishes and lovely, often funny, replies, and ask you kindly to forgive the lack of individual answers. It can only happen when the opportunity arises technology-wise. But you are all in our thoughts, and it is so lovely to know that you are travelling with us.

Nick and Angela xx

DAY 26   GOUDEREEDE – OUDE TONGE
26 km; even warmer; 19°C

We set off with many warm wishes from Harald and Willeke in our thoughts having left them with hugs for their gracious hospitality. I found that the battery on the pedometer had gone flat, which was annoying, as it meant resetting it at zero. Funnily enough it had stopped at 374.7 miles, which is within a whisker of 600 kilometres. I reset it to calculate the distance in kilometres from then on, and we went off through the village to find the Deltapad, a long-distance footpath which goes across the Maas/Rhine delta towards Antwerp. We had been advised that it went through an area called the Slikken, which until 1971 was a large mudflat and salt marsh influenced by the tides. After the building of the dams, it became dry land populated by scrub, bushes and small trees, but the path took us through a kind of primeval swamp. We had to take our boots off and wade in the water, which soon became knee deep for about two kilometres. It seems that at high tide – or perhaps at exceptional spring tides – the water is pushed up above ground level. In any case it wasn't rainwater as it hadn't rained for weeks. A unique biosphere is created: the pools contained quantities of frog-spawn, and who knows what was lurking in the mud underfoot, but we pressed on, thinking "this must surely end just around the corner". We had been warned not to wander into the undergrowth beside the path for fear of catching Lyme disease from ticks, but no-one had mentioned the fact that we would have to negotiate this replica of the Florida Everglades!

After emerging from the swamp with freezing fizzing feet we walked beside reclaimed land next to herds of semi-wild Fjord horses, deer and oxen which have been introduced over the last 30 years to graze upon the recently sown grasses. We finally came upon a sea-dyke we could walk upon with our faces to a stiff breeze, past whirring wind turbines, looking out over the inland sea on our right. We passed the bridge over to the next island and found our way to Oude Tonge, a fishing village, where we looked for a place to stay and discovered a little hotel in the main square.

There we stopped for the night, after having a beer at The Goat, where various members of the landlord's family and friends engaged us in conversation and gave us useful tips about travelling in southern Holland while a 70-year-old African parrot cackled hilariously in the background.

DAY 27   OUDE TONGE – BERGEN-OP-ZOOM
27 km; warm, less wind; 19°C

The next morning we were offered a lift back to the bridge – which we had already walked past the day before – by the hotel owners' daughter, who was looking after the place while they were away on holiday. She had recently come back from spending a year in the Antipodes so was well versed in the art of backpacking, and gave us a potted history of the local area before dropping us off at the bridge, which was actually two separate bridges with a total length of about two miles. On the other side we found ourselves going for a long way past a beautiful panorama of lakes and wooded islands, punctuated by sluices and the gigantic locks through which huge freighters pass on their way out of the Rhine Delta to the Atlantic or North Seas. Nature reserves abounded, full of wildfowl, including one flock of migrating geese, hundreds strong, which settled just across the road from our picnic spot.

The afternoon was much less interesting, and after tramping another ten or twelve miles to what we thought was the outskirts of Bergen we found we were still some miles short. Having taken an early lunch-break we were beginning to flag when we spotted a bench next to a lone house beside the busy main road we were forced to walk alongside. Angela was exhausted and was bending over to ease her back when the woman of the house spotted us out of her kitchen window and came bustling over. I thought she was going to tell us to make ourselves scarce, but she asked with concern whether we were OK, and said: "Yes, please do sit on the bench. That's what it's there for! Do you need some water? Here, I'll fill your bottles. Would you like an apple?" It was the most delicious and restorative gift and the gesture of an angel!

Finally we made it along a ring-road past factories and warehouses to the middle of Bergen-op-Zoom, which has a grand old centre full of fashionable shops, and found a cheap B&B run by a former art student who generously left us to help ourselves to whatever we could find in the kitchen and gave us a good breakfast in the morning along with home-made bread and little pots of jam to take with us.

DAY 28   BERGEN-OP-ZOOM –
OSSENDRECHT
16 km; still warm and clear; 19°C

To make up for the massive effort of the day before, which had furthermore been entirely on tarmac or concrete, today would be a jaunty stroll of about ten miles to the abbey of Ossendrecht, where we had booked a room. The path led us a merry dance alongside a major road then into a beautiful forest full of sun and shade, over some fields and through more forest in a sandy landscape on the edge of what is known as the Brabantse Wal, a Dutch version of the Wolds. Local historians and geologists are very proud of this unique landscape of hills and dunes which scarcely rises above 100 metres, but in relative terms that is high in western Holland! The Abbey, when we finally located it after a prolonged battle with our meagre map, while still operating in part as a working seminary, had also been tastefully done up as a visitors' centre, available for conferences, weddings, hiking groups, etc. We had a basic room at a reasonable rate but the place was rather empty apart from a small group of conference-goers. It was strange to think that the following day we would already be in another country. We were on the verge of speeding through Holland in only five days of actual walking!

DAY 29   OSSENDRECHT – KALMTHOUT
19 km; cooler, sunny intervals; 15°C

"The most lonely places are the most lovely."

The dunes we had walked upon as far as Ossendrecht gradually turned into the Kalmthoutse Heide, which is a large stretch of heathland, an unusual mixture of deciduous and pine trees scattered among sand dunes scoured by the wind and peat bogs interspersed with small black pools (*Fig. 8). In places the previous summer's drought had obviously caused fires to break out and devastate large expanses of moorland scrub and dry grass, and we saw few people across the empty heath, only a couple of runners and a serious walker with poles – going twice as fast as us, possibly in training for the Olympics in June. At the far side we came to a wood, in the midst of which was a small group of local hikers looking lost Somewhere around here was the Belgian border, but there was no way of knowing exactly where as there were no signposts, let alone a sentry-box or customs post Making our way through the woods to Kalmthout we were early – it was only about 4 o'clock – and we'd got out of the habit of being indoors during daylight hours, so we sat outside a roadside café and had coffee and cake and stared at the cars, then explored the town of Kalmthout which looked pretty big on the map but was actually just several villages strung together along the road, so it had no real centre but was very long from one end to the other. There didn't seem to be anywhere to eat other than a very pretentious and rather expensive Italian *ristorante*. We had booked ourselves into a guest house on the edge of town at the end of a country lane, an English-style villa which had been built a hundred years ago by a Swiss man who had somehow been an officer in the Dutch colonial army in Indonesia and subsequently become a follower of Annie Besant, Rudolf Steiner and the mysterious Madame Blavatsky. The present owners were more interested in Steiner's later indications on anthroposophy and biodynamic gardening rather than his earlier studies on theosophy, but seemed rather disillusioned with the current state of Europe as a whole and were talking about moving – perhaps they would end up in South Africa, or maybe the destiny of the house's owners would go full circle and they would move to Indonesia!

DAY 30   KALMTHOUT – ZOERSEL
32 km; much colder, cloudy; 9°C

"Everything we meet is equally important or unimportant."

We hit the road early with the prospect of a long day's walk ahead of us. We had rather a shoddy map we had picked up from a Tourist Information Office which had a lot of cycle-tracks and footpaths on it, including the GR5 which is a section of the international E8 leading east via Luxembourg. We didn't want to go through Luxembourg but rather along the northern edge of Flanders to Aachen, which sits at the meeting-point of Belgium, Holland and Germany. The problem with our map was the place-names. We soon realised that the names on the map didn't correspond – or at least not in the way we are used to – to the names on the ground. You would get a small blot on the map called something, say Noordwijk, with a few villages dotted around it, so you'd imagine it would be about the size of a small market town and would have a centre with a church and a square and some shops and a garage and a café or two: a nucleus. Then you'd get within about five kilometres and find a sign next to the road welcoming you to Noordwijk. "Funny!" you'd think. "I can't even see the church spire yet." Then you'd go through a village which might or might not have a sign up with a different name, and finally half an hour later arrive at the church and find it's on a long straight stretch of road with houses on both sides interspersed with the odd shop or garden centre or hairdresser's salon quite randomly, and this arrangement might be scattered along the road for a couple of miles for no apparent reason. The outskirts of some of these places were disfigured by American-style strings of diners and warehouse-style supermarkets and car salesrooms, which seemed somehow exaggerated here when we had just been out in open country and forest for most of the past couple of days. At least it had the advantage of discouraging us from hanging about, as we might have been tempted to do in a quaint cosy little town square, and we tended to press on through these Flemish strip-towns. The other thing we noticed about this particular part of Belgium was the number of houses, both new and old, which were detached, and often surrounded by a large high hedge and usually a ditch, like a miniature moat. There were many new-build ecohouses too, with solar panels and labour-saving devices like robot lawnmowers but virtually no windows. Many of the people we met on the road looked suspiciously at us and scowled a greeting if they had to reply to one, although sometimes their faces would light up at the surprise of being greeted at all.

We walked a long way on roads and concrete cycle-tracks, then through some woods full of people randomly sawing tree-trunks, trudging quickly to keep warm as the temperature had suddenly dropped dramatically and it felt almost wintry again. We had found a Youth Hostel marked on our map, and finally arrived there at about 6 o'clock after ringing in the morning to be told that it was a very long way and they were not sure we would make it that day. We were welcomed by a couple of cheerful women who were greatly surprised that we had walked so far: they showed us to a dormitory which we would have to ourselves but told us that we'd missed supper, although they then found some bits and pieces we could finish off and all was well.

DAY 31   ZOERSEL – OEVEN
25 km; cool, cloudy, occasional drizzle; 11°C

Today was the worst day so far. We had to traverse many miles of boring flat land, much of it alongside main roads with no footpath or with a cycle-path rather than a pavement which meant that we constantly had to make way for bad-tempered Lycra-clad demons speeding along in training for the next Tour. The Belgians are big on cycling, unsurprisingly as the land is so flat, but not on walking. It seemed unheard of, the idea of walking any distance when you could be on a bike! The weather was grim and the sky like an upturned pewter bowl above the brown fields. There were some patches of woodland but they were all rather manicured and full of signposts for cycle routes.

We had arranged to stay with Tanja, a young woman who was a member of Hospitality Club and lived on the outskirts of Westerlo, but the further we went the more painful my left shin became, starting as a dull bruise and turning into a sharp stabbing pain at every step. I tried putting my weight on the outside of my foot, then the inside; the toe, then the heel; all to no avail. By the time we got to the edge of Westerlo my leg was screaming to STOP WALKING!

Tanja rented an old farmhouse with her boyfriend and they made us most welcome although it was the first time they had hosted anyone and they were a bit unsure how to proceed. I went to bed with a sense of dread thinking that my leg might be worse in the morning and I may not be able to carry on.

DAY 32   OEVEN – WESTERLO
4 km; sunny intervals; 13°C

My leg was slightly better, so we decided to go as far as we could. We left the house with Ed and Tanja and their dog to walk down to the abbey at Tongerlo, which is one of many in this part of Belgium which have been standing since medieval times and supplying the population with their beer. Ed told us that most of these monkish breweries have been taken over by multinational companies in recent years, and in many cases the beer is no longer brewed on site, although you would not guess it by looking at the bottles. I hobbled along for another kilometre or so before deciding it was getting worse again and we would have to stay another night here, this time at the Youth Hostel, to ponder the future. I became very distraught at the idea of possibly having to give up, and we turned over all sorts of ideas before giving up speculation and going out for a meal in a *brasserie* which looked very ordinary from the outside but was furnished with an extraordinary collection of Art Nouveau and Art Deco mirrors and carvings and stained glass windows.

DAY 33   WESTERLO – DIEST
26 km; mostly sunny; 14°C

Since the leg was no better in the morning we decided to look for a hospital, so we asked at the Tourist Information Office. "Oh, no, there's no hospital here." "Medical centre? Clinic?" "No. I'm sorry. But there is a doctor's surgery just round the corner. He's the football team doctor, and it's a big team which plays in the Premier League and has foreign players so I think he speaks good English." That sounded good. I went and made an appointment in an hour or so, and returned to see a young woman who was a physiotherapist specialising in sports injuries. After I had explained the circumstances she told me I had an inflammation of the muscle: "Take this ointment twice a day, these pills three times, and rest for two or three days, and you should be able to continue your walk."

We had arranged several days earlier to stay with a Servas family in Diest, so in order to keep our side of the bargain we decided that Angela would walk there while I took a bus and a train. We reasoned that as long as at least one of us kept up a continuous trail to Rome we would have stuck to our intention, and I could always make up the difference by walking around Rome when we got there (which I did!). When we met up in Diest Angela told me she had enjoyed walking alone through forest, where she had spotted jays, woodpeckers, cranes and tree-creepers. That evening Johan – a social worker – and his wife Katja fed us well and their son Xavier entertained us with an impromptu concert of music on various forms of piano-accordion. He was an interesting young man who had been diagnosed with fairly severe autism but managed to drive himself to work as a gardener for the council, which he loved. They then took us to the Begijnhof (*Fig. 9), which throughout the Middle Ages served as a refuge for wives whose menfolk had been called up as soldiers or were itinerant workers. The women lived together in a walled community as temporary nuns, within the city but apart from it.

4th April 2012

Dear friends,

All of a sudden it feels like a long time since I wrote to you with an update on our travels, so much so that yesterday someone sent me an email saying "You've gone quiet!"

In order to let you catch up I need to give you brush strokes of Holland (or more correctly: The Netherlands) and Belgium.

When we left our dear friends Harald and Willeke, we had partied with them, we had entertained their visitors with our growing little repertoire, and we had been granted a very welcome break from the daily miles, so much so that we had to work at it rather to get back in the swing again!

Then we traversed the island coast lines along the 'Delta Pad' as much as we could manage to stick to it. At one point we followed the little wayside symbol for it and ended up wading through a wetland wilderness up to our calves in moorland brown water, often on mossy ground, but often feeling with our toes through twigs and branches, for about two kilometres. We felt like real jungle explorers!

It was really striking that this kind of real wilderness was there in Holland of all places, a country so marked by a kind of ruthlessness of orderly structure, where most of the land has been sculpted and used to purpose by mankind, and where so much of it reminds one of a giant Lego set. And yet there is an openness which sees no need for net curtains; a playfulness and a mostly quite tasteful charm: people are friendly and greet you, they stop in their tracks on their way to work just to find out whether you are lost and whether they can help you find your way. However, you can see there is no hesitation to make the environment conform to human purpose; even the trees are forced into pollarded contortions and militaristic rows.

Again we walked along ridges with water worlds on one side and flat drained agricultural business space on the other. Momentarily I had visions of walking along the central bridge of a brain with the two halves, one very rational and one wild and lateral and unpredictable and full of wildlife. I can hear you thinking that Angela has too much time on her hands!

Well, we entered Belgium by the back door, so to speak, as we opted to walk through a wonderful nature reserve of different kinds of woodland, boggy marshes and heath land, where again we enjoyed the unfolding of spring with the business of all the little creatures nest-building, and filling the air with such an incredible multitude of calls. I haven't been drawn into any more counting games, but had I done I imagine the woodpeckers would give the skylarks a run for their money. We've heard veritable percussion performances. So, we are in Belgium, and what an enigma this place is! Our first impression was of Kalmthout, where it struck us that every house was different, there seemed a complete absence of homogeneity, everyone seemed able to create their own castle, and indeed a fortress-like quality seemed the only thing most of them had in common. The people look different to those in Holland, and often we were the ones to greet first, but then when a smile did meet us it was like the sun breaking out from behind a cloud!

The orderliness of the Dutch landscape had given way to a much more random view altogether, less structured, less organised, with a closer intertwining between wooded nature and domesticated life. The impression of place can change from moment to moment, you can get taken by surprise as to where you are, town or country.

I still want to ponder this country for a long time, but I should tell you of our disastrous news too. Well, I hope you will still think of our trip as a complete trip to Rome, even though Nick has been stricken by an inflammation of the shin muscle and had to go and see a doctor who told him to rest his leg for 2-3 days. The way we are working it at the moment is that I walk the distance, Nick travels to the same destination by public transport and we meet up and find the place we are staying.

We have been the guests of some absolutely delightful people. Tanja and Ed in Oevel were most welcoming: both in their early 30s; she a primary teacher in a 'free school', he a factory worker for Estee Lauder; both active football players and good fun. Last night we stayed with Johan and Katja, closer to our age, whose son Xavier gave us an impromptu concert on accordion, melodeon and concertina. Johan and Katja took us round the old city of Diest, an absolute jewel of a place with a most picturesque historic town centre. They both praised how much care the English take of their heritage and bemoaned the fact that in Belgium the intention to renovate and restore is hardly ever followed through with the deed, mostly due to lack of money.

Dear All of you, I have to find an end. You have probably long since stopped reading, I am welling over with impressions and thoughts. I am over the initial howling when it became apparent that Nick had to stop at least for the time being, and we will arrange ourselves according to need. His health is more important, and I just hope you will accept the task as done if one of us keeps the thread going?

Averil has kindly agreed to forward these missives to you as the tablet just will not do group emails. Thank you for continued good wishes and your mails. It is a great comfort to receive them.

Next time will be sooner and shorter, promise!

Much love from us both

Angela and Nick xx

DAY 34 DIEST – STEVOORT
22.5 km; mostly sunny; 15°C

Angela and I parted company on the outskirts of Diest She went off towards Hasselt and walked through a pleasant landscape on various paths signposted as *fietspad*, although they rarely strayed far from a road, while I phoned around for a B&B in that direction. I found one in a village south of Hasselt, and made my way there by bus, meeting Angela in the *brasserie*, which had a pool table and a dart board and a couple of old soaks at the bar. At one point a heavily-tattooed character came in and started showing people pictures on his mobile phone – "Here mate, want to see some dirty pictures?" Down the street was an attractive-looking restaurant, but it was closed for a fortnight for a holiday break, so we checked in to the B&B and asked where we could eat, as we were both getting hungry. The owner was an interesting Dutch woman who was in the process of converting a barn into an art gallery full of pictures and wooden sculptures and *objets trouvés*. She had previously been the curator of a big art museum in the Netherlands so she knew her onions, but had recently lost the roof of the barn in a gale, so was grateful for a bit of extra cash from doing B&B. She told us we would have to go to Hasselt to eat, but there were plenty of buses, and they were free. It seems that a few years ago the residents of the city elected a socialist mayor who was full of good ideas, including having a free bus service to and from all the surrounding villages. It took about half an hour to get there, by which time we were famished and stumbled into the first eating-place we saw, which turned out to be a former warehouse called The Palace, which was filled with long curved staircases, chandeliers and huge mirrors. The waiters, who had obviously been chosen for their boyish good looks, scurried about from floor to floor looking purposeful and elegant, and they served small portions of fancy food so we had the cheapest, most filling dish they could recommend and wolfed it down surrounded by people who had dressed to the nines to go out to this place for a special occasion. It reminded us of a sign we had seen outside Westerlo saying: "Wilkom te Crass Vegas!" We got the bus back, but this time it took about an hour as it went a long way round to drop people off near their houses, like a taxi service really.

DAY 35   STEVOORT – MAAS MECHELEN
41 km; cloudy, colder; 10°C

The longest day so far, for Angela at least We had arranged to be able to stay with a Hospitality Club member called Gerda, who lived off our track somewhat but sounded friendly on her profile and in the email she had sent us, saying that if we made our way to Maasmechelen she could pick us up. So we decided that Angela would walk and I would once again travel by bus as far as Lanaken, where we would meet up at the end of the afternoon. Luckily we both had mobile phones with us, which were old and chunky but did the job, albeit too expensively to use them often. I managed to negotiate my way via Hasselt without too many problems and arrived there at about 1 o'clock. After hobbling around the town, which was very uninspiring, a couple of times and having a sandwich from a shop which I ate in the rain outside a little shopping mall, I texted Angela who said it was further than she had thought, she was only about halfway there and wouldn't arrive until about five o'clock, so I went for another slow walk up and down the main street then retreated into a homely *brasserie* which sold good coffee and good beer and tried to read a Flemish newspaper for a couple of hours. I could get the gist of the headline stories and the sports scores – although it mostly seemed to be about minority sports like cycling and handball and water polo – but the editorials and political comment were beyond my ken. I did find out that a lad from Westerlo had won the Tour de Flandres, as they quaintly called it in French, which Tanja and Ed would be pleased about.

When Angela finally turned up she told me she had completed an epic day's march of about forty kilometres, mostly along the canal past the industrial heartland of Genk, flat but hard going. She was exhausted, and I determined to get back to full health as quickly as possible so that we could get back to walking together. We met up with Gerda who took us to her house on the bank of the River Maas (again!), from which you could look over into another part of the Netherlands which hangs down like a sock as far as Maastricht. The house had been renovated to make it all one big room with curtains and staircases and bookshelves dividing it into separate areas for cooking, eating, sleeping and sitting, all around a central wood-burning stove. She invited us to stay for another night when she saw how tired Angela was and heard about the state of my leg, and we accepted since we weren't in any hurry and it was such a comfortable place to stop and relax. On top of that, it was raining outside, cold and windy.

DAY 36   MAAS MECHELEN
0 km; cold and wet; 6°C

In the evening, after a lazy day pottering about, washing and drying clothes and cooking, we were joined by Gerda's friend and neighbour Luciano, whose parents had moved to Belgium from Italy after the war to work in the coal-mines nearby. He told us all about the history of mining in the area, especially the nature of the model housing which was built for the miners. Luciano was an interesting character, a large man of about fifty with large features and large hair tumbling down in curls to his shoulders. He had just flown back from China where he had been to a carpet exhibition and sales fair, and was suffering from jet-lag so needed to be up talking and drinking wine. This idea of staying with random strangers is growing on us.

DAY 37 MAAS MECHELEN – VALKENBURG
30 km; cool, cloudy, sunny intervals; 12°C

We left Gerda's homely house together, with the idea that I could walk as far as felt comfortable, along the riverbank. We had found out that, unusually, both banks of the river belong to Holland. Allegedly the Dutch offered one bank to the Belgians, who declined as they didn't want to be bothered with the maintenance. Consequently we followed a path on the Belgian side which wandered in and out of Holland. After crossing on a bridge we avoided Maastricht and cut across country, stopping quite often for cups of tea and snacks, including an icecream at a dairy which made their own in an old farmhouse with a courtyard, where one corner was taken up by an aviary full of parrots and canaries. When we got to Valkenburg we discovered it to be a pretty town which has been a tourist destination for Dutch people for generations. Nestling on the edge of the highest range of hills in the Netherlands, its castle perches like a falcon on a steep rocky outcrop above the walled town, but the walls were bursting at the seams with the number of bars, restaurants, hotels, clubs and casinos, and the streets were heaving with people later in the evening, mainly drunken visitors. We found a hotel with a room where we were offered a cheap rate, although we were finding that prices in Holland were generally pretty expensive.

DAY 38   VALKENBURG – AACHEN (25 km.)
Cold, occasional showers. 8°C

My leg had begun to hurt again towards the end of the previous day, and I was beginning to worry whether I was going to be able to carry on. I decided to get a bus to Aachen, rest up for another couple of days and rub a lot of ointment in, while Angela would walk and meet up with my brother Anch on the way. Anch has been called that in our family since he was a toddler, and that's his *nom de plume* as sub-editor of a well-known weekly magazine. He often enjoys cycling holidays on the continent, so a weekend walking in Belgium was no big deal for him. I arrived in Aachen first and after a little gentle exploring settled down in a bar near the Dom to await their arrival and sample the local brew. A friend of ours in York had contacted us on our way to give us an introduction to Iain, an Englishman living there, and through more recent contact by email he had offered us a place to stay for a night or two in his flat, so there was quite a gathering when he turned up at the bar shortly after Angela and Anch, who were thirsty and needed to try the local beer. Angela had much to tell about her walk through beautiful countryside along the riverbank avoiding the showers; climbing a steep path to a forest; and the difficulty of keeping in touch with Anch by phone because they were both so close to the convergence of the borders of Holland, Belgium and Germany that the phone servers kept on changing. They told us how they had eventually met each other at a strange café called the Black Madonna full of religious kitsch next to a 'Jesus and Mary' museum. Of course we were also obliged to have a beer with Iain and his German girlfriend Daniela, then we had to walk across town to the flat…

It was a beautiful flat on the fifth floor with a fantastic view over the city and surrounding countryside, and they left us to it, going off to Daniela's house in a village nearby, saying we could use the flat for as long as we liked. Iain is a quiet self-possessed man who gives off an air of calm and lack of haste, and his flat is representative of his character: neat and tidy without being obsessive, full of interesting books and little bits and pieces without being over-stuffed, the kitchen small but efficient with a minimum of fresh food but all good quality, no waste.

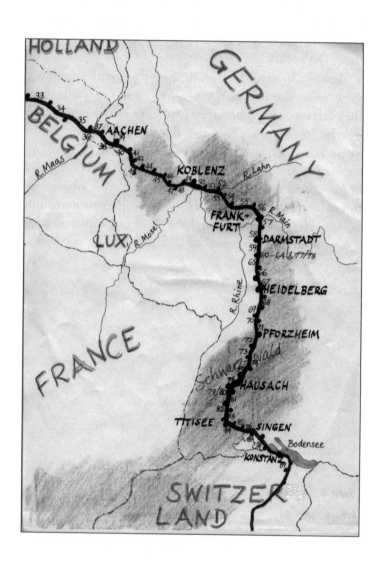

UP AND DOWN IN GERMANY

DAY 39   AACHEN (AIX-LA-CHAPELLE)
0 km; cold wind, sunny spells; 10°C

Today was Easter Sunday, which seemed an entirely
appropriate day to be in Aachen. We arranged to meet
up with the others at the famous Dom (Cathedral) –
Anch was staying at a hotel round the corner from us
with his bike, which he had brought on the train from
London – but when we arrived first we could hear
sweet music leaking out through the massive West
Door, which was firmly closed. Angela wanted to go in
for the next service, but was disappointed to find that
the choir and orchestra had packed up and gone home.
Meanwhile Anch and I went to look round the Treasury,
which contains many ornate baubles from the 11th to the
16th centuries. Even if one is not a fan of the exhibition
of colonial plunder by the Catholic Church there is a
certain fascination in seeing how power was solidified in
the Holy Roman Empire by ostentatious wealth from its
very beginnings. Charlemagne, King of the Franks, who
founded this cathedral and created a court at Aachen
which attracted artists and scholars from as far afield as
Rome, Byzantium and Northumbria, was crowned Holy
Roman Emperor – or governor of Western Christendom
in temporal matters – by the Pope on Christmas Day
800 AD in St Peter's Cathedral, Rome. When he
returned to Aachen he had a throne brought to set upon
the balcony overlooking the whole interior of the Dom
and facing the altar. Unfortunately on Easter Sunday

2012 the Throne Room was locked. We had to go to the reception desk at the information office dealing with ticket sales for the Treasury. "Look," said Angela, who was thoroughly fed up and got to the desk first: "We've walked almost a thousand kilometres to see this throne, we're leaving early in the morning and we need to see it now!" A young guide rather sheepishly unlocked the door for us and led us up the ancient stone staircase to see the throne at close quarters. What is striking is how primitive it is. The Emperor would have been sitting up there wearing his golden crown, looking down with pride at the magnificent altar and his courtiers in their finery, but his throne was not finely carved and embellished with symbols of reverence or grandeur. It was made up of several slabs of roughly hewn marble from Rome and Byzantium, the armrests polished by the hands of many emperors and scratched by their rings or armour-clad wrists. It would have already seemed ancient and this in itself would no doubt have symbolised the history and greatness of centuries of Empire which was now being taken over by a new dynasty: quite a statement!

That evening Iain and Daniela came back to the flat with us. Before they left they agreed to meet us in the morning in Daniela's village, when we could give Iain back his key. "You must go and look at St Joseph's Church on the way out of town", said Iain. "It's on the main road leading east, so it's on your way," and off they went. Ten minutes later Angela's nephew Silvano phoned. He is not the most communicative lad and had never rung her before in all his 19 years, so it was a surprise. He went straight to the point: "You're in Aachen, right? Have you ever heard of St Joseph's Church? I'm coming up there in the morning so I'll see you there at 10 o'clock, OK?"

DAY 40   AACHEN – ZWEIFALL
22 km; drizzle, grey; 10°C

We set off to walk from the beginning of the alphabet
to the end, full of curiosity. We knew that Silvano was
doing some research into columbaria for his college
course in joinery. A columbarium is a building with
tiers of niches for holding funerary urns, and when
we arrived at St Joseph's we discovered that that was
exactly what it was. Within the original church building
a miniature town had apparently been created, with
streets and blocks of flats, which on closer inspection
were towers of niches full of urns. Through the middle
runs a stream, and the modern stained glass windows
have a watery theme. The columns of hewn granite and
their simple design had caught Silvano's imagination
and gave him ideas of how he would create his own
version in wood. It seemed a rather morbid subject for a
teenager to choose, but it had come up since the mother
of a friend of his had committed suicide, perhaps as a
process of redemption. It was a pleasure to see him and
his girlfriend: we looked around the church carefully
then went for a drink and a chat before they joined us to
walk out of town through a grey drizzle.

Leaving them and Aachen behind at the city limits
we strode off to meet Iain and Daniela, who also walked
a few kilometres with us, far enough to give us directions
of how best to continue. We had bought a local map of
the northern section of the Nationalpark Eifel, which
covers the route from Aachen to Bad Munster Eifel, but
soon got lost and had to ask the way from various people
out walking their dogs or Bank Holiday hiking. After
so many days of rest in the last week or so it felt good
to be back on the road again – the medicine was finally
working and I was no longer troubled by the shin pain,

especially after doing some ankle exercises first thing in the morning, which became an essential part of my routine to prepare for each day's walk/work.

We had to get to a place called Vossenack, somewhat less than halfway to Abenden where Harald and Willeke had invited us to stay at their German house. This whole section of the route from Aachen to Koblenz was off any long-distance paths so we had to make up our own itinerary. In addition it is a little-populated region of forest and moorland, so difficult to find anywhere to stay the night. We had trawled through our various hospitality sites in Maasmechelen and found one host from Couchsurfing, so we'd been in touch and arranged a date when we would arrive. As it happened we only got as far as Zweifall, a logging town surrounded by beech and pine forest. We had an argument just above Zweifall as to whether we had to walk along the road, which was busy and winding, making it difficult to see traffic coming, and had no footpath alongside it, or whether we could cut across the heather on a footpath which seemed to peter out at the top of a steep hill. There were times – not many, but there were some – when we fell out at such moments, especially when they came at the end of the day and we were both tired, and this was one of them. On this occasion we tried to follow the little footpath and it did actually continue as a sheep-track all the way down the steep incline to the town, which was actually not much more than a few large timber-yards clustered around a bridge with a couple of streets' worth of houses and a small church. But it did have a café! We sat down for a coffee, made up, and phoned Janis, who was the lad of 19 who had posted something on Couchsurfing to offer a spare bed at his house. Actually it turned out to be his mum's house, but she had been happy to let him advertise the space for weary travellers. We were their first guests, in a new house which Connie (the mum) had designed herself, one of a group of detached houses scattered over the hillside outside town with a fantastic view across the hills and forests to the east They came and picked us up from Zweifall with a promise to take us back there in the morning, and introduced us to the rest of the family – Connie's younger son (16), and a boy of seven whom she has fostered after he had had a very difficult start to life. He seemed very chatty and well integrated but we were struck by her bravery and commitment in taking on such a responsibility. What a boost it gave us every time we met people who were **positive**, whether in wishing us well or in their own – often troubled – lives!

DAY 41   ZWEIFALL – ABENDEN
27 km; brighter, chill wind; 11°C

We started in the morning where we had left off, outside Zweifall, to go back through the alphabet almost to the beginning again, and walked through an empty silent forest to a point where we could take a small path off to the side and cut a corner. It soon stopped being a path and became a brook, which tumbled down the steep hillside over difficult terrain. At the bottom we had no idea which way to turn, and must have made the wrong choice as we got hopelessly lost wandering around a part of the forest dotted with signposts pointing to a 'historic walk around the battlefield'. We found out that this particular corner of the forest was the site of the Battle of Hürtgen Forest, the longest battle ever fought by US troops. It lasted from September 1944 to February 1945, resulting in a defensive victory for the German army and killing or incapacitating over

60,000 soldiers. The centre of the fighting was between Vossenack and Schmidt, which we were heading for. When we finally stumbled out onto a main road we found we were not at all where we had expected to be and had to walk seven or eight kilometres along the side of the road to Schmidt, but at least we hadn't stepped on a mine. We phoned Harald to let him know we were still some way off – were they at Abenden? Yes, they were, but were going back to Holland that evening. Yes, of course we could still stay the night. We wouldn't have to pick up the key from the neighbours, he'd come and pick us up. Since we had already walked 27 kilometres that sounded like a good plan, although we had to think about it for a while. Would we be cutting miles off the distance to Rome? In the end we decided that a) we must have added several kilometres to the direct route between Vossenack and Schmidt; and b) we could start the next leg from Nideggen (further north) which would add a few kilometres as well. We spent a few hours with Harald and Willeke at their house, where they spend a lot of time, before they had to set off, and then decided to stay the following day and meet Fynn, who would be coming to the area from York to visit his mum.

DAY 42   ABENDEN
0 km; cool, showery; 11°C

We spent a lot of time looking for a WiFi spot where we could hook up our tablet and send emails or look at hospitality sites to plan our next few stays with a decent amount of notice. In Abenden village all the pubs, hotels and cafes were either closed or had no connection. In the end someone said: "You could try the architects' office up by the old watermill," so we went and knocked on their door and were greeted most amiably by all the staff. Once they had heard our story they set us up with one of their computers, gave us a cup of coffee and wanted to know all about us then left us to it. It felt like a fair exchange – we were able to find what we needed and we gave them a surprise to brighten up their office day.

In the evening we were joined by Fynn, who brought a copy of his latest book of poetry and ate with us. We talked until late, as is often the case when Fynn comes to visit. As well as being a eurythmist who works with children and also with adults who have special needs, he helps his wife run a vegetarian restaurant in York and is a master of words who writes poems in German and English. We swapped travellers' tales – he told of times he had cycled to Athens and studied in Romania – and agreed to meet the next morning.

DAY 43 ABENDEN – KOMMERN
22 km; cloudy, some drizzle; 11°C

Fynn turned up (an hour later than expected as he was still running on British time) and took us to meet his mum. She was living with his sister and brother-in-law, who run a motorbike accessory shop and diner near Monschau. We had breakfast and talked of angels with this fragile and beautiful lady to the strains of Country & Western music as a succession of burly bikers came and went then Fynn gave us a lift to Nideggen and we walked across open country to Kommern. At one point near Vlatten the road – a straight single-track paved way flanked by chalky fields of beans and linseed and wind turbines – went over a rise (*Fig. 10) from which we could see a long way in all directions, with the Rhine valley in the distance on our left, and the great expanse of sky was full of rainclouds rushing to and fro in the winds. Down the hill to our left a rainbow emerged, and straight ahead large black clouds were raining heavily upon the next villages on our path, with a single sunbeam lighting up one church spire. Remarkably, the storm moved off before we arrived, and we went on through a small village where we found a massive Baroque *schloss* surrounded by a moat on which sailed a majestic swan. We got to Kommern miraculously dry to meet Angelika, whom we had met before in England at a summer camp. She had decided to support us practically by walking with us and paying for us to stay a couple of nights on our way, so came with her husband Uwe and met us at an old coaching inn in the main street of the town, which is full of ancient half-timbered houses. After booking in we wandered along the cobbled street looking for a non-smoking restaurant – still a problem for some in Germany – and found a good Turkish pizzeria.

DAY 44   KOMMERN – BAD MUNSTER EIFEL
19 km; warmer, sunny intervals; 12°C

We left Kommern for a short and interesting day's walk. Not far outside town we followed a footpath past an ancient tree which was billed as the Thousand Year Oak. The man who lived next to it said: "Actually it's only 900 years old." So it had only been there since about 1100 then, round about the time that the Teutonic Knights were going on the First Crusade. The four of us just managed to hold hands around its massive trunk. Further on as the forest grew denser we went past a Roman irrigation project, which had involved building an aqueduct and a series of small canals along the hillside. Near Wachendorf, on the other side of the *autobahn*, we diverted from the road to visit the Bruder Klaus Kapelle, as recommended by Fynn. This extraordinary building (*Fig. 11), less than ten years old and standing in a cornfield a good walk away from the small village, is dedicated to a medieval mystic from Switzerland who was renowned far and wide for his ability to converse with wild animals. It was the brainchild of a local farmer who decided, with a Swiss architect, to build this memorial to give thanks for a life graced with good and fruitful work. Together they erected five walls of uneven length out of bricks which they made of straw mixed with cement and laid around a scaffold of angled pine logs to a height of about fifty feet. The logs were then burnt away to leave a structure which looks roughly cuboid from the outside, but inside tapers to a small hole in the top in the shape of an eye or a fish. On the floor below a slate dish is set into the beaten earth to collect the rainwater, while the walls are pierced by many hollow rods which let in light. The effect of the whole is startling, and it is rapidly becoming a well-known site of pilgrimage for visitors both religious and aesthetic. We dawdled around and inside for some time and ate our pack-ups nearby, then continued to Bad Munster Eifel, which is a charming walled town in a steep valley on the edge of the Flamersheimerwald, full of old stone houses packed alongside the river, somewhat similar to Kommern but obviously more likely to be found in tourist guidebooks. We found a café with many old photographs on the walls, of the town as it used to be a hundred years ago: quite similar, really, apart from the present-day profusion of gift-shops and hiking-gear shops and cafés, and the absence of grubby urchins. We bade farewell to Uwe and Angelika who were going home, about 100 kilometres to the north, and made our way up an extremely steep hill to the Youth Hostel, which was quite full of families as this was still Easter holiday time.

DAY 45   BAD MUNSTER EIFEL – ALTENAHR
30 km; cool, rain in the afternoon; 15°C

We'd booked ourselves into another Youth Hostel tonight in Altenahr, which we knew would be quite a long haul but proved to be also one of the most pleasant to date. We began by climbing on a steep footpath up through the forest to a height of about 500 metres. When the path hit a road we came across a little chapel dedicated to St Anthony of Egypt, who is apparently the patron saint of motorists. Perhaps he was originally the patron of camel-drivers. At any rate his shrine is well-maintained and had several candles burning. When we crossed the road we got lost in the forest briefly but refound our way and followed a cycle-path until it stopped at the boundary of two provinces and we had to find an unsigned path down hill and over dale to Binzenbach, where we ate a hearty lunch at a pub for once then joined a trail called the Sahrbachtalweg (or Sahr Valley Way) which must be the most beautiful path in Rheinland-Pfalz. It was clearly signed, led through beautiful countryside alongside a bubbling rivulet and was well maintained. We met a couple of volunteers painting the woodwork on a bridge which ran across a wetland meadow full of buttercups and darting with dragonflies. They were very pleased to meet us, saying that it made their work worthwhile to see it used by long-distance walkers. Whereas at the top of the hill in the morning we had traversed much open landscape with rolling vistas of heavily wooded hills unveiling themselves one behind the other in the distance, we had now dropped down into a cleft between the nearest of these hills. All along the path we came across traces of settlements from the past: Stone Age, Roman and Templar. The last few kilometres to the hostel from

Altenahr – a jolly holiday town at the end of a railway line from Cologne and Bonn, full of caravan parks, casinos and gambling arcades – were hard going, but at least it wasn't at the top of a steep hill for once as most youth hostels seem to be in Germany. This one nestled at the bottom of the valley in a loop of the river, and again was largely full of families.

DAY 46   ALTENAHR – SPESSART
22 km; cool, light rain; 11°C

The only thing was that sooner or later we'd have to climb up the hill on the other side of the valley, and it was seriously steep, the hardest hiking yet. At the top we made a little detour along a friendly path between shrubs and bushes to the sort of place I've never seen in England, a mixture of hikers' watering-hole and country restaurant. It must have originally been a forest ranger's house or maybe a hostel for the local hiking club – an old-style wooden chalet in the middle of nowhere at about 1,800 feet above sea level at the end of a long and winding single-track lane for drivers or the afore-mentioned steep track for walkers. Inside, at about 11.30 on a Sunday morning, the place was packed with groups of friends and families who had obviously got in early for their Sunday lunch and were tucking into venison stew and jugged hare with no frills. We had some *Kaffee und Kuchen* (too early for our lunch) and enjoyed the view and the warmth. Outside it was cold and threatening rain. We were given a local map, which was in tatters but was up-to-date and proved very useful as we negotiated our way through the forest for a few more hours before finding a bar open in Ramersbach. When we asked the people in the bar whether we could get to Spessart by going straight down the hill and through the forest they said: "Yes. Go straight down there past the llama farm, round the bend and through the woods, over the hill and you can't miss it." We did wonder at one point if we'd got it right, but trusted the directions and arrived at the village where we had arranged to stay in what was in fact the only place to stay, a large hotel in the middle of the village, inasmuch as there was a middle. All the original buildings had been demolished to make way for new houses, and the only shops sold heating systems and tractor parts. We were made heartily welcome at the hotel with a complimentary glass of local wine, and later had a good meal in a bar full of friendly locals, travelling salesmen and visitors. Judging by the amount of wildlife we saw nearby this must be a hunter's paradise: kites and sparrowhawks, deer, wild boar and a possible sighting of a polecat.

15 April 2012

Hello dear friends, new and 'old'. Easter has been and gone, and certainly was impactful! I thought of all of the music lovers amongst you when I clapped my ear to the great gate of Aachen cathedral (the Dom, which goes back in structure and some of its parts to Charlemagne) on the morning of Easter Sunday to hear the most moving, rousing orchestral and choir music swelling against the ancient portal from within. Later, after I had been to the second mass, which was nothing like it – alas! – we visited the history-soaked place as tourists. Having looked forward to standing at the foot of the throne of many Kaisers of the last 1200 years, I could not help kicking up a fuss when it seemed as though I should be prevented! Well, fuss paid dividends for once, and a pleasant young man rose up, picked up a key, and gave Nick and myself a private tour in the throne room of the cathedral! The seat of Charlemagne, the creator of the European idea, you might say, was a simple roughly hewn structure of marble slabs with seven steps leading to it, some sandstone, some shiny black marble, with dells trodden into them by Ottos and Lothars and all those crown bearers who shaped this continent. Their hands had gripped the armrests of the seat and scratched them white: an amazing sense of the presence of history's pulse. By the side of it would have stood Alcuin, who had met with Charlemagne in Rome in 800, and there through the sympathy between the two men he had been recruited from York, where he had been a wise and much sought-after teacher, to the court in Aachen to teach the emperor's courtiers and family. We were guests of a very generous and sweet young couple, he being a friend of friends in York, an Englishman in Germany who just left his flat to us for two days! Oh, I am learning I hope! Nick's brother Anch came to see us for that weekend, which was lovely, and so did my nephew with his girlfriend, who on hearing where we were came to meet us at another extraordinary location, a burial church or 'columbarium'. His interest lies with the forms of the stacked granite urn-shelves, something he wants to translate into wood and glass for his apprenticeship piece. He and his friend walked with us for a couple of kilometres in the drizzliest weather yet. But still we have not been drenched, most lucky! Spring is simply beautiful here, and we seem to have benefited from the soft white powdering of thorn-blossom for weeks now. Here in the Eifel we are revelling in the wooded high hills of the landscape, forests whose quality changes every few hundred metres. There is majesty in the tall stands of silver-grey beech trees whose little ones have held on to autumn's brown foliage and give a pink blush to the forest floor with it. There is an eerie stillness in the pine-stands under whose dark-needled roofs lies the softest mossy carpet. We wander around forests for hours at a time, mostly happily soaking in air and bird chatter, occasionally losing our way for ages, having a truly Brothers Grimm time of it. A couple of days ago we met Fynn, our friend, colleague and poet-eurythmist from York, here in the Eifel, as he came to visit his former home and his dear mother. It was a very strange brush with another world to be in such close contact with York! He told us of another unmissable place along our way: a chapel created in thanks for a good life, done in the shape of a giant haystack! Light streams into the cement structure through many tubular shafts, each capped with a little glass seal. It is open to the roof, and in it the architect created a most moving and reverential space. On that day we had the company of two people who felt like walking along with us (hint hint!). It was a particularly lovely day's walk and culminated in a very pretty town, medieval and beamed, with a small river running through the middle of the street. There we stayed in the youth hostel compliment of our friends! Generosity is overwhelming! Should just tell you of the skylark concert on the way to the aforementioned chapel: large fields with spring sprouting greens had our path meandering around its edge, and the air was literally shimmering with the trill of about 20 larks! It lifted the heart and gave wings to our souls, and not least made us smile…

Dear friends, I have now gone beyond my one thousandth kilometre! We are near the river Rhein, and we are still in one piece, body, mind and soul. We hope that you are all well, and you don't mind passing these emails onto our friends who may not all get this. Much love to you all, and think whether you may come and walk with us at some time. Nick is walking again, thank goodness. Thank you all for your lovely messages, keep them coming, it is wonderful to hear from you!

Angela and Nick XX

DAY 47   SPESSART – MARIA LAACH
23 km; cold, North wind; 6°C

"Pools, walls, solitary trees, are natural halting places."

We stayed in the hotel until 11 o'clock since the manager told us it would only take a couple of hours to walk to Maria Laach, and did some emailing, planning, etc., then set off to walk through the woods to Kempernich. An elderly lady hiker we met on the way told us: "If you walk that far you'll live to be a hundred!" We thought we could get some money out of Angela's bank account at Kempernich, but she was told it was only valid in Dieburg (200 kilometres away). At the same time I discovered that to take any money out of the wall with my card was going to cost €10, which seemed rather excessive. We cleared out Angela's Post Office account, which had €180 in it, then went shopping for some necessities and set off rubbing our hands – it was colder now than at any point on the journey so far and felt like snow. We got lost on the way to Weibern by taking the wrong fork at a point which had no signposts, and felt the first snowflakes as we trudged through a turnip field on the brow of a hill. Weibern, we discovered, was the centre of the tufa-quarrying industry in this volcanic region. All the houses were built of the soft pale stone, and as we climbed out of the town we passed more signs of ancient volcanic activity with traces of lava and pumice among the shards of stone in the fields. The region is full of round- and flat-topped hills, some with groups of wind turbines gathered on the summit, creating a strange dreamlike atmosphere. Near the top of the steep track leaving Weibern we found the perfect place to stop for a bite and a drink of water as the sun came out: a bench next to a little shrine in memory of a local walker who had loved the view from that particular spot. In Weibern itself we had been looking for somewhere to stop and have a warming cup but everything seemed to be closed, as was often the case on Mondays on the continent. Just as we'd given up hope we saw some people coming out of a *gasthaus*, which said it was closed, but among them was the landlady, who let us in when she saw our bags and cold noses. It was an ancient house with old photos on the walls of men with felt hats and knickerbockers, pocket-watches and clay pipes, digging, hacking and cutting huge slabs of the porous local stone.

On the way down from the wind turbines we took another wrong turning and ended up stuck on a major road not knowing which way to turn, but finally figured it out and eventually found ourselves for the first time on the Jakobsweg – a branch of the Camino de Santiago which originally took pilgrims from the North and East of Germany, and perhaps from Poland and even Scandinavia too – to the Kloster of Maria Laach (*Fig. 12).This extraordinary monastic site was founded in 1093 by a local prince. Unable to have children, he and his wife decided to give the money they would have saved for a dowry to create a place of prayer and learning. It has been extended over the centuries but at its heart is the original Romanesque church and abbey completed in the 12th century. Standing on the shore of a picturesque circular lake (originally a volcanic crater) it has a fairy-tale quality which was enhanced by our meeting with a large hare in the surrounding forest It stood stock still on its hind legs for a long time as we stared at each other.

Angelika had arranged for us to stay the night, and when we knocked at the door we were introduced to Pater Viktor, who was the monk in charge of staying guests and spoke excellent English with an Oxford accent. He showed us to our cells, which were simple and calm, looking out onto the huge courtyard in front of the church door. Supper was served in the refectory to a group of about a dozen visitors including a group of priests and a pair of women from Karlsruhe who make regular visits for "peace and prayer" and invited us to stay if we went near where they live.

DAY 48   MARIA LAACH – KÄRLICH
27km; cool, cloudy; 10°C

When we were ready to leave in the morning Pater Viktor gave us heartfelt blessings for the remainder of the walk, refused to accept any money for our stay, and offered another night's lodging if my leg was still troubling me. Fortunately it was feeling much better and I resolved to carry on and keep on taking the tablets! Angela on the other hand was beginning to feel an abdominal muscle strain more and more strongly – the result, she felt sure later, of some shocking news – and while we had been hoping to push on to Koblenz, we decided to stop when we got to Kärlich. We had received word in the morning that a good friend who had got herself into debt had been charged with tax evasion and given a prison sentence which could end up being at least a year, despite having in the meantime paid all the money back. Along the way we met a couple of walkers on a hillside near Kettig, where the countryside began to change into a land of rolling orchards: apple, cherry and plum trees in full late-April blossom. Despite the leaden clouds and chilly wind, it was an inspiring sight, but Angela was struggling with her sore muscle and it was heavy going climbing that hill. Arriving at Kärlich, which looked like a reasonable-sized town, we found there was nowhere to stay apart from an expensive hotel which wanted to charge us €100 for a room. The owner gave us a 10% reduction after asking to hear where we were going, and when we had looked around and found no alternative we decided to bite the bullet and accept the offer, since Angela was feeling sore and tired. We *thought* the offer was because we were doing it for charity, but as we were beginning to realise many more people in Belgium and Germany than in England had no idea what we meant when we said we were being sponsored by people so that we could raise money for a charity, and we often had to explain it three or four times before people understood. On this occasion a customer came into the bar as we were waiting to eat who turned out to be English. He spent much of his time working at a local engineering plant producing aeroplane parts, had a flat in Kärlich, and was a regular in the hotel bar. He helped to break the ice with the other locals and we had a long conversation about the state of the world.

DAY 49   KÄRLICH – KOBLENZ
24 km; cloudy, showers; 11°C

In the morning we had a hearty breakfast and made a pack-up from the remaining rolls and cheese. We had a long discussion about Angela's muscle and decided she should rest it as much as possible for the next few days. After all we were fast approaching a much more testing time: in a few days we would be crossing the Taunus

Mountains and climbing to 1,000 metres for the first time, and the weather was still cold. Maybe there would be snow at the top, or fog…Angela decided to take the bus to Koblenz while I would walk down to the river – a couple of kilometres – then along the towpath and meet her at the "Deutsches Eck".

I went down towards the river past a big gas holder and not far from a nuclear power station but through more orchards until I crossed a busy highway and came to some houses just before the railway line. I knew I had to cross the railway but wasn't sure exactly where, so I asked an old woman who was out sweeping her front step the way to the river. She looked at me blankly. "Maybe she doesn't speak German," I thought. "Or is it my pronunciation?" I tried again: "Excuse me. How do I get to the Rhine?" "O, der Rhein!", and the explanation was immediately forthcoming. In Germany the rivers each have a name, a gender and an individuality that perhaps only the Thames has in England. When I got to the towpath I first passed a huddle of police cars on the riverbank with a small group of inquisitive passers-by watching a helicopter trying to scoop something out of the river, failing, then repeatedly circling and coming back to try again. There was something terribly sad about the scene, as the policemen stood in the drizzle gazing into the muddy waters. At Kaltenengers I stopped at a bench and was joined by an elderly woman who told me her life story, all about how she had moved here from Holland to marry a bargee. We sat and watched as the barges floated heavily down towards the delta, and now I could picture where they would dock near Rotterdam or Hoek van Holland. At St Sebastian it began to rain properly just as I arrived at a little park with a statue and some flower-beds. A young man with the look of a Turk or North African beckoned me over as he was walking in the opposite direction. I was expecting him to be wanting something from me, like some tobacco, but he thrust a small blue plastic package in my hand, muttered something about the rain, and strode off. When I looked more closely I saw it was a rain-cape.

Further along, the path left the riverbank and went through an industrial estate, then doubled back and approached Koblenz through a park. Spotting what looked like a little ferry-dock I headed towards it, thinking I could save myself a few miles' walk by going directly across the river to the very spot where I had arranged to meet Angela instead of walking the long way round, but I found the way barred by a couple of bouncers who told me the ferry wasn't operating and I'd have to go round by the bridge. There was a throng of people standing around looking excited, and a pistol shot suddenly rang out. Several people in suits ran around a group of police cars and more shots were fired: an episode of a TV series was being filmed. Just across from the park was a spit of land jutting out between two rivers – the Rhine and the Mosel – and on the spit an enormous statue of a Kaiser on horseback. This is the spot known to all Germans as the Deutsches Eck (German Corner). I went round over the bridge and through the old city of Koblenz and met Angela at a café near the statue, and we looked across the Rhine at the massive fortress on top of a cliff which dominates the city. "That's where we're staying tonight," said Angela. "It's the Youth Hostel!" "How are we going to get there?" I asked, not having noticed the cable-car dangling 200 feet or so above the river.

We had to negotiate a way of getting through the castle without paying the full visitors' price, which was complicated, but finally managed to get to the Youth Hostel and were assigned a room with an amazing view looking out over the city and far beyond (*Fig. 13). The castle was first built in the 10th or 11th century and it is hard to imagine how it could ever have been overrun, but it was besieged by the French in 1799 and subsequently taken apart stone by stone, only to be rebuilt by the Prussians as part of an immense system of defensive fortifications around the city.

DAY 50   KOBLENZ – NASSAU
26 km; cloudy, showers; 13°C

Angela said her strained muscle was much better after a day of rest and a good night's sleep. I wasn't entirely convinced, but took her word for it that we could at least try it and see how far we got. We set off early, through the silent empty courtyards of the castle and took a path downhill and up, past a golf-course and through civilized forest full of orderly signposts for local walkers and cyclists until Bad Ems came into sight a long way below us in the Lahn valley (the Lahn comes down from Limburg to flow into the Rhine just above Koblenz). Coming to a fork in the road we had to decide whether to stay on the curving, zigzagging road with the odd car or motorbike or go straight on following a single-track road which our map suggested petered out just before Bad Ems. Taking a gamble we carried straight on, and it paid off, as we were assured it would by a well-dressed hiker out with her dog about halfway down. Arriving at a farm, the road did stop, but around the back was a tiny footpath which meandered steeply down through narrow terraced vineyards inhabited by a herd of goats.

Coming out in the town with sore knees after such a steep descent, we made our way to the river, marvelling at the great number of ornate and luxurious hotels, civic buildings and casinos dating from at least a century ago, including hotels dedicated to the English, the French and the Russians. As we were to discover, in its heyday in the second half of the 19th century it was one of the most popular spa resorts in Europe, and was regularly visited by anyone who was anyone in the social hierarchy of the age, becoming the summer residence of such as the Tsars of Russia, Richard Wagner and Dostoyevsky. There has been a spa here since Roman times, when a fortress was built here on the Upper Germanic *Limes* (pronounced leemess) – the boundary of the Roman Empire to the north – and the baths were rebuilt in the middle ages by the Counts of Nassau and the splendidly named Counts of Katzenelbogen (Cat's Elbow). The other face of Bad Ems is its history of mining for metal ores: the hillsides are dotted with holes and tunnels dating back to Roman times. We walked along a riverside footpath with steeply wooded hills on our right past some of these caves to Nassau, where we would stay the night and whose name sounded very familiar. Apart from being the capital of the Bahamas, wasn't there some connection with the Dutch royal family?[4] We had been greatly looking forward to getting to Nassau as it was the place where we would be able to pick up the E1 Long Distance Walking Path which we could follow all the way to Italy. The town itself is small and unpretentious, with a castle perched above it in the woods across the valley, and we found an excellent B&B and a *gasthaus* where we could drink some excellent German beer and use their computer for hours, gratis.

---

4   To get a taste of the labyrinthine politics of Western European history, google 'The Principality of Orange-Nassau' or 'The Duchy of Nassau'.

By the way, the capital of the Bahamas was named Nassau in honour of King William III of England of the House of Nassau-Orange, which also explains the colour of the Dutch national football team's shirts and the Loyalist flags in Northern Ireland. Strange connections!

DAY 51   NASSAU – BALDUINSTEIN
32 km; cloudy, warmer, showers; 14°C

Finally we had met up with the famed E1 Long Distance Walking Path and could use their route guide, which comes in the form of a little book, small enough to fit in an anorak pocket and spiral bound so you can pull pages off when you've finished with them and send them home. The first day following the path was pretty straightforward – a well-signposted walk along or parallel to the river Lahn, mainly in forest, with many ups and downs as the valley became more and more steep-sided the further upstream we went, with a lot of little streams to cross. It reminded me of walking in the Wye Valley, and we did come across an abbey, or *kloster*, after a couple of hours; although unlike Tintern Abbey it sits perched upon the hillside above the river. We also saw some rather more exotic wildlife here, including red squirrels, lizards and boar. Oh, and mice in abundance, rustling the dead leaves above their nests or darting alongside the path where we also saw some bizarre natural sculptures which we named The Mossy Throne and The Babies (*Fig. 14). In another spot near Balduinstein castle we came across a herd of large-horned Hungarian cattle, which looked very unfamiliar. As for people, we met one solitary long-distance walker, who was walking from Limburg to Koblenz in a long weekend. He looked the part with a stout staff and a long red beard. I realised after we had chatted and parted company that we should have warned him about the seriously steep path we had just slithered down, holding onto saplings to break our fall, but it was too late, he had disappeared round the corner. Coming down into Balduinstein village was also dangerously steep in places – at least, it was with a ten-kilo pack – but we managed it and took a train a couple of stops up the valley to Diez, where we stayed at another Youth Hostel in another castle. Definitely worth a visit if you like railway journeys!

Another person we met on the path was Norbert, who was on his way home to Nassau by bike after taking his car to Diez for repairs. A former sports teacher at a secondary school, he had interesting views about Facebook, saying he never uses it and discourages his children and pupils from doing so. As he pointed out, who knows who might look at your Facebook page now or at any time in the future and see that you won Best Bum of Bad Ems 2012? He had similarly trenchant views on the value of hikers' walking poles, which are extremely popular in Germany. He had done much research on the matter and concluded that they are likely to give you repetitive stress syndrome, and even the highly sprung ones can overstrain your carpal tunnels and other points on your arms. We had been debating whether to buy some ever since we left York so this was an interesting point of view which we had wondered about but had never heard spoken by anyone.

Having arrived at Diez we walked from the station into the old town and up a long flight of stone steps to the castle. How good it is to have these medieval castles turned into something useful for the people rather than always an expensive hotel or a conference centre for senior managers! Having said that, we enquired at several Youth Hostels along the way and were told that they were full of school parties, which is obviously their target market: this has knock-on effects. For example it was impossible to get onto any social websites such as Hospitality Club from any Youth Hostel. Most said they had no idea why it didn't work, but one warden thought it may have been blocked along with many other social sites to protect the young teenagers who are the primary users of their WiFi. This made it difficult to plan our accommodation ahead, as we had intended to do on our day off at Diez.

DAY 52   DIEZ & LIMBURG
0 km; cool, rainy; 10°C

In fact we caught the train to Limburg, just a few kilometres away, for the day. Whereas in the 12th or 13th century Diez was more powerful, it is now little more than a suburb of Limburg, which is a large industrial city with its own old quarter which is actually much more tourist-oriented than that of Diez, so much neater and tidier. The interesting little cathedral is on a hill above the river, and stands out with its colourfully painted walls and towers. Inside are many frescoes dating from the 12th century, and we explored inside it as well as the surrounding streets, where we found some delicious cake. Angela went to the cinema but I didn't fancy it and took the train back for a middle-aged nap. Later, in the evening, we went looking for somewhere to eat in the cobbled street at the bottom of the steps. Everywhere was closed apart from a little bar, or *kneipe*, which seemed to be in a time warp. It was like going into an old lady's parlour, with a couple of tables and a bench, and a tiny bar in one corner. The old lady, who had been running the bar for fifty years, was remarkably incurious at our arrival and at us speaking in English, and we left when she started cursing the Turks from the greengrocer's shop down the road in blatantly racist terms to her only other customer.

DAY 53   BALDUINSTEIN – MICHELBACH
24 km; warmer, showery; 13°C

We had needed a rest day after not having had one since Abenden, ten days earlier, and set off refreshed for the next stage – three or four days' walk to Frankfurt through the Taunus Mountains. First we had to take the train back to Balduinstein then climb the hill up to Schaumberg Castle, which we'd seen from the other side two days before. Just below the castle we were not at all sure whether to take an unmarked path off to the left from the road and went back to ask at the only inhabited building we'd passed, which was a large house that looked like a former monastery or convent and was now in use as a meditation centre. As we rang the bell and looked again at the words on a plaque on the wall, it dawned on us that this was the very place that a friend of ours had visited and spoken about. Robert, a respected traditional acupuncturist, musician and Oxford graduate, who was passionately interested in the meeting of mind and spirit, had recently succumbed to cancer in his sixties, but for many years been inspired by Mother Meera, an enigmatic figure who is revered by many as an incarnation of the Divine Mother. Born in India in 1960, she has been living in Germany since 1982. Despite never having courted publicity she is visited by people from all over the world seeking her *darshan* – the gift of grace and light bestowed by her gaze. When the door opened and a slight figure in a sari regarded us with curiosity we found ourselves saying: "Can you help us please? We have lost our way," only to be treated with utmost courtesy and given the right directions, for which we are still grateful.

The walk was beautiful, through woods and glades with occasional stunning views of the Taunus ahead, and the weather was getting warmer. When it did rain in the afternoon we managed to avoid it as the clouds rolled away in the wind leaving the top of a rainbow's arc stuck momentarily to the hill ahead. We came out of the woods at Michelbach Hütte, which was not just a collection of huts but a large iron-smelting works a couple of kilometres from the town of Michelbach where we were booked to stay the night at the only *gasthaus*. When we phoned on the way to confirm the booking a man answered and said his wife had just been taken to hospital with a stroke, but to come anyway and knock on the door of the house opposite for a key. The *gasthaus* was large and more like a pub than a guest house, but entirely empty, and a couple of times we got lost and couldn't find our way out. It was remarkable, looking back on it, that he let us stay at all when we could have cleaned up the contents of the bar or walked off with articles of furniture, but he clearly trusted us enough and had other things on his mind. The town has a population of several thousand but there was nowhere to eat apart from three take-away pizzerias, only one of which had a small table where we could sit and shelter from a mighty downpour. It had apparently never been a market town, and only had a couple of shops to serve all the people who must have come in from outside to work at the iron foundry. However a large new supermarket had been built far enough outside town for people to have to go by car to shop.

DAY 54   MICHELBACH – HEFTRICH
29 km; sunny intervals, showers; 11°C

This little corner of the country definitely didn't feel like a tourist destination, especially next to the autobahn and the industrial estate near Idstein, although Idstein had a 'historic centre', like so many German towns, which was neat and well-ordered. One could imagine many visitors stopping in the summer to sit in the wide main square or go to the Hexenturm, or Witches' Tower, where a plaque commemorated 43 people, mostly women, who were put to death following a series of trials in 1676. We walked on another five or six kilometres to Heftrich so that we would have less distance to cover the following day, having ascertained that there was a place we could stay when we got there. The weather was perfect for walking, apart from a few showers, as it was so fresh, and we strode along briskly past a gliders' airport then in and out of woods. We heard a strange unidentified noise at one point which at first sounded like the deep-throated grunt of a pig, but it was so regular that we begun to think it might be a bird, although we couldn't imagine which. We kept on hearing from friends in England that the weather had been awful and it had hardly stopped raining the whole of April, so we felt lucky and were quite prepared to put up with the few showers we had experienced so far. When we reached Heftrich we found the *gasthaus* was also the village butcher's shop, the kind of old-fashioned country inn which had changed little since the days when it was on the stagecoach route from Cologne to Frankfurt. We had a simple but tasty meal of salmon with *kartoffelpuffer* (potato dumplings) and horseradish sauce.

On the way, as we were walking on a typical wide gravel forest path quite near a village, since we hadn't seen a soul for about half an hour and Angela couldn't wait, she went off the path and was just unbuckling herself 'to answer a call of nature' when a car drove up behind us and stopped about ten metres away. Our eyes rolled upwards as two women got out and started loading tree-stumps into the boot of the car, looking around shiftily as if they were doing something illegal, which they probably were. The collection of timber is highly organised in rural Germany: you have to apply at a certain forestry office to buy a tree in your local forest, which you then have to have felled, cut up and taken away to be stacked outside your house to be used for winter fuel. Throughout our journey we often saw gigantic heaps of felled tree-trunks with the owners' names marked on each one in red paint.

DAY 55   HEFTRICH – NIEDERURSEL
26 km; cool, heavy showers; 11°C

In the morning we followed a track called the Alter Burgmarktweg, which is to say the Old Town Market Way. Local people would have taken this path until fairly recent times, a couple of generations ago, to take their produce to Frankfurt market – their geese, sheep, carrots and onions. Up through the woods we met a woman in her seventies outside her house who asked us in for a drink then told us all about her family – her son and daughter had both been national judo champions – and the history of the village, particularly its position on the Roman *Limes*, the limits of the Empire. Here we were on the edge of the known world as far as the Romans were concerned, an edge which went east as far as Syria and Judaea, beyond which there were only wild lands inhabited by barbarians. We followed the line of the boundary straight up a very steep hill to a spot known as Rotes Kreuz (Red Cross) then continued past a Roman fort and an ancient well-spring to the top of Grosser Feldberg (870 m) where we climbed a tower (a further 165 steps!) and peered through the clouds at a 360° panorama including Frankfurt city. Going down from the peak the path, which on our map should have gone back up over the top of the Alte König (790 m), was closed and a diversion sign had been put up which made us think we would go around the mountain, avoiding another steep climb, but in fact it took us halfway round then up a (mostly) dry stream-bed over large boulders and tree-roots into a misty drizzle which rapidly became a rainy fog. By the time we were near the top the path ran out into a myriad of smaller animal tracks and the E1 signs we had been following disappeared. It became very dark and the cloud we were in disgorged itself with gusto as we struggled to don our rain-capes. I left Angela sheltering under an overhanging branch and went off to find the path, then returned squelching through the mud with my mind full of images of the opening sequence of 'Gladiator' where Russell Crowe and his legion are trapped in a misty forest by Germanic tribes. We finally made it to the top and stood dripping in the middle of a circular grove. The rain stopped, and as we started our descent the sun forced its way out, the mist and steam began to rise, and a huge rainbow appeared across the hills and plains which stretched far into the distance below us (*Fig. 15).

From there it was downhill all the way to Hohemark, the outermost limit of the urban trains in the Frankfurt area. We hopped onto a U3 for a dozen stations, walked round the corner and we were at Edith's house. She'd told us where the key was and said she'd be home later. She was back late from the theatre, but made us most welcome in her tastefully decorated flat in Niederursel, and we spoke at length in the morning about philosophy and religion and the price of bread.

DAY 56   NIEDERURSEL – CENTRAL FRANKFURT
25 km; warmer, overcast; 14°C

"Walking is not so much romantic as reasonable."

We took the train back to Hohemark and walked towards Frankfurt city centre, first through a municipal forest, where we saw some wild boar grazing very close at hand, then alongside fields, beside a river and through various parks, following the E1 signs all the while. The closer we got to the city centre – the financial hub of Western Europe – the more ingenious the path became in avoiding busy roads. From a large council estate with many tower blocks clustered around a shopping mall we were led past the Roman settlement next to the railway then along leafy back lanes and alleyways, through allotments and graveyards and parks, until we arrived at a landmark I recognised from our only previous visit: the Opera House. From here we took a train to Neu Isenburg, promising to return in the morning, and were met by a delightful man called Bodhi, an animal trainer who had travelled the world. He stood out from the small crowd outside the station with his dungarees and Santa Claus beard – as I suppose we must have with our rucksacks and windswept looks – and after introducing ourselves, he loaded our stuff into the back of his pickup truck and off we went to the circus, where we met Elfi, who had invited us to stay in one of their caravans. Elfi has known Angela's brother Michael for many years, and now runs this small children's circus with Bodhi and Matze, their assistant and expert diabolo juggler.

When she heard we were coming near the circus site she instantly wrote to invite us to stay, and when we arrived she phoned the local paper and got a reporter out to interview us.

DAY 57   CENTRAL FRANKFURT – DREIEICHENHAIN
19 km; chilly wind; 13°C

We slept well in the caravan despite feathers leaking from our sleeping-bags and constant noise from the autobahn. In the morning we had breakfast in the Big Top – well, Little Top, actually – then watched the show with a group of schoolchildren, during which Fridolin the goat jumped through hoops of fire and balanced on a plank and the children went to meet the ponies, sheep and llamas. We got a lift back to the station with Bodhi, who was going to collect some straw, and went back to the Opera House. It was surprisingly easy to walk out of Frankfurt going south, especially since we had been able to leave most of our luggage at the caravan. We crossed the River Main and went through the Sachsenhausen district for a couple of kilometres and we were in the ducal forest. We did have an argument about which way to go after asking directions from someone which proved to be wrong so we ended up walking through a museum and a building site, but it was soon forgotten as we became more interested in the deer, red squirrels, boar and hares we saw. Beyond the forest the land began to rise slightly, enough to be able to look back and see Frankfurt in the distance looking small and insignificant beneath the majestic mountains we had crossed only two days before. The E1 at this stage was following a country lane which led past a field full of solar panels – at least two acres' worth – and a walk-in sculpture made of wooden poles arranged in a pyramidal shape, then downhill to Dreieichenhain (the place of three oak trees) which only had two left but had a castle and a little walled town centre. We met up with Elfi, who lives there with her octogenarian parents, and a choleric Irishman who was about to go back to Ireland after having problems with his temper at the circus, and went for a Turkish takeaway – vegetarian kebabs for us! – and got a lift back to the caravan for the night.

DAY 58   DREIEICHENHAIN – DARMSTADT
23 km; warmer, cloudy; 19°C

We got a lift back to Dreieichenhain Castle in the morning with Bodhi and his hay-trailer and set off to walk a long way through the forest – mostly beech – until we came to the Baroque Grand Ducal hunting lodge of Schloß Kranichstein. Beside the stables there was a small lake, and beyond that a long avenue of saplings of different trees, each with its own label – there must have been fifty different species there, which would be worth another visit in twenty years' time! Beyond the avenue there lay the main road to Darmstadt and the Oberwaldhaus café /restaurant where we met Angela's brother Daniel and his partner Dani, along with a reporter from the Darmstädter Echo whom Daniel had alerted, along with a photographer. Several strands were coming together now. Angela grew up in Dieburg, only 15 kilometres from here. Daniel lives in the Odenwald, south of Darmstadt, as do her mother and two other siblings (Michael and Jorinde), and they all wanted to help out in some way. In addition we had contacts in the area through Michael's involvement with anthroposophical ventures such as biodynamic farming and the Camphill communities which provide independent/sheltered living and working spaces for adults with various special needs. One such community was on our list of hosts' addresses, and as it happened was on our path just a few kilometres down the road. The Hofgut Oberfeld occupies an old farm estate formerly belonging to the Grand Duchy of Hessen/Nassau-Darmstadt (them again!) which would certainly otherwise have fallen into disrepair, and is a thriving community including a busy farm shop, a café and a market garden. We met our host, Jens, on a tractor across the road from the buildings coming home from the fields with his 4-year-old son on board. Jens and his Swiss wife Katrin have been living and working there for a few years. They told us it's very hard work but very rewarding and they love it. We met one of the residents whom Angela had met before on a previous visit, and he proudly showed us his little flat, where he lives quite independently after previously having been in a shared house supervised by 'houseparents'.

DAY 59   DARMSTADT – WALLHAUSEN
27 km; very warm, sunny; 26°C

"A stick of ash or blackthorn, through long use, will adjust itself to the palm."

Suddenly it's summer! It's April 28th and the temperature has shot up. As we walked through the forest to Ober Ramstadt we heard two cuckoos and saw two deer and a hare at the same moment. We met a man out walking who told us he was in training for the Jakobsweg then a tractor came towards us pulling a trailer full of men on a works outing who looked as if they each had an already half-empty hip-flask of schnapps. Walking up from Frankenhausen in the midday heat on an exposed country road the temperature passed

25°, and after having been served a lemonade in a pub courtyard although the pub was closed – and finding we were sitting next to a barn full of swallows' nests – we overshot the mark following a long discussion about whether to turn off the path given a total lack of signposts to Stettbach. In the end we walked across someone's field and crashed through a forest, losing the path entirely. When we'd scrambled down a steep slope and crossed a stream, I tripped over a branch hidden under a pile of dead leaves and tumbled over rather neatly, thanking my stars that I hadn't sprained anything. From the road outside the village of Stettbach there is a single-track lane which goes off to the right, signposted only with a street name: **WALLHAUSEN.** Winding its way uphill beside a small stream for a kilometre it arrives at two houses and turns into a track disappearing into the forest. We walked into the farmyard with the large rebuilt house before us and a couple of barns to the right, one of which houses the four cows while the other stores quantities of bottled apple juice. To the left stands a patio made of thick poplar planks laid on concrete blocks so that the kitchen garden is some eight feet below on a slope, which continues down, through a meadow which serves as pasture for the cows and as a small orchard, to the stream. Hills covered in trees and grazing land rise steeply on all sides so that the view from the house is of nothing but sky and greenness. We arrived very hot and dehydrated, to find Michael and Eva sitting out on the balcony with a group of friends, one of whom, a trained doctor, is working to make Steiner schools available in Zimbabwe, while another is a Brazilian who makes a living as a musician in Frankfurt. We stayed there for several days in beautiful late spring weather, spending one day at a local Spring Fair where we helped Michael sell his own-brand apple juice made from the apples at his own orchards. Another day we went to the dentist in a nearby town and I had a tooth pulled out, which was not so pleasant but needed to be done and didn't give me too much grief. Another day we went to Darmstadt – less than an hour by car compared to a day's walk! – where I got a new pair of boots, as mine were falling apart. The stitching had come undone on one and the soles of both had huge cracks in them: I don't know whether this was the cause or the effect of my shin inflammation but having tried a few cobblers there seemed to be no remedy unless I was prepared to wait somewhere for a week or more to have new soles sent from Italy, so I took a deep breath and splashed out on an expensive German pair and hoped they would last the whole way to Rome. On the Sunday there was a singing workshop in Roßdorf, which had been planned for about four months and drew about 15 people who contributed generously to our MSF funds.

We spent a lot of time sitting on the patio looking out at the fields and hills, watching the cows (*Fig. 16) grazing in the orchard and listening to the deer barking in the twilight. We went for little walks to keep in practice and one day cut some hazel sticks and whittled them ready for the day we would get back on the road: good stout sticks with a bit of spring in them, enough to feel connected to the ground. After a total of five days of rest and relaxation in this idyllic spot we were ready to continue.

1st May 2012

It has been a while again since you heard from us. Allow me to assure you then that we are hale and hearty, even if Nick had to leave a tooth at my dentist's practice! He seems to not be too knocked out by the experience, and hopefully this will now remove one niggle out of our walking experience.

We are staying with my brother Michael and his family, who have put a beautiful house in the most idyllic spot in Germany, and whose business is the production and promotion of the most delicious fruit juices, biodynamic and gorgeous! It so happens that their home lies about one kilometre off the E1 Long Distance Path, the one we have now decided to stay on, contrary to initial intentions! I will mention this again later.

For many days we have walked through Germany's forests, and in all its subtlety and glory observed the changes of the world of trees and forest creatures with the advance of the seasons. With the consideration of the most finely developed spirit, beech trees, who cannot but bud their foliage early, spread carefully from the bottom upwards, so that all the small growing things are able to gain enough strength and sunlight. Also these first leaves give a magical light to the forest at lower level, and the sun is still able to stream in from the top. This is not to say we had only sunshine, far from it! But light penetrates the forest until the trees have spread their upper leaves, by which time the lower ones have slightly darkened and 'toughened' and the May time richness moves in. In the forest we have come across glades with blossoming wild cherries, and carpets of anemones and violets. Now the woodruff is scenting the woods, and the willows are blowing endless little tufts of fluff through the air. Here it is now very warm with the promise of rain and cooler weather to come, and many days we traipsed through a damp and drizzly chill, but miraculously we never got really soaked! Once, when we had clambered up a very steep bit at the end of a tiring day, and the path annoyingly led over rather than around this mountain, we found ourselves in a cloud at the top and couldn't find the little way sign anywhere in the midst of the crossing of five or six paths. Nick asked me to stop at the very point where we'd felt lost while he searched the terrain for an indication of which way to go. After a moment's panic suddenly the cloud lifted, the sign became apparent, the sun streamed in and we found ourselves only a few metres away from a ledge from which we could view the entire plain below in the most glorious colours, with a stunning rainbow spanning the whole picture. All exhaustion fell away, and we were glad to have chosen this path after all! In the other direction, behind us there was a dripping glassy silvery fairytale forest with every droplet sparkling in the newly returned sun. It was truly magic!

Coming down from the Taunus Mountains and walking into Frankfurt was quite an experience in itself, not least because it defied all expectations. We stuck to the E1 (our trusty path) and were led through Frankfurt on a leafy, lush route through allotments and parks, along brooks and rivers, through backways and byways, and really did not have too much exposure to the overcrowded traffic of the city. We also were hosted by friends and friends of friends, from a lovely house where we found the key in a boat and soup ready on the stove to a circus caravan with a llama peeping in through the window. The latter was an enterprise for children, who are invited to learn circus skills but in many cases simply gain confidence, being drawn out of themselves by spending time with unthreatening animals. They are involved and engaged in a beautiful way by Bodhi, the trainer, whose calm and centredness could inspire many a teacher.

We were invited too to be guests of a young couple who are farming and baking in a farm community on the edge of Darmstadt together with people with special needs, and who produce lovely food and create a special place in the world, full of good ideas and lovely energy. Forin, the toddler, really hit it off with Nick, reminding me of how wonderful he is, and has always been, with young children.

Walking away from there we heard two cuckoos (one after the other)! I really celebrated that day, knowing how rare they have become. And on that same day we watched a couple of swallows swooping in and out of a stable block, where they were building a nest and then sitting in between all the hard work preening themselves. To complete the exhilaration I discovered there are plenty of maybugs around this year, reminding me that their 4-year cycle used always to fall together with leap years and Olympic years. But I had not seen as many since I was a child. Their numbers have been increasing since the cutback on pesticides began some twenty years ago.

As I am searching my mind what I might last have written about to you, I realize that I have not told you about staying in the monastery of Maria Laach, where to our amazement we were treated as dear guests by the monks, who had been told by our friend Angelika that we were going to Rome and could we stay the night? It was as we were leaving there that I had a phone call telling me about one of my very dearest friends having been put in prison (for tax fraud, although she had already paid back the money she owed!) The shock and worry rocked us, but I am reassured that all of her other friends, some of whom are receiving these mails, are with us in sending unconditional love and support to her, and have no need to pass more judgement. We will all be welcoming her back with open arms, open hearts and every help to come back into our midst, ready to pick up where she left off.

Dear friends, I was going to briefly tell you of the change of plan regarding our route: we pondered for a long time to leave the E1 around Heidelberg and walk across the rest of southern Germany, further east then straight south through Stuttgart. Now that we know how well researched the choices are, that determine the path, and having spoken this through with people who travel much in this area, we have decided to stay with the path, which means we are no longer going via Stuttgart. This means some embarrassment towards those of you who have created some lovely contacts for us, invitations of people we are very sorry not to meet now!

I can only apologise to you and them, but the proliferation of motorways and the need to buy more and more maps to cobble together our own route through this densely built-up area of Germany has persuaded us that it is better to go the scenic route.

Today is the first of May, a day which is traditionally celebrated here with many fairs and 'grill parties'. My juice-producing brother gathered all of the family to one particular fair to sell his wares. Now everyone has returned back to his home, from where we are setting off again on Friday after almost a week's worth of 'attending to needs' and a break, and they want to have dinner. So I have to go!

I hope you are well, and I look forward to receiving some mails from you. Please remember that it's not unbotheredness (quite the contrary!) if you don't receive an answer, it is technical limitation! It means very much to get your news, your contact, your thoughts!

Much love to all from

Angela and NickXX

DAY 65   WALLHAUSEN – NIEDER LIEBERSBACH
30 km; clear, warm; 19°C

We left with Michael, who wanted very much to be part of the whole thing and spend a few days walking with us, and went up onto the El, which at this point is synonymous with the Bergstrasse, the old way along the edge of the Odenwald looking down often onto the Rhine plains spread out on our right. Nowadays the Bergstrasse is a mixture of narrow lanes and wide gravel paths winding its way across open country and in and out of forest The day was glorious, a perfect temperature for walking, and everything around was in full springing growth. After only a few kilometres we found ourselves at the top of the hill we had seen from the patio at Wallhausen, and the other side of the hill we were suddenly in a wonderlandscape (***Fig. 17**) of huge boulders left behind by a glacier. You're clambering down the side of what seems to be a stream-bed, but it's gigantically bigger than it should be. The boulders are each about the size of a room, making broken tree trunks look like match-sticks, and the woods round about are littered with the remnants of Roman quarrying operations. Coming out at Reichenbach at the bottom of the hill, we followed the lane alongside fields full of dandelions and grasshoppers then entered another large forest, where we stopped at a silent spot where several logging tracks crossed and had a picnic.

Thirty kilometres was a bit far for Michael on his first day, and when he staggered into Nieder Liebersbach down a steep path with wooden half-steps built into the hill his knees were in bad shape. We managed to get to the house where we had been kindly offered a flat to stay the night by a friend of Michael's who was away for the week, then freshened up and went for a good meal of fresh local food at a bar just across the road.

DAY 66   NIEDER LIEBERSBACH –
WILHEMSFELD
18 km; cloudy, heavy showers; 16°C

We went together as far as Birkenau, where we left Michael to make his way home, not before he had knocked on someone's door to ask about the history of the old pigsties in their courtyard. Up and down we tramped through a beautiful green light in beech woods and along old drovers' hollow ways which have been gradually trodden into the sandstone over the centuries, or millennia, by human and animal feet. At Nieder Flockenbach it began to rain, and by the time we got to Wilhemsfeld it was pouring and we were soaked. On the way we had phoned Fritz, a Servas member who lives on the outskirts of Heidelberg, who gave us detailed instructions how to get to his house from Wilhemsfeld. We dried out for a while in a café then caught a bus down into the valley followed by a couple of trams. At first Fritz was rather cool – we hadn't given him much notice – but warmed up as we chatted and decided to take us to the city centre, where we treated him to a Chinese meal. An interesting character, he is involved in film-making projects, principally with 'voiceless' people such as refugees from conflicts abroad, and also works on local history at the city archives, so was a very well-informed guide to the old city of Heidelberg. In the morning he made us an excellent breakfast and we retraced our steps to Wilhemsfeld.

DAY 67   WILHEMSFELD – GAIBERG
19 km; cloudy; 15°C

From Wilhemsfeld we had a long walk down to Ziegelhausen, on the Neckar several kilometres upstream from Heidelberg. It stands at the crossroads, or rather the crosspaths, between the E1 and the E8, which had come that far from somewhere near Cork and was on the way to the Black Sea via the Danube. This momentous coincidence was marked by a notice-board erected by the good burgers of Ziegelhausen, along with a signpost saying something like PERUGIA → 1680 KM, which was encouraging, as Perugia wasn't far from Rome, so we were going the right way and it couldn't be far if it was already on a signpost; and discouraging, as the distance involved began to sink in: it was certainly going to be further from here than we'd already done. And that was going the short way along the top of the Apennines. We still hadn't definitely decided whether to go that way yet. We stopped for lunch at a traditional *gasthaus* and ate *Spätzle*, a kind of fried pasta dish rather like macaroni cheese, then walked slowly uphill for an hour or so before coming across another landscape of strangely massive rocks lying about in the woods: huge blocks of sandstone which had apparently been split off the cliff-face above us by ice getting into cracks about 10,000 years ago, or so the sign said. I'd have thought it would be more like 20,000 but I'm no geologist

Arriving at Gaiberg on the other side of the hill, we were given an address to stay at a farm outside the village, which also did catering for events and special occasions. In fact we arrived in the middle of a wedding party, so dropped off our bags and went back to the village pub for a bite to eat and to use their WiFi, which worked fine but the Hospitality Club site was frozen, meaning that yet again we were unable to contact prospective hosts in advance.

DAY 68   GAIBERG – ÖSTRINGEN
26 km; cloudy, showers; 15°C

As we were leaving the village early, we came upon a little glass cabinet beside the path, containing a book to be signed by walkers on the LDWP (Long Distance Walking Path), which was a nice touch. The first few hours were quite muddy and wet, with odd showers, and it was definitely getting cooler every day since we'd left Wallhausen, but we both had red hooded rain-capes now (Angela had been given one in Heidelberg) so we didn't get too wet, although we did look like a couple of pixies. The landscape was changing now from the steep wooded hills of the Odenwald to the gently rolling fields and vineyards of the Kraichgau. In Rauenburg we looked for somewhere to stop for a coffee break but everything was closed. We spoke to a couple in the street who said we'd have to go to Mühlhausen. By the time we got there we were feeling tired and sat for a long time outside an ice-cream parlour beside the main road in an open space beneath the town hall, which was all very 1970s in style and atmosphere. At the table next to us was a group of hairy bikers and punks in provocative T-shirts, including a Goth who looked like she was the mum of one of them. Going out of Mühlhausen into a forest we met an ex-professional footballer who had survived two heart attacks and was a keen walker. He engaged us in a long conversation about cycling and good health, praising the local region for its fabulous climate and rich and fruitful soil. He wished us well on our journey, asking us to give his best wishes to the Pope. At Östringen we went to the Rathaus (the Town Hall) to ask where we could stay the night and were told there was nowhere except the big old Östringer Hof, and after walking around the town just in case, we accepted it and went in. The charming old man at the desk gave us a knockdown price and a free glass of the local sweet wine, and in the morning made us fried eggs for breakfast The restaurant he recommended, which was next door, had an interesting menu with fantastic vegetarian options, a good ambience and excellent music – one of the culinary highlights of the whole trip!

DAY 69   ÖSTRINGEN – GOCHSHEIM
23 km; warm, clear; 22°C

The E1 led us across more undulating farmland where we saw red kites (or milans) swooping and chasing one another. They seem to revel in that kind of landscape at about 500 metres above sea level. As we went in and out of swathes of woodland we heard several cuckoos and also repeatedly the song of what we became sure was the golden oriole. It sounded lower than the call of a blackbird and had three notes, up a major third and then a sixth down. They are extremely elusive, spending almost all their time in the tree-tops, and despite hearing them occasionally over a period of about a month we only ever saw one once. We walked through ever-changing agricultural land, with fields of barley, peas, beans, beet and hops, with orchards here and there, and spotted a large lizard and two snakes. At Odenheim we stopped for a long break at the railway station, which was at the end of a short line called the Katzbachtal Bahn from Bruchsal. By now the sun was beginning to feel hot and we sat and wrote postcards and dozed until the time came to set off again. There was nowhere to stay in Neuenberg (where a man called out to us from his back garden next to the path, inviting us in for a drink and wishing us well) nor in Münzesheim, where we joined a path running alongside another railway track for a few kilometres as far as Gochsheim, which we entered through an industrial estate full of warehouses and chemical factories: an unprepossessing welcome to what was a beautiful old town on the ridge of a hill, with a defensive wall, a castle, and old half-timbered houses, many of which had expressive paintings on the walls from Reformation and Baroque times. At the bottom of the hill we found an old-fashioned coaching inn to stay the night, a place where Napoleon supposedly lodged. The menu was not vegetarian-friendly, but we ate a delicious cream of asparagus soup – with fresh local asparagus – and icecream with hot raspberry sauce.

DAY 70   GOCHSHEIM – BRETTEN
12 km; warm, cloudy; 18°C

I was so taken by the unpretentious little town that I got up early and took photographs of interesting buildings before breakfast (*Fig. 18) then we set off to go to Bretten, a short walk to catch a train to Heilbronn, where we had arranged to meet up with old friends. We walked all morning through rolling waves of wide fields, rapeseed crops, pinkish soil, edges packed with buttercups and odd thin lines of trees. We arrived in Bretten at lunchtime, but spent an hour in a little mobile phone shop where a young German-Turkish man was serving with great assurance. When it was our turn (after the Italian woman who was translating for a young Brazilian) he was very helpful, calm, and not at all condescending. He tried to set us up with active 'maps' on our tablet, but it proved impossible. We chatted about life balance between technology and other needs, walking and forests. After that we caught a *stadtbahn* to Heilbronn, a journey of about an hour. The train journey was funny. It stopped every few minutes and was full of very noisy seven-year-olds who had obviously been out on a class trip somewhere accompanied by a bunch of very young teachers who were pandering to their charges yet had little impact on their high decibel exuberance. Sitting next to me was a man with his face painted like a pierrot whose peculiar outbreaks of gesture and smile rehearsal seemed to betray a mime artist mentally rehearsing his act, while by the door a bearded young man was avidly reading *The Lord of the Rings* in German. When we got to Heilbronn we first met up with Martin and Claudia, friends and colleagues whom we have known since their school and ours forged a connection many years ago, and who had prepared afternoon tea for us. We sat in their garden in the spring sunshine. Fired by enthusiasm and poring over the large map of Europe which Martin had tacked to the yard wall, Claudia began to think of people she knew on our way. She had an old friend living near Lake Constance, she said. She'd get in touch with her and see if we could stay the night. She also told us much about Rome: being one of several art historians we encountered on the way and having visited many times, she could give us tips on where to go which might not be at the top of the list of tourist attractions. They gave us a lift to the outskirts of town where Uli and Karin live. We have known each other for twelve or fifteen years since our daughters became penfriends, and have all continued our friendship over the years, often meeting up in England, Germany and Corsica. Uli is a great chef, and had decided to cook a meal in honour of my birthday which happened just before we left York. After desserts Karin, a professional masseuse, gave us both a wonderful foot massage whilst we sipped wine and enjoyed each others' company. We then retired to the garden and continued in the balmy night air with our catch-up of news and traveller's tales.

DAY 71   BRETTEN – PFORZHEIM
27 km; hot; 28°C

This portion of the journey seemed to have a gastronomic theme: stopping for lunch at a *gasthaus* south of Bretten at a place called Stein – after an early start we were already halfway to our destination by noon – we settled down to a fantastic dish of walnut and spinach dumplings with mushroom and cheese sauce. After an appropriate pause to digest we braved the heat to complete the walk to Pforzheim. The path again wound its way over hillsides and beside some long lush meadows, with the blue mountains of the Schwarzwald beginning to loom closer ahead of us. We paused for a while on the way at a small chapel dedicated to a St Wendelin to sit under a tree in the shade and sort out where we were going to stay the night. The receptionist at the Youth Hostel said they were full but that there was a B&B next door which had a vacancy, so we phoned them and booked a room for the same price. Just then a farmer arrived with a bunch of flowers for the chapel and spoke to us at length about hay-making and pruning fruit trees and the size of fields. We continued towards Pforzheim, which turned out to be a large modern town, rebuilt in various stages after having been bombed to smithereens during the war. The most recent stage was the creation of a huge concrete shopping mall in the middle of town, surrounded by a lot of open space, also made of concrete, which was something of a shock after the quantity of greenery we had been seeing all day. There were no public taps in sight and no cafes where we could ask for water to refill our bottles, and by the time we had walked through the town and out the other side for a few miles along the riverside I was becoming bad-tempered with dehydration, and was beginning to rant about the blooming Youth Hostels, and how they are often in the most fantastic castles or ancient houses but their priority is always to fill the space with parties of schoolchildren or conferences, who travel there by bus or car. Walkers are now at the bottom of the list, and there's no longer any idea of a few beds being set aside for hikers or cyclists who may turn up unannounced! My mood was not lightened when I went to the Youth Hostel later to see if they had a map or information about how to get back onto the E1 in the morning, and the girl at the reception desk told me she knew nothing about walking, she went everywhere by car with SatNav. As it happened we ended up in a pleasant guest house with a great view over the Rabeneck gorge: we were indeed at the gateway to the Schwarzwald now, where the Hohenweg originally began,[5] and the next week or so would be hard going, according to our guidebook.

---

5   The Black Forest Society was established in 1864 specifically to campaign for better walking trails through the Black Forest. In 1900 the Society created what is perhaps the world's first purpose-made, fully waymarked long distance

DAY 72   PFORZHEIM – DOBEL
23 km. Hot. 30°C

At breakfast we overheard an elderly gent telling another guest that he was walking to Rome, but had to take a break for a few days to go to a grandchild's christening in Stuttgart. He seemed to be an experienced hiker and was very lean and fit for his age – he must have been in his seventies. He told us he was a widower and was doing this walk for his wife and passed on some useful information about accommodation along the way. We left Rabeneck to make the ascent to Dobel (689 m), and almost immediately found ourselves climbing an incredibly steep hill through a field. The sun was already hot at 9 o'clock as we emerged, out of breath and sweating, into a half-built new suburb where people were driving about or catching buses as though they lived on flat land. We soon came to a forest, criss-crossed by paths and gravel roads along which occasional cars were out collecting wood. At one point we passed a carved stone commemorating the tornado which decimated the forest in 1968. As we went on, the forest became older and more picturesque. We pushed on through Weissenstein, where the path took us past an ancient church and down the equally ancient steep cobbled road leading up to it from the village, and stopped at Neuenbürg at lunchtime for a spring roll at a Chinese restaurant, everything else being closed. Soon afterwards, after another massive climb, the path flattened out and meandered through more forest with another Ice Age rockfall. A couple of kilometres into the

leisure walking trail with the opening of the Hohenweg, or high level route, which later became the Westweg – 203 kilometres between Pforzheim and Basel. The Mittelweg followed in 1903, the Ostweg in 1904.

forest we met a well-dressed man out for a walk with a child in a pushchair, which was a rare sight so far from urbanisation. He was very calm and matter-of-fact about it, which made us wonder why more people don't take their toddlers out for walks in the country like that.

As we approached Dobel we found a sequence of panels beside the path, about 100 metres apart, each with a painting and a quote about angels, such as:

"For every twenty devils there are at least a hundred angels. If this were not so we would have long since perished." (Martin Luther);

"Unless you learn to dance, the angels don't know what to do with you." (Aurelius Augustus, 4th century bishop).

The B&B in Dobel was cheap and cheerful, run by a sweet old lady who loved having different people staying at her house and sent us a Christmas card six months later! We went looking for a place to eat and sat outside on a terrace overlooking the mountains as the thunderstorm which had been brewing for a while finally broke. Lightning flashed all around and the heavens opened as we ran laughing back to our lodgings.

DAY 73   DOBEL – FORBACH
27 km; very cool, showery; 10°C

Dobel is a one-horse town which is not really on the way to anywhere and doesn't attract many visitors unless they are on foot, but in the summer it must be busy, as so many Germans love hiking. This section of the E1 is well-trodden, being the Westweg to Basel, one of three long distance paths leading south from Pforzheim through the Black Forest (the others being the Ostweg and the Mittelweg). This became clearer as we started to bump into many weekend hikers, including a couple of noisy groups and a pair of married couples who had decided to walk the Westweg together in small chunks, one weekend a month, and thought they might get to Basel in a year.

After the previous night's storm had cleared the air it was decidedly chilly, and we walked along quickly to keep warm through high forest, along a path (*Fig. 19) which led past the Ski Club headquarters in a little wooden chalet up to a look-out tower built around 1900, the top of which was over 1000 metres high. We had fallen in with the two couples and wandered along with them chatting about work and plans and children and things which make you take stock of your lives. From the top of the tower there was a fantastic view over the wide plains beyond the Rhine to the mountains of the Vosges in France, and in the other direction to the Swabian Alps.

A long steep descent followed to Forbach (331 m) at the bottom of the valley, which boasted a railway station and a few shops. I had phoned ahead to the Youth Hostel two or three days earlier and been told it was full, so we asked around in the little town, to be told there was nowhere else to stay. We had something to eat with Heinz and Vera, Hartmund and Karin – the two couples we had walked with – which reminded us what a pleasure it is to meet people who spend most of their time in a completely different world from us, and considered our options. None, unless we got a train to somewhere bigger; but Angela decided to ring the Youth Hostel again on the off chance that someone had cancelled and was told they had plenty of empty beds... We had to walk uphill a couple of miles to get there, but it was small and welcoming and just had a few families staying. There had been a misunderstanding about the date, allegedly, when I phoned them before. We had a room of our own and – the best thing about Youth Hostels – a buffet breakfast where you can eat as much as you want and sometimes even have enough left over to make a packed lunch. Of course the WiFi connection didn't work, so we couldn't plan ahead, but at least we were given the address of a place further down the Westweg that we could phone.

DAY 74   FORBACH – OCHSENSTALL
22 km; cool but clearer; 12°C

We set off on another cold morning to rejoin the E1 at the top of the hill near a reservoir, meeting an old couple in their eighties dressed in very old-fashioned hiking gear – or was it just their traditional Sunday best? – on their way down towards Forbach. The track continued to wind its way up and up: when the sun came out it was quite warm but very chilly in the shade. And there was a lot of shade! Occasionally the path, which was a gravel track wide enough for a forestry vehicle, would emerge from the dense dark canopy of the pinewoods and a wide panorama would unfold on our right hand side. There were a lot of groups about again – "Sunday walkers," we caught ourselves smirking once – some of whom seemed to have to shout at each other even when walking very close together, and many off-road cyclists who spent a lot of time whizzing downhill and not much time struggling up, as far as we could see. The path ran alongside the main road, the picturesque Schwarzwaldhochstraße (Blackforesthighroad) to a bikers' caff, where a delightful narrow footpath veered off to the left into the woods up to Ochsenstall, where an amazing old wooden chalet-type bunkhouse, specially built in the early 1900s for summer hikers and winter skiers, stands next to a couple of other wooden houses and a ski-lift. The walls of the large café/common room downstairs were covered with old photos of tanned men climbing sheer rock-faces in plus-fours and fingerless gloves, or ladies standing on skis with long dresses covering their ankles, with captions like "OCHSENSTALL, 1908". The place is now run by a young couple, and she said she'd cook us whatever we fancied since we were the only guests. However as it was getting dark another walker arrived: Konrad, a German of about 35 or 40 who spoke Russian and Polish and had done a lot of farm-work all over Europe. He was walking on the Westweg heading north from Basel and told us there were quite a few cheap places to stay the next night in Kniebis. He said he might set off with us in the morning and go down to Mummelsee, which is a small lake famous in German folklore.

DAY 75 OCHSENSTALL – KNIEBIS
24 km; warmer, clear; 19°C

Konrad did join us after breakfast to walk up to Hornegrinde, at 1164 metres the highest peak in the northern part of the Schwarzwald. The morning was very fresh at that altitude but became warmer as we started to go downhill in the sunshine. We arrived at the Mummelsee, which was a very small lake, epitomising the ancient qualities of the silent all-hearing forest, only to find it surrounded by rows of shops and stalls and tourist coaches. We parted company with Konrad, who was going to take a more easterly direction and maybe complete a circular route back to his home near Basel. We took an uphill path to Darmstädter Hütte, which had been built as a bunkhouse for the Darmstadt branch of the Schwarzwaldverein – the equivalent would be something like the York branch of the Scottish Highlands Club (which as far as I know doesn't actually exist) building a large bunkhouse near Glencoe for their members to stay at – and also functions as a café during the day for passers-by. There was then a long walk along a gravel road as the sun rose higher in the sky. The temperature was just below 20° but the sun was strong and we were soon getting burnt, especially on the right hand side. We began to see storm damage on this section – looking up to the left we could see that huge swathes of forest were missing. As a result of Hurricane Lothar on the evening of Boxing Day 1999, millions of trees were destroyed and there are still just stumps remaining. Further on there was a swarm of 'dragon flyers' – people who had hurled themselves off the mountainside to float on the winds and surf the thermals with hang-gliders. At the end of the track we got a free bus ride to Kniebis along the busy main road: every time we stayed at a B&B in the Schwarzwald region we were charged a small tax which was refundable on any form of public transport when displaying our 'Kurtax' card – what a good idea to encourage people to use the local buses and trains as well as hiking or cycling! We found a cheap and tidy B&B in Kniebis which felt more like an Alpine village than anything we had seen yet, with many large wooden houses, often with roofs reaching down to the ground. We went looking for a place to eat in the village instead of sitting in our room with a handful of dried cranberries and a crust of stale bread each. Appropriately (or oddly) enough, we found a Swiss restaurant called the Schwyzer Hüttli, which was run by a Swiss man and did serve Swiss food, which we ate ravenously, and drank a toast to having passed the thousand-mile mark!

DAY 76   KNIEBIS – BAD GRIESBACH
14 km; cooler, cloudy, drizzle; 14°C

After breakfast we walked back to the place where we had caught the bus, passing a Tourist Information Office (closed) on the way, then continued on a marked track off the Westweg down to the bottom of the valley to the spa town of Bad Griesbach (*bad* means bath or spa, by the way, not **bad**). It was hard to believe we had climbed up this far; we seemed to be going down for hours, with amazing views across the valley. We came down past a large hotel and a *kurhaus*, or therapeutic centre, and made our way to the railway station. We were going back to Wallhausen, having been asked to put on a singing workshop in a nearby village hall. The thing was, we had had to give them a date before we even left England so they could advertise it, and we had said we'd probably be there in the middle of May, so call it the 15th. Of course we'd actually arrived at the end of April and walked on another 300 kilometres since then, so we had to go backwards to fulfil our obligation. Would it be worth it? Well, it only cost us about €70 to travel to and fro between Bad Griesbach and Wallhausen as we could use our Kurtax cards for some of the journey, and we were hoping to raise much more than that for MSF, and I suppose we were due a day off by that stage anyway. This was to be the fourth such workshop after Barton, Goedereede and Roßdorf.

DAYS 77-78   WALLHAUSEN
0 km; cool, overcast; 15°C

Well, it was worth it in terms of having 25-30 people who all made a contribution to MSF and was thoroughly enjoyable to boot. We received €375 in generous donations. The next day was spent relaxing with family members and friends who came to visit.

17ᵗʰ May 2012

How different the seasons feel now, not quite a fortnight after the last time I wrote to you. During the five days' break we allowed ourselves, the forest had taken a huge leap forward; the ground was covered in a dense tussle of things winding around each other in eagerness for life and light. The translucence of the early leaves had given way to a lush full deep green presence on earth. When we came out into meadow-scapes the grasshoppers were chirping in their dozens, giving suddenly a very southerly feel to our surroundings. We walked the first day with Michael, my brother who sadly could only manage the first day. But perhaps he will join us again in the Alps. We still wandered through the Odenwald, Germany's best-kept secret, a wonderful expanse of partly volcanic mountain terrain, densely wooded, with valleys of farmed land in between the undulating tops.

I grew up in the plains to the north of it, and many a time looked towards the Odenwald with longing during my childhood. I will continue to think of it with the longing of a deeply wonderful experience from now on! Once we had crossed the river Neckar, we spent an evening and a night in the historic and romantic university town of Heidelberg at the home of a Servas host of theatre- and film-making pedigree, then we spent a few days getting accustomed to cooler and damper weather, while we became acquainted with the Kraichgau, an area I had no knowledge of whatever! It is so fertile and well-favoured in its attributes that the locals call it "The German Tuscany". They seem to be able to grow anything there including vines and hops.

Vineyards meant the occasional unpleasant noseful of sulphur, I'm afraid, since we were caught without escape in the spraying efforts of the 'conventional' farmer. But particularly in this area we heard the cuckoo again, and also the golden oriole, a most tropical-sounding bird who lives in the tops of trees entirely and is very difficult to see. Needless to say I stood and stared for a long time squinting and cricking my neck – no, I didn't see it either, but we heard quite a few of them!

We entered the Black Forest shortly after crossing through a very modern town called Pforzheim – modern on account of having been badly destroyed in the war – and we delighted in the fact that we were in the forest, with a mixture of deciduous and coniferous trees. But soon enough we became aware of the Black Forest's tragedy: vast hillsides of needle tree monoculture, which were swept bare by a particularly vehement hurricane in 1999, and many more trees in a skeletal state from being literally poisoned during their cleansing work of the polluted air and by the chemical cocktail they imbibe through the water from the ground (*Fig. 20). Prevailing westerly winds bring lots of it from the Rhine plains and France. The ray of hope lies in the beautiful fuzz of the new and young generation of little trees which cover much of the abused areas, and they are far from the monoculture look of the 'old' Black Forest picture. Here again we met so many people to chat with, even several to walk with. And we ever more appreciate the pace and openness of walking as opposed to any other means of transport. We are being talked with by so very many people!

Tomorrow we will travel back to the Black Forest and pick up where we left off a couple of days ago (after eleven days of uninterrupted walking!). This was the first time we returned somewhere, again to my *brother's house, but the promise of giving a workshop here had been standing for a long time. It had been fixed in accordance with when we had expected to get here, which you may remember we pipped by about a fortnight! I should tell you, the workshop was lovely! There was a big group of people, all of whom were really taking part with gusto and made a lovely sound together. Seemed like they enjoyed themselves, and they were very generous in their donations to Medecins Sans Frontieres, which of course we celebrate. We also celebrated our 1,000th mile the night before we came here again, and I am still wearing my first pair of boots!!*

Dear Friends, thank you all very much for the lovely emails and messages and encouraging words. It means a huge amount to us, and we are by now working quite hard to get through the daily stretch as the terrain has begun to cross the 1000 meter mark. You can imagine then that we are not just climbing up there once and then walking on flat land. Oh no! It goes up and down considerably on a daily basis now, and we are definitely keeping our breaks to a minimum just so we don't get out of the swing of things. I still notice every feather along the way and acknowledge it with thanks as one of the many good wishes I feel going with us, as this is the idea our Bolivian neighbour in York set us going with. Joy over every feather, these are good wishes on your way!

It will be some time again before you will hear from us, but we will read anything you send as we approach Lake Constance on our next stage!

Our best wishes to you all, and lots of love from

Angela and Nick XX

We were up early and got a series of trains to Bad Peterstal, the town next to Bad Griesbach. From there we climbed steeply for two or three hours until finally at the top we rejoined the E1, only 4.5 km from Harkhof, which we'd had recommended to us by Konrad. The atmosphere was beginning to get warmer and heavier, but it felt good to be walking again after a somewhat enforced break. Now that we had notched up the thousand-mile mark we felt that we must have passed the halfway point, which was immensely encouraging, as were the good wishes we were still receiving from friends and strangers alike. Shortly after we got back onto the E1 it dwindled from a wide gravel forestry road to a rocky footpath and finally a sandy way flanked by blueberry bushes. Coming round a mountainous outcrop we suddenly had a fantastic view of verdant meadows and distant snowy peaks, and just below us a large farmhouse which was our destination. The farm had been adapted to cater for hikers and cyclists, and had a bunkhouse with three rooms full of bunks, a restaurant and its own butchery. The view from the balcony was somewhat marred by the smell of the slurry being spread on the field below, but the bunkhouse was fine, if a little cramped. Our room had two pairs of bunks, but one pair was wide enough for five people to sleep next to each other in sleeping-bags on each level, so there was technically enough space for a dozen sleepers in a normal-sized room, although there were only seven that night: us, two Dutch couples and a quiet older man who spoke German. We found out from chatting to the Dutch people that it had snowed quite heavily while we were away for those two or three days, although there was no trace remaining, and they proved it by showing us their noses, sunburnt from the reflected glare. We had a drink with them on the balcony and were getting on well: Henk and Anneke lived in The Hague while Dirk and Carla lived in Vienna, but they had decided to get together twice a year for a week to walk the El from Nassau to Genoa. They invited us to eat with them (*Fig. 21), and we walked with them for chunks over the next few days, sharing some good conversation and laughter.

DAY 80 HARKHOF – HAUSACH
14 km; mild, becoming stormy; 21°C

"For the right understanding of a landscape, information must come to the intelligence from all the senses…"

After it rained heavily overnight the sun was shining in the morning and the view over the mountains had changed into a landscape of mist rising in scraps and wisps, gradually uncovering the greens and blues of the forest. We had breakfast with the other resident of our bedroom, who said he was called Hans and lived in Schonach, a couple of days' walk further on. It turned out he had been a doctor there until his retirement a few years earlier, when he had spent six months crewing on a tall ship out of Cuxhaven to the Caribbean before turning his attention to long distance walking. We discovered over the next two days that at 68 he was at least as fast as the Dutch couples who were about twenty years younger. He invited us to come to supper at his house with the Dutchmen when we got to Schonach.

We embarked on a long and beautiful stroll through the heart of the Black Forest, an enchanted, ever-changing landscape which entirely disproved my speculation beforehand that it would be boring, just a succession of pine trees by the million: sunless, sightless, soundless, lifeless and charmless. On the contrary. This day somehow encapsulated the essence of the walk insofar as we were constantly having all our senses tickled by the sounds of birds and breezes, the smells of moss and bark and sap, the tastes of ozone and distant snow… The regular snaps between focusing on the mountains or valleys in the distance and the hanging branches over the root-strewn path, the switches between looking outwards and thinking inwards, all of these were clarified. After a couple of hours walking we had just been talking about fairy tales, and how perhaps in the past lone forest-dwellers would have been banished or exiled from their towns or villages because of some eccentricity or unusual physical condition, giving rise to the idea of witches, giants or dwarves living in the depths of the forest. Or is the stuff of fairy-tales something more archetypal? Suddenly we saw smoke curling from a chimney in a tiny house by the side of the footpath, looking out over a dramatic view about 2,000 feet down a steep hillside. A little old lady stuck her head out of the doorway and invited us in, and once we had dismissed our immediate thoughts of a gingerbread house, we accepted. The reality was that she and her friend operated this resting-place for passing walkers on behalf of the local branch of the Schwarzwaldverein. They had walked up from Wolfach in the valley at the foot of the mountain (several miles uphill) that morning with tins full of cakes in their rucksacks, lit the stove and started making coffee, which they offered to all and sundry for a nominal sum. All the people we had seen on the path over the last few days, and some new faces too, seemed to be stopping there simultaneously:

Henk, Anneke, Dirk and Carla; Hans; Jens from the Odenwald and Jane from Lincoln; two sisters from Zurich; and a Swiss man with a huge dog and a 20-kilo pack who looked as though he'd been walking non-stop for years. People set off again in dribs and drabs and we stopped for our pack-up at a high vantage point where we saw a swallow-tail butterfly, then dropped down steeply about 500 m to Hausach. By the time we got there the air was very heavy and it was starting to rain great fat drops as we passed an old man trimming the hedgerow to keep the footpath clear. Luckily we didn't have too long to wait out in the open next to a large road crossing the river before we spotted our host for the night, Matthias from Servas. Or rather, he spotted us, as he was looking out for two people with large rucksacks. He gave us a lift to his house in Haslach, about five kilometres down the valley. A small neat fellow of our age with an attentive manner, Matthias told us this was his childhood home. His father had been a tailor, with a workshop on the ground floor, where his mother lived now, while Matthias lived upstairs with his bright and lively wife Uta. She arrived home from a cycling tour after we had accomplished our post-walk ritual: shower, wash clothes and look at any incoming emails. Matthias cooked a delicious meal involving a lot of asparagus and we went to the local church where he is a verger to see a concert of classical music played on the piano accordion by a Ukrainian maestro. We walked into the old town centre and visited Uta's studio, where she works as a music therapist among dozens of musical instruments, and after an impromptu jam session went to the main square where about two hundred people were gathered at long tables eating sausage, drinking beer and watching a football match on a big screen TV. Bayern Munich were playing Chelsea in the Champions' League final, which inspired much enthusiasm. I seemed to be the only person there who was not German, so I kept my head down. We went back to the house at half-time and sang some songs together, then watched the end of the match – penalty shoot-outs and all.

DAY 81   HAUSACH – SCHONACH
22 km; warm, sunny intervals; 20°C

"Climbing uphill, the horizon grows wider; descending, the hills gather around…"

This morning was an important day for Matthias and Uta, being their sixth wedding anniversary, which was their excuse for preparing an excellent breakfast. They took us back to Hausach where they saw us off with many good wishes and we exchanged the hope to see each other again, and next time for longer. From there we began to climb up again. We knew this would be a hard day's walk: there was no steep downhill walking involved but a lot of uphill, from 280 m ASL (above sea level) to over 900 m by lunchtime, which was heavy going in the humid atmosphere. Once we got to the top it was fairly flat all the way to Schonach, where we arrived together with the Dutch Four to be met by Hans. After about an hour's climb we met an apple-cheeked young woman in her late twenties wearing a Turkish-style headscarf, who was coming downhill: it was an unusual and welcome sight to see a woman out walking alone in those parts. The path went across moorland on the top and passed by a couple of "eagles' nests" with stunning panoramas. We stopped for a bite to eat on a blasted heath surrounded by hurricane damage, but on the whole the path led through relatively unscathed forest, and the day's walk ended at a large café at the top of the hill outside Schonach, where we met the Dutch contingent again. We managed to phone Hans, who had gone on ahead, to tell him where we were, and he and his wife Anita immediately jumped into a car each and came to fetch us all. Hans took us to the Youth Hostel, which was in fact several kilometres further away than we had expected, so we were glad of the lift. The hostel was almost empty, and while we had a shower and washed our clothes he went away, then came back to pick us up to take us to his house for supper. Anita had prepared a good walkers' meal, and we chatted about our histories before going back to the hostel. What a kindly couple!

DAY 82   SCHONACH – FURTWANGEN
16 km; mild, heavy, thundery; 17°C

"Of the many ways through a landscape, we can choose, on each occasion, only one, and the project of the walk will be to remain responsive, adequate, to the consequences of the choice we have made, to confirm the chosen way rather than refuse the others…"

In the morning Hans came and picked us up again and took us to see the waterfall at Triberg, near the Hostel, which is apparently the highest in Germany. When we started out on the footpath again we decided to take it easy as we were only going to go as far as Furtwangen. The question had been: "Should we continue on the E1 which goes a long way round over the highest peak in the Black Forest; or should we cut across and pick the path up again at Titisee?" The former would be more challenging, and we had an address from Michael of a farm we could stay at near the Feldberg, but weren't able to get a response from them by phone or email, and the weather forecast was not brilliant. On the other hand we had the address of a Hospitality Club host in

Furtwangen who had been sending us emails almost daily for a fortnight asking when we were going to arrive. We decided to go to Furtwangen, home of the cuckoo clock, to stay with Heinrich. The route took us through a peat bog, past a toxic lake which had a sign next to it saying that it was naturally as acid as vinegar. We went beside and through meadows full of lush grass and dandelions waiting to be cut for hay. We came around corners to see sloping glades full of campanula (which Angela assures me are not the same as English bluebells) and aconites, or ploughed land or grazing cattle. We passed by what felt like a Stone Age settlement in the midst of a shady beech forest, or perhaps it was another Ice Age forest: it seemed as though the boulders had tumbled down at some point in the distant past. In fact they have always been there. A mixture of sandstone and granite, they have been subject to what is known as Woolpack weathering and the forest has grown up around them only in the last fifty years or so. Among the huge rectangular sandstone blocks one had been carved with an "In memoriam" epitaph several feet high in beautiful Gothic script, at least a century old, which made us wonder.

Our Dutch companions had set off just ahead of us in the morning, and though we saw them once in the distance we didn't catch up with them again. They were expecting to cover about thirty kilometres to reach their car at the endpoint of this section of their journey. Although Dirk had a longstanding limp, they covered the ground pretty quickly and we thought they'd have no problem getting as far as the Mediterranean. We decided they represented the four ancient Greek temperaments (subsequently forgotten in Western Europe until the Renaissance and then overtaken by ideas based on individualism and genetics): Henk would be the choleric, Anneke melancholic, Dirk phlegmatic and Carla sanguine. Henk reminded me of a cowboy and was always the one striding out ahead, beating the path. He was in charge of the coffee machine so he decided when to stop for a break. Anneke was the quietest, serious and tranquil and most likely to be nostalgic; while Dirk was the solid and dependable type who prepared all the routes in advance, kept the accounts and made sure everyone had enough to eat. Carla was the one who skipped along bringing up the rear, being distracted by this and that, having a headful of ideas at the same time as seeing everything fly past.

After the fork to Furtwangen took us off to the left of the E1/Westweg, we dawdled and sauntered along, feeling under no pressure to keep up with any fellow hikers, and stopped at a café near the Martinskapelle, an ancient and tiny chapel built next to the source of the Danube. A signpost next to it says it is 2,888 kilometres to the Black Sea – roughly the distance we would be walking in total from York to Rome. The path rose and fell at about 1000 m for some miles, and passed by the Brend tower (1130 m) from which one can allegedly see the Jungfrau and the Eiger on a clear day. Today wasn't clear enough, but it was exciting to look out over the hazy distance towards what might be the Alps. A thunderstorm was brewing: when it erupted we were luckily on the edge of the forest within sight of a *gasthaus* on the road into Furtwangen, and after an hour of hearing the rain batter down on the roof and watching it pour down the driveway towards the front door, an old man at the next table asked where we were going. He recognised Heinrich by name, and said: "I'll give you a lift to his house."

Heinrich and his wife Elsa were both very large people. They lived in quite a small house with their 11-year-old son, but he was the youngest of eight, the eldest being about 30. It must have been a full house ten years earlier, before all the other children had moved out to work or study elsewhere. Heinrich was a journalist who worked from home, being particularly interested in local history and folklore, and was obviously more conversant with his PC than with his walking boots. He cooked an enormous meal for us of macaroni cheese followed by massive bowlfuls of blancmange. He was very helpful, printing out reams of information about the best route to Switzerland, while Elsa showed us albums full of photos of their children. The pile of notes that Heinrich printed out for us proposed a completely different route from the one we had envisaged, going in more of a southerly direction via Schaffhausen and the Rhine Falls to Zurich rather than via Konstanz then south to Wil. As it turned out we took neither option, but decided for the time being we'd get back onto the E1 at Titisee and head east towards Konstanz then play it by ear.

DAY 83   FURTWANGEN – BERGHÄUSLE
20 km; sunny, becoming overcast; 17°C

Elsa accompanied us up the hill out of town for a little way before she ran out of puff then we continued upwards over ground made increasingly muddy by the evening's downpour. The weather was pleasantly mild and the landscape became less densely forested with many meadows full of the vivid yellow of dandelions against the deep blue of distant wooded mountains. At one point we looked down at Freiburg, at another to the snow-covered peak of Feldberg (the highest in the Schwarzwald). Walking beside a main road then turning off to the right we went through woods again, firstly on quite a civilised well-signposted track then increasingly a path for more adventurous walkers, which was not always easy to follow. We were thinking of stopping at a place called a *Berghäusle*, or Mountain Hut, which according to our guidebook was run by the SWV (Schwarzwaldverein), but hadn't booked anything as we thought we might want to continue to Titisee. However as the afternoon wore on it became cooler and began to threaten more heavy rain. I saw a notice nailed to a tree, advertising:

HIKERS HOSTEL & RESTAURANT → 1 KM.

We got there just before the rain and discovered it was in fact the same Berghäusle. The boss seemed pleased to see us and offered us bunks in a room with enough beds for six, while the chef said he could make us a tasty vegetarian meal. As the evening wore on it became clear we would be the only guests, although a group of local people turned up who had just come to have a little stroll in the forest and something to eat and drink. They were very jolly, and we ended up singing songs to each other before they left shortly before 9 o'clock. At 9 the man in charge, whom we had taken to be the SWV warden, said he was locking up and disappeared. Two minutes later there was a knock at the front door but nobody came to open up. I called out for the warden but there was no answer – I didn't know whether he was even still on the premises but suspected he had a flat behind the main building. Another knock on the door…I looked out though the window in the door and to my astonishment saw Konrad. What a pleasant surprise! I turned the key and opened the door. Konrad came in and told us where he had been and that he'd phoned ahead to say he was coming this evening, so I told him he'd better go and find the guy in charge; I thought he was round the back in that flat. Off he went, leaving his rucksack with us. The next thing we knew the boss came in with Konrad and told him: "Take your bag and go! Get out and don't come back!" then chased him down the drive with a stick. He turned on me: "What did you think you were doing, opening the door? Is this your house? No! You have no right to unlock the door of my house and let in any stranger!"

"Yes, I'm sorry," I replied. "Enschuldigen sie bitte. But we know this man…"

"Yes, you know him, but you don't know he is deranged. I've worked for years in mental hospitals and I know the signs. I could tell from his tone when he telephoned. He's crazy!"

"Well, we haven't seen any sign of it. He seems quite normal," I answered in poor German. "Anyway, you've got room for him to stay. He could stay in our room…"

"Who are you to say whether or where he can stay? I've taken this place over from the SWV; it's up to me to decide who stays. I am responsible!"

He was a big man, thick-set and bearded; his face was reddening and his eyes bulging with apoplexy. Flecks of spittle flew out of his lips. For a moment he was on the verge of throwing us out too, and we were on the verge of walking out: we had begun to wonder whether he had been a nurse or a patient. The problem was we had already paid; we were stuck in the middle of the forest, and it was becoming very dark outside. Konrad had already left and we probably wouldn't catch up with him by the time we'd packed all our stuff including our wet clothes. Your man obviously wasn't satisfied with my apology, and in the end Angela stepped in and said sorry in some more polite and acceptable way which defused the situation for the time being, and we all went to bed. We were worried that Konrad might have got lost or not been able to find anywhere else to stay the night, but at least we knew Titisee was only a few kilometres away and he seemed to know his way around the area better than us.

DAY 84   BERGHÄUSLE – SCHATTENMÜHLE
22 km; warm, becoming thundery; 18°C

We rose early and went downstairs with our bags packed ready to leave when the bearded giant appeared and offered us breakfast. He'd apparently forgotten the whole episode, and when we brought up the subject he reiterated his explanation more soberly. He seemed to be quite convinced that he was in the right so we ended up shrugging our shoulders a lot and eating a hearty breakfast. The forest was shrouded in mist as we resumed our journey and descended towards Titisee, passing a memorial stone erected in 1858 to remember a travelling salesman who was murdered there by brigands. We stopped long enough in Titisee to get some cash and book into the only hotel between there and the other end of the gorge we were about to enter, some 20 kilometres away. The town, which is on the shore of a fairly large lake, was a hive of tourist activity, full of people from all over Europe despite it being a foggy Wednesday morning in May, but we did pass a couple of little guest-houses with "VACANCY" notices in the window, which boded well for Konrad's chances of having had a good night's sleep. We pressed on up a steep cobbled road which led into the forest and over the hill to Kappel, where it became a footpath named "The soul-health path" leading to a small chapel, incongruously dedicated to St Anthony of Padua, who made a name for himself in the Middle Ages as the scourge of the Cathars in the South West of France – another massacre perpetrated in the name of religion. At the bottom of the hill we were at the beginning of the Haslachschlucht (*Fig. 22) and the footpath became ever narrower as it wound its way alongside the river leading out of the Schwarzwald through a crack in the bulk of the mountains. At times the path climbed high above the steep gorge, where it had been cut out of the cliff, and often you had to hang onto cables screwed into the stone as you clambered over ancient rockfalls. The extraordinary geology of the place – on the border of several different kinds of rock – meant that there were always new sights to be seen round every corner: a wide variety of plants, some of them exclusively found in this small region; waterfalls; or fantastic colours and patterns within the rock strata. The whole valley seemed to be humming with life: butterflies fluttered around our heads and lizards scuttled around our feet. Meanwhile the air was full of tension as the thunder rattled around the echoing walls of the gorge. When we were still four or five kilometres short of our destination the thunder finally turned into rain, but just a few of those heavy drops which seem to have been squeezed from a giant sponge. By the time we reached the inn it had passed by and the skies were clear.

The last week or so had been an eye-opening experience of the world of the rambler, a world we had only dipped our toes into beforehand. For a long time after leaving York we had been long-distance walkers who were persevering with our task because we had undertaken to do it, but in the last couple of weeks it was becoming more and more of a pleasure to get up in the morning and be outdoors all day whatever the weather, revelling in it! Walking through the landscape at the end of May we had been almost constantly enveloped in green. Layer upon layer of forest and field in all directions and dimensions stretched away from us or embraced us in every conceivable shade of green. stepping out of dense forest into rolling fields merely changed the variety of greens upon the palette and added some blues, whites and greys from the sky, while inside the forest there were moments when the all-pervading greenness was only shifted by the play of light and shade in the air.

DAY 85   SCHATTENMÜHLE – BLUMBERG
21 km; still warm and thundery; 19°C

Leaving the Schattenmühle – an old watermill at the bottom of a steep dark valley – we made our way along the footpath which leads through the Wutachschlucht for about ten kilometres. Practically speaking it was much the same as the day before: absolutely stunning scenery, muggy weather, difficult footpath, amazing geology. Actually it was more so, on every count. The path was quite dangerous at times and in places it may easily have been impassable a couple of weeks earlier because of snowmelt and rainfall swelling the river and flooding the path – or even a couple of days later. The rainfall was so intense at times that it felt like you could get washed away by flash floods, or at least that's what we thought when we got stuck behind a couple of visiting day-trippers from Israel who were out for a pleasant stroll by the river in their summer casuals when we all got caught in a sudden downpour. After sheltering under a tree in our capes for a while it began to feel like not such a good idea with so much lightning about, so we pressed on. The Israelis were trying to negotiate a slippery rockface which sloped directly towards the rushing waters of the Wutach, which at this point had become about five metres wide: wide enough to drown in anyway. Actually it wasn't that difficult even with packs on – there were ropes and cables and poles to hold onto at strategic points – but the woman was panicking, and they just weren't mentally prepared. I mean, we had been walking through this thundery rainy weather for five days, while they had driven up from Munich that morning. So we helped them over the hardest bit and walked through the forest with them for a little way. "Will you be coming back for a longer walk?" Angela asked innocently. "No," he answered with a wry smile and a glance toward his partner. "Never again!" We left them waiting at a bus stop with twenty or thirty other people who had appeared from nowhere and were sitting at a roadside kiosk in the middle of the forest, sheltering from the rain and waiting for a bus to arrive and take them to wherever they'd left their cars.

Up to that point we had spent most of the day in the gorge. Heinrich had given us copious notes about the history and geology of the Musselkalk gorge, so we were somewhat prepared, and would otherwise have missed much of the detail. As it was we found cliffs of limestone, shale and chalk, often with the underlying strata visible so that the prehistoric folding could be clearly seen. We saw ancient trees, often draped in creepers and moss; more butterflies, and beautiful flowers in shady glades full of bluebells and wild garlic or in sunny corners with violets, aconites and orchids peeping out. There were other tricky spots on the path too, where we had to clamber over boulders, pull ourselves up by tree roots, wade through streams, and sometimes avoid falling down the side because of rockfalls and mudslides having taken away chunks of footpath (*Fig. 23).

Having emerged from the gorge at the kiosk we continued in more open country, walking through woods and meadows then along a quiet country lane with "Spring Poems" pinned up on notice-boards at regular intervals. We decided to carry on through Achdorf and look for somewhere to stay in Blumberg, which meant negotiating a very steep, narrow and rarely used footpath around and over a mountain. Arriving at the town we checked in at the Kaktus Kafe, which was run by a moustachioed Mexican. We sat around and talked to the locals, who were a pretty lawless bunch. A toothless ex-merchant seaman bought us a drink and told us about the rise of far-right extremists in the area, as various shady characters cruised around the high street in 4x4s. We slept well despite the thump of the jukebox from beneath us.

DAY 86   BLUMBERG – ENGEN
26 km; warm and breezy; 21°C

In the morning we got up early, showered, packed our bags and had breakfast at the posh hotel across the road as the Kaktus Kafe was strictly for night birds and didn't offer breakfast The weather had changed completely with a stiff breeze blowing the clouds away. Following the map in our guidebook and the E1 signs we took a path which went off in the wrong direction then circled around and over another large mountain. When we finally emerged an hour and a half later at a road on the other side we found ourselves next to a sign pointing to another footpath and saying:

DIREKTER WEG → BLUMBERG 1 km

Shrugging this setback aside we followed the path across the road and up the hill past a lot of signposts saying something about historic railways. We saw viaducts in the distance then tunnels and a station, all laid out as neatly as a model railway set. We walked along country lanes under trees fully in leaf then around a corner suddenly a panorama of volcanic hills unfolded, with a distant view of Alps, and we wandered through it on the Alte Postweg past an old battleground from the Napoleonic Wars. We spoke for a while with a retired bricklayer who was out for a spin in the forest in his electric wheelchair. He told us all about the battle, and also said that much of the forest in these parts had been felled and taken away to Switzerland as a form of compensation after World War II. It was a long walk, but invigorating in the warm breeze, heading for Engen, where we had arranged to stay the night with someone called Sigfried. We gave him a ring. He said he'd meet us in town then he just needed to go and do a bit of shopping at the supermarket – oh yes, and he could introduce us to this English friend of his on the way – then we could go home. So we all piled into his little car and had a quick tour of the town centre then knocked on the door of the Englishman, a young man who had accompanied his German wife, a doctor, to her locality and been left to look after the children during the day and do up the dilapidated old townhouse by himself, which he didn't have time to do as he had his hands full of nappies and shopping and toys and cooking, which seemed to be weighing him down a bit.

At Sigfried's flat, which stood in a suburban street in a village which had become a dormitory town for Engen and Singen, we met his wife Fatima, a cheerful Moroccan. They had met when Sigfried went on holiday to her home town on the Atlantic coast, and seemed a most unlikely couple. He is about 45, she about 28. He is serious and thoughtful, she is giggly and frivolous. He is stocky and no pin-up, while she is pretty and girlish. He is interested in world affairs and ecology, while she likes lying in bed drinking Coke and watching bubblegum TV. And yet – or maybe "and so" – they get on very well together. We slept on the couch in the front room and were invited to stay another night; since we hadn't had a rest day for about ten days we accepted.

DAY 87 ENGEN & ENVIRONS
0 km; warm, clear; 23°C

So in the morning, a Saturday, we went to town and had a haircut – it had been three months and it was starting to get warm, particularly for Angela who had had her hair long for about the last twenty years and was feeling the heat – while Sigfried went to finish a job at the garage/workshop he co-owns with a mate. We pottered around the town a bit as well: it is built on a ridge and has a lift going down to the car-park near the river at the bottom of the cliff. The town is full of sculptures and well-groomed houses, specialist shops and cobbles, reminding me of a small version of Luxembourg. "Klein aber fein," as a hiker we met outside the garage told us.

Sigfried had suggested going to see a friend of theirs who lives near the famous Rhine Falls near Schaffhausen

145

(which Heinrich had wanted us to see), so we went shopping for BBQ ingredients and set off in their car. We asked whether we'd need to take passports as we would be going into Switzerland, but were assured that no-one ever gets stopped at the border, they've been that way about forty times and never been stopped, but we took the passports anyway, and sure enough the Swiss border police stopped us and wanted to know how much meat we were taking over the border.

""That's OK, you're allowed to import less than 10 kilos." As our contribution to the barbecue was strictly vegetarian the combined total was well under the limit.

We pulled into a lay-by and looked down over the Bodensee (known as Lake Constance in English) with the Alps in the distance, while behind us a plateau stretched out towards Blumberg dotted with volcanic cones. Sigfried said at this point: "Oh, I ought to mention that the friend we're going to visit, Marion, used to be a man." We probably would have guessed straight away as she is about 6′4″ with hands like shovels. She has almost finished building her own house – and I mean building it herself brick by brick. She also had several cars and camper vans out the front which she's working on, and is very interested in the history of railways and industrial engineering as well as having been a professor of art history. We sat outside on the patio and had our barbecue and drank beer in the hot late afternoon sun after visiting the falls, which are really more a set of rapids at a point where the river has just come out of the lake and started to flow downhill quite sharply. It is indeed impressive as the river is already wider than the Thames in London, say, and goes rushing straight at a small island, not much more than a rock with a set of steps carved into the side, which is served by a little ferry which plies to and fro across the calm pond below the torrent, taking people who want to climb the steps and feel the spray.

On the way back to Engen we stopped at a covered wooden bridge which crosses the Rhine further downstream and gazed across to the medieval houses on the other side (*Fig. 24). Angela took a photo of Sigfried but he said "Don't publish it on Facebook!"

DAY 88   ENGEN – HORN
30 km; cloudy, mild; 20°C

In the morning we set out early to walk to a farm whose address we had been given by Michael as a place which has WWOOFers (volunteers who help World Wide Organic Farmers) to stay. They had told us we could stay the night in a caravan there, but we looked at the map properly and realised it was less than ten kilometres away, so on reflection we thought we should maybe stay with those friends of Claudia's that she had told us about in Heilbronn, the ones who lived near the shore of the Bodensee. We gave them a ring, and spoke to Anne, who said she'd never heard of us but yes, of course, if we were friends of Claudia's we were welcome to stay the night. That altered our original plan considerably as we then had to cover quite a long distance to get to Horn, so we'd have to get a move on. We walked a long way at first on cycle paths and pavements into and out of Singen, and as far as Böhlingen, after which we found footpaths but were led a long way round by signposts and ended up in Bankholzen when we thought we would have been in Bettnang, then found ourselves in what must have been the communal forest belonging to Horn but didn't know which way to go at a crosspaths. When we phoned Anne to ask her which way we should turn she said: "Ah, I know where you are. I'll come and find you now. We're all looking forward to meeting you," and hung up before we could object. They have a beautiful house five minutes' walk from the lakeside and we spent a delightful evening with her and Wolf, a bearded art teacher who had much to tell of life working at a secondary school ("gymnasium") in Germany. We also met Sabine (16) who had spent a term at a school in Northern Ireland, and Maria (18) who was practising for a clarinet competition the next day in Stuttgart, open to young people from the whole of the state of Baden-Württemberg. They were so welcoming, we were sorry to retire early after what had turned out to be a long day's walk of thirty kilometres: mostly on the plateau at about 500 m, so fairly flat, and by the side of the volcanic plugs rather than over them, but it had still felt like a long way.

28th May 2012

Dear Friends, all of you, most recent and longstanding friends,

Summer advances, we think, in that we seem to be hot and sweaty most days most of the time, but that means nothing since the terrain certainly has given us plenty of exercise! The Black Forest, announced to us as possibly a rather boring expanse of nothing but coniferous trees, turned out to be every bit as varied and surprising in its many faces as anywhere else we have been so far. To give you just a couple of pictures: coming out of the woods, in which we would have clambered up very steep rocky paths with the roots of trees lending a series of uneven gnarled steps, we would find ourselves among mountain meadows ever more rich with flowers of such variety and scent!

Wild carnations, several varieties of buttercups, many purple shades of flowers some of which I can only name in German (sorry), most of which I cannot name at all, buzzing with bumblebees and full of butterflies. Little meadow blues with their intense sky blue wings in many shades and in their dozens, fritillaries with bright orange spotted wings – a sea of colour and joy.

Another picture – and I will admit to nearly welling over when I stood there gazing – before us such a meadow-scape with one singular old-fashioned Black Forest house at the meadow bottom, some young cattle friskily frolicking behind it, and suddenly from behind the house on a narrow strip of brown earth appears a strongly built horse, copper brown with a golden mane, followed by a plough held by an old man. They were working together in such peaceful concentration and with such attuned energy, it was spellbinding! A young lad skipped around behind the course of the other two picking up some grassy clods to clean the 'morrow' – the strip of land you can plough in such a fashion during one morning.

Another picture: scrambling down and along a very narrow path down through a gorge, and due to its remarkable geology, which has laid strips of different kinds of rock sideways, the environmental circumstances changed frequently as we walked along. One moment we were in a prehistoric world, the plant life reminding us of those school book fantasies that made us expect to see a dinosaur appear at any moment; the next moment I was spotting orchids; the next I was clinging to limestone rock, admiring caves overhead, and minding my step not to join the water in cascading to its depths. The sound of the water, roaring one moment, gurgling and chattering the next, was our constant companion. Thunderstorms chased us along, stimulating my adrenaline, but bothering us hardly at all. Having reached some shelter we sympathetically watched those arrive who did get caught out!

I would love to tell you more, but as ever I am snatching an opportunity to use a real computer, in the house of a lovely family who yesterday morning did not even know we existed! They were a contact given by a friend here in Germany who promptly forgot to tell them she had given us their address, and when we rang it came completely out of the blue. Just to show what lovely people they are, they there and then said on the phone of course you can come. What a wonderful world!

And so here we are, five minutes away from Lake Constance and in half an hour we will bid our farewells and board a ferry to take us to the other shore, from which we shall walk today in another country – Switzerland! So, dear friends, those of you who would like to join us on the walk somewhere, better polish up your walking boots and get out your rucksacks. We are approaching the big mountains, having spotted them for the first time in the distance three days ago.

When I can I will write again, and I thank all of you who have written to us. It is and will always be a joy to get messages from any of you. Another time I will have to tell you of our various wonderful encounters with people from many different places, walking along with us for some time, or short stretches of the way.

Much love to you all from

Angela and Nick XX

OVER THE TOP

DAY 89   HORN – LANGRICKENBACH
26 km; very warm, sunny; 26°C

We walked down the hill with Wolf to the ferry dock to cross over into Switzerland, We were the only customers at first so it felt as though we had a slight but definite personal relationship with the skipper/ferryman, who was very proud of his craft, a river-boat with enough room for about twenty passengers. Disembarking at Steckborn we drew some Swiss francs out of the wall and knew we were in another country after being in Germany for almost six weeks. The weather was better than fine, it was clear and hot – allegedly 26 ° – and the first footpath we found led up very steeply past a vineyard then gave us a panoramic view of the whole of the Bodensee as far as Konstanz. The volcanic cones we had walked past over the last few days now looked far away in the distance. By the time we stopped for a very expensive cup of hot chocolate at a lakeside café we were already feeling quite sunburnt on the right-hand side. We followed the path by the railway track to Kreuzlingen where we went back into Germany briefly due to the vagaries of the border hereabouts. We had a thorny problem to overcome at this juncture. We had tried to book accommodation through the Internet a few days back, which meant going through an agency. We thought they had booked us into a farm B&B in Langrickenbach, in Germany north of Konstanz, who offered sleeping in a hay-barn at €25 for both of us.

Unfortunately we didn't get the confirmation back from them until after we had changed our route to go south via Horn, at which point we discovered they had actually booked us into another village called Langrickenbach in Switzerland, east of Kreuzlingen. This Langrickenbach was too far to walk in one day, but we decided we would honour the reservation and go there anyway although it was some way off our direct route, which lay on the E1 from Kreuzlingen south to Wil. The most sensible option was to get a train to Altnau then walk the six or seven kilometres to the farm. A cyclist's bike fell on my leg on the train, causing a nasty cut and swelling on the same shin which had given me trouble in Belgium, which was a bit of a worry. We walked up the hill away from the lake and stopped halfway at a village hostelry for some lake fish and what they called *Aelplerrösti*, which are the Swiss version of chips, but more like sautéd potatoes. When we arrived at the farm we found that they were no longer offering the option of sleeping on hay bales in the barn as there was a nationwide scare about ticks and Lyme disease, but they had a big room full of mattresses which was cheap and clean enough, and had a great view over the snow-capped peaks to the south. The farmer was very welcoming and we spent some time chatting to him in the cowshed and to his nine-year-old daughter who was doing her English homework at a table in the farmyard. We had walked 26 kilometres and felt tired and sunburnt, so slept like logs although the surface was quite hard. Someone else arrived after we'd gone to bed, snored a lot then left before we got up – maybe a farmhand who'd been out for a drink.

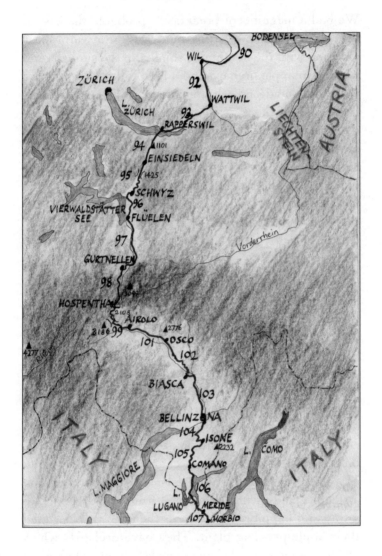

We had a magnificent breakfast – probably the best of the whole journey – sitting outdoors on a warm clear morning with the mountains shining in the sunlight and nearby an apple orchard and a field full of cows. There was home-made muesli and bread and jam, and eggs from their chickens… a delightful change after so many days when we had set off with nothing but a croissant inside us, longing for some oats, which as all walkers and horses know are the best form of slow-burning nutrition. We hoisted our packs on our backs and left the farm behind with a spring in our step, wandering along quiet country lanes past apple orchards and strawberry fields to Riedt.

At Riedt the roads no longer corresponded with our map. We needed to get to Wil to rejoin the E1, so we'd have to make up our own way across country. We asked a crew of road-menders the way to the next village and got a long explanation of how to get there and a warning that it's probably ten kilometres away, which didn't seem right. After walking up the hill a way we turned back to find a second opinion. An elderly man who was coming out of his yard on a moped stopped and said he could give us directions but why didn't we come in and have a rest and a drink first? He parked us on a couple of chairs in the courtyard and called out: "Two glasses of apple juice if you please!" whereupon a small twinkly woman emerged from the kitchen with a tray and happily chatted to us then showed us round their apple-pressing plant. They have orchards which produce enough apple juice to make a modest living but supplement it with odd bits of casual work. He was just about to go off to a place in Germany to collect a trailer-load of timber for some neighbours. His wife Ruth volunteered to show us the way and led us up a very steep and almost invisible footpath through a vineyard and an orchard to a small village, then she just kept walking with us, asking about our journey, telling us of her family and village life, pointing out landmarks, for about two hours until we arrived at Bischofszell, where her daughter lived. After having a coffee break together we parted company and she went off to see her daughter while we wandered around the pretty town with its ornate Baroque town hall (*Fig. 25). Round the corner we found a labyrinth laid out in the churchyard, and walked round it in preparation for the next leg of the day's journey.

There was a footpath to follow along the riverside towards Wil, and we walked for a couple of hours along that, mostly upon freshly laid gravel which became hard on the feet. We met a few local ramblers and passed many signposts informing us about the local wildlife, particularly the beavers which have multiplied in recent years. We wanted to stop at Oberbüren which was a large village, but found no lodging and were told there was nowhere to stay in that valley apart from Unterbüren, which we'd already passed some time ago. The day had been hot, it was getting late and we were beginning to feel we'd walked enough already. In the end we decided to take a bus to Uzwil, an ugly town where the only places to stay were the hotel next to the station, which was closed, or a posh one in the centre which was far too expensive, so we got on a local train to Wil, where we were told there were plenty of hotels and guest-houses. There were, but unfortunately they were all full. Or so I was told, after I'd left Angela sitting on a park bench with our luggage and gone trekking off into town. I was beginning to think perhaps my unkempt outdoor appearance was putting people off, as the town didn't appear to be heaving with visitors, and as darkness fell the streets became quite empty. I had been to every lodging-house in town except one, the Gasthaus zum Ochsen, a battered old coaching inn in a cobbled square just outside the city wall, and luckily they had a room. We snapped it up, and were feeling so exhausted we booked it for two days. Across the little square stood the old city, perched on a ridge. We rode a lift up to the church at the top of the citadel then looked over to the snowy peaks of the high mountains glowing pink and orange in the sunset.

DAY 91   WIL
0 km; warm; 22°C

It had only been five days since the last rest day with Sigfried, but we needed to stop and do some Internet research for accommodation: judging by our experience so far it was going to be difficult to find cheap B&Bs in Switzerland. We went to the library in the old quarter and logged onto the Hospitality Club and Couchsurfing sites for a couple of hours with mixed results, mostly inconclusive, but later in the day had a message back from someone called Hannah, who had advertised as able to host travellers in Wattwil, our next port of call. It transpired that she'd since gone to Geneva to study, but she said she was sure her parents would have us to stay in Wattwil. Angela phoned and spoke to Hannah's mum who was very encouraging, and said they would see us the following evening. It was sometimes uncomfortable contacting people like this with only a few days' notice: this is certainly not recommended by the various hospitality group sites, especially Servas, but we had no alternative other than to say: "We would like to stay with you in about a fortnight's time but we're not sure whether we'll be there then or not," which we did sometimes but once or twice had to subsequently cancel because we had had to change our route or we were just not going to get there that quickly. Anyway it's not very helpful to the host to have such a vague idea of when, or even whether, someone will arrive. They want to know when they'll need to be at home to receive their guests. However people were remarkably spontaneous in response to our requests at short notice, and we came upon nobody who said they could have put us up but it was just too unplanned.

DAY 92   WIL – WATTWIL
26 km; warm, sunny; 22°C

Leaving Wil on the last day of May, the weather was still warm and we walked though farmland speckled with small villages and crossed the river Thur several times. Angela was feeling under the weather with a griping stomach so we took it easy and stopped at a little medieval town called Lichtensteig for a break. The centre was almost unchanged since about 1700 apart from paving the road, and the main street was lined with arcades, but the open town square had obviously lost many older buildings which were being replaced by a supermarket, which revived an old debate: is it better to deface old towns like this in the name of progress or leave them in aspic while hypermarkets are built outside town to which people have to drive? As we sat pondering this question anew, Hannah's father Karl rang up to ask if we'd like a lift to Wattwil. We thanked him but refused the offer, as that was part of the bargain with our sponsors and ourselves, and said we'd be there in an hour or so. He excused himself, saying that he had to go out to a school play for which he'd written the music, but that his son would be at home to greet us. We stopped on the way into Wattwil at a mobile knife-grinder's workshop, whose owner honed my penknife blade for free. Sixteen-year-old Thomas made us some food, chatted with us in English then went off to practise his clarinet. We met the parents briefly but they were both busy people: all the more remarkable then that they agreed to put up a couple of foreign strangers. Karl gave us a tip for the following night: "Rather than stay at the Youth Hostel in Rapperswil, why not try the Pilgerherberge? Rapperswil is on the pilgrims' way – the Jakobsweg – from Eastern Europe to Spain and there's a small pilgrims' bunkhouse there." We rang them to book in for the night and cancelled the Youth Hostel.

DAY 93   WATTWIL – RAPPERSWIL
33 km; cooler, cloudy; 19°C

"There are walks in which I lose myself, walks which return me to myself again."

We set out early, knowing that we'd have a long haul ahead of us, a hilly walk of at least 30 km. We marched off down a steep hill from their house and up the other side of the valley to the castle we'd seen from our bedroom window the evening before, illuminated amid the darkness of the forest It began to drizzle. We continued to climb up to the 1000 m mark through the cloud, at which point there was also a sharp wind blowing. Then began a long descent, and by the time the lake (Lake Zurich) hove into view a watery sun had begun to break through and the wind had dropped. Near St Gallenkappel we met an itinerant cowherd from Austria who spends the time in between jobs walking the great pilgrimage routes, and had almost reached Einsiedeln, his present goal and the seat of a famous Black Madonna. We walked together for a while, talking of cows and hay and suchlike. Angela told him how we had spent most of a summer in the east of Switzerland on a farm high up in the Alps many years ago, helping Michael look after a herd of cows at their summer pasture, and agreed that for cattle to be fed on silage is much worse for them than being fed on fresh grass and hay – it's the equivalent of us eating sauerkraut every meal every day, and must affect the quality of their milk and cheese. We would no doubt be having more conversations about milk in Switzerland… Taking a short cut down to the lakeside path that runs alongside the railway line we found a remarkably quiet and rural scene with few habitations once we were out of Schmerikon, which stands at the eastern end of Lake Zurich and from which a little steamer goes to Lachen and Rapperswil. At Bollingen we stopped at the village hostelry which was hosting a wedding reception in their lakeside garden. Nobody seemed to mind us sitting on the balcony above the party to enjoy a lemonade and a cup of tea, and we spent a while there easing our aching muscles and admiring the happy couple along with the merry throng surrounding them in the foreground, while behind them lay the lake, speckled with sails, and the heavily wooded hills on the far side. The bride was a beautiful young black woman who had a few relations present in full African dress but spoke fluent Swiss German and after a while a yodelling choir struck up just beneath us.

Walking on we met a fellow traveller who appeared from a nunnery saying there was nowhere to stay there. Hearing of our destination in Rapperswil she said she would join us. She was of a very nervous disposition and chattered away as we walked. She shared some cake and water with us, but there was something annoying about the way she accompanied us: some people join in the existing rhythm while others blunder along clumsily, taking no account of the width of the path or the speed at which others are walking. Catherine was of the latter sort, but for all that she was a funny old stick and we were disappointed to find that when we arrived at the address we had been given she muttered something and vanished. Perhaps it was just as well as there had been a misunderstanding somewhere along the line and the place was already full, although we had been told there were plenty of beds left. The lady in charge was most put out but said, with a conspiratorial wink: "Actually, don't tell anyone, but there is an emergency bed in the breakfast room. Will that be OK?" At that point we'd have settled for sleeping in a broom cupboard, so yes, thank you very much. She took a shine to us once we told her we were on the way to Rome and explained that this hostel was run by volunteers who were all pilgrims or long-distance walkers themselves. They had a room with bunks for about ten people, showers, minimal cooking facilities, and cheap bottles of beer. She recommended a pizzeria round the corner and gave us pilgrims' passports, which she said would be invaluable on our way. After eating we strolled about the old town, up a cobbled lane to the castle, which has fantastic views to all sides. Rapperswil stands on a promontory halfway along the narrow lake, with a bridge across to Pfäffikon which has been there since the 14th century to serve merchants and pilgrims. Looking across from the castle walls as the sun was setting, we could see the hills on the other side growing blacker as the glowing sun splashed an intensifying sheet of light upon the water and picked out every window and church roof with flashes of silver and gold.

DAY 94   RAPPERSWIL – EINSIEDELN
16 km; clear, sunny; 23°C

In the morning we had to be up early to allow the room to be free for breakfast We chatted with several pilgrims who were all on their way either to Einsiedeln to visit the Black Madonna or further on towards Santiago – a long long way distant, but most people approach it in stages, say a fortnight at a time. Ahead of us lay the bridge across the lake and then a steep climb up from 400 m to about 1100 m. The bridge carries road and rail traffic across the shallow waters to Pfäffikon, with a wooden footpath running alongside. We walked over with Catherine from Munich who had reappeared saying that she tried every B&B in town but they were all full so had ended up in the Youth Hostel (probably taking one of the beds Angela had cancelled). The town had been so full because it was the venue for an extreme sports competition called the Iron Man which involved swimming 1.9 km, cycling 90 km and running 21 km. Astonishingly, the winning team completed the entire course in under four hours! Since the field comprised entrants from all over Europe it was not surprising that all the beds in town were taken. We'd been wondering why the town centre had been full of determined-looking, lean and wiry types cruising the streets on their racing bikes looking for large steaks until we saw the banner strung up next to the Town Hall.

On the other side of the lake we were confronted by the steepest footpath we'd ever seen, partly zigzagging, partly cut into timber-clad steps, which rose up the mountainside beside ridiculously steep vineyards and pastureland into the forest, where it continued to climb over roots and boulders to St Meinrad, where there is a chapel to commemorate the 9th-century hermit who had withdrawn to that wild and beautiful spot. There is also a restaurant with scenic views all around where we fell into conversation with an Austrian who was walking from Salzburg to Geneva as the first instalment of his pilgrimage to Santiago. He left with a slightly older woman, a teacher from Zurich, to follow the E1 to Einsiedeln but we decided we would take a short cut and follow a lane past the Teufelsbrücke or Devil's Bridge. This was an old bridge with a wooden roof to protect it from rockfalls which led across a gorge next to the house where Paracelsus (1493-1541) was born, according to a plaque nearby. [6]

It was a hot June day and the sun blazed down from a clear blue sky. Although the temperature didn't rise above 23 or 24°, the sunlight was much more intense due to the altitude and we were becoming sunburnt again. We met up with two sisters aged about 40 who were heading our way. Andrea from Schwäbisch Gmund in the heart of Swabia was on her third or fourth stage of the Jakobsweg, which she attempts a week at a time whenever she has a break from work. Her sister, a physiotherapist from Munich, had joined her on this leg after promising for years to accompany

---

6   Paracelsus stood at a crossroads in the history of medicine, representing the growth of medical knowledge at the time of the Renaissance when alchemy became less of a search to create gold from base matter and more of a study to find the complete medicine – the elixir of life – which led to many discoveries as alchemy became chemistry and the alchemist became an apothecary or pharmacist.

her. We walked into Einsiedeln together, across an open plateau (*Fig. 26) which made up for what it lacked in sources of fresh water and shade by the magnificent views of the mountains ahead of us. We saw the huge abbey of Einsiedeln from a distance, with the little town huddled around it, close to the shore of a small lake. As we drew closer we began to hear the sounds of a brass band, and arriving at the enormous square in front of the abbey church steps we came across a succession of bands marching about playing popular tunes in a national competition, all dressed smartly in variously coloured uniforms. All around the square were hotels, restaurants, cafes and shops selling religious knick-knacks. The hotels looked rather faded, as if they had seen better days before the invention of the motor-car, but the cafes were doing a roaring trade in cold drinks and ice-creams. Judging by the number of coaches in town we were expecting our hostel, which was run by the Swiss equivalent of the YMCA, to be full, but there were hardly any other guests. Perhaps the bandsmen ands their supporters had just come for the day. We checked in, using our pilgrims' passes for the first time, then went to sit by the lakeside and stared out at the mountains beyond, spotted with little farms and cowsheds among swathes of forest.

DAY 95   EINSIEDELN – SCHWYZ
22 km; cloudy, heavy; 18°C

"Is there anything that is better than to be out, walking, in the clear air?"

In the morning we paid a visit to the Black Madonna, which we found curiously unsettling: a beautiful image of Mother Earth, but imprisoned in a golden cloak which rendered her incapable of movement.

We set off briskly as we were expecting it to be a hard day's walk – not so long, but with a lot of ups and downs. We were already at almost 1000 m but would be climbing to 1400 m then descending to about 500 m at the end of the day. The first few kilometres were flat, going along a road at the bottom of a valley, but we seemed to be heading for an impasse as the mountains closed in until suddenly a path went off to the right and climbed very steeply up a boulder-strewn track which looked as though it had been a rushing stream a month or two earlier. We had fallen in with Christiana, a young traveller we had met the night before at the hostel. She was on her first solo venture with a backpack and struggled to keep up with us on the steep uphill stretch to the top at Haggenegg (1414 m), which was the highest point on the Jakobsweg in Switzerland and made us think the Alps were not so daunting after all – the highest pass we would have to traverse was only another 600 m higher than this. We stopped at the top and had a picnic, feeling the fresh air course through our veins, and Christiana caught up with us as we were getting ready to go again so we continued together to the next habitation, where the E1 went off on another long detour along the crest of the mountain range and we took the direct way downhill towards Schwyz. For the first time up here on the high plateau we had been in true Alpine country, surrounded by emptiness, with the whistle of marmots in the distance and fields of lush grass growing to feed the cows which had been brought up for their summer grazing. A collar of magnificent mountain-tops surrounded us as the path led inexorably downwards through meadowland with crickets chirping, past ancient quarries and into a dense wild forest garden full of exotic flowers. The weather began to curdle as

1. Bungalow Farm, North Newbald,
in the morning fog.

2. Near Boston.

3. Near Fosdyke Bridge, Lincolnshire.

4. Wisbech: the B&B car park. Some real Goths.

5. The Suffolk troll.

6. The Stour Valley near Dedham.

7. Goedereede, late March.

8. The Kalmthoutse Heide, almost in Belgium.

9. The Begijnhof, Diest.

10. Avoiding a thunderstorm in the Eifel.

11. Bruder Klaus Kapelle, Eifel, the giant haystack.

12. Kloster Maria Laach, two days' walk from Koblenz.

13. View from our bedroom window, Koblenz YH.

14. Root beings in the Lahn valley.

15. On top of the world!

16. Smells like sweet hay!

17. 'Das Felsenmeer', literally: an ocean of rocks.

18. One of the typical old houses in the Kraichgau.

19. Our cup was never half empty.
A well in the Black Forest.

20. Damage from storms and acid rain.

21. The Laughing Cavaliers.

22. Haslachtal.

23. In the Wutachschlucht.

24. The Rhine between Gailingen and Diessenhofen, or
between Germany and Switzerland.

25. Bischofszell Baroque.

26. Shelter beside the path near Einsiedeln.

27. Approaching the lake near Schwyz.

28. The looming peaks across the valley from
Gurtnellen.

29. The Old Road to the Gotthard Pass.

30. Almost there!

31. At the top, June 7th.

32. On the Strada Alta.

33. Daniela's arty staircase, in Meride.

34. ... and the view from her balcony.

35. A grand, yet crumbling villa at the side of the
Naviglio Grande.

36. The first rice-field, near Escalate.

37. We're off to Rome!

38. That evening in Cassio.

39. Siesta time.

40. Ponzano Superiore.

41. "I can see the sea!"

42. Tuscan colours.

43. Aaah, LemonSoda!

44. The towers of San Gimignano

45. Sunflower scene.

46. Siena in the afternoon - stand in the shade!

47. A sheep shop in Siena.

48. The granary - interior.

49. Porcupine quills.

50. The church at San Quirico.

51. Welcome to the Wild West!

52. An alleyway in Acquapendente.

53. Bench outside someone's house.

54. Looking for a lost passport.

55. Chris looking out over Lake Bolsena.

56. The Cathedral at Montefiascone.

57. Stairway in Viterbo.

58. Lake Vico.

59. 3 0 0 0 kilometres!

60. The public wash-tub, Sutri.

61. Part of the Etruscan necropolis in Sutri.

62. Passing the finishing line.

63. Crossing the square.

64. At St Peter's Square

we descended towards the lake (*Fig. 27) until we arrived at the bottom of the mountain and emerged onto a suburban street in the middle of a cloud, which soon began to shed its load. We reached the hostel we were heading for just as it began to bucket down and rejoiced at our good fortune at avoiding a soaking again. The "backpackers' hostel" was actually very expensive, but we met an interesting local farmer there who had been born and bred in the USA, where there is apparently a well-established and thriving Swiss community in a corner of Washington state. I seemed to remember that Ruth from Riedt had told us one of her sons was living in that part of the world too. We had another frustrating evening with the tablet: we could get online but it refused to send any emails. We did manage to book a B&B in Flüelen at a reasonable price though for the next night.

DAY 96   SCHWYZ – FLÜELEN
24 km; rainy, sunny intervals; 16°C

The news from England was that the bad weather had continued throughout April and May. The latest Test match against West Indies in Birmingham had been ruined by rain and 3 out of 5 days had been completely washed out. It had seemed impossible when we were up on the top of the Haggenegg, but this morning the previous night's storm had not cleared the air entirely and we were in the middle of a misty Monday morning drizzle.

Schwyz is the heartland of Old Switzerland, the home of the founding of the Confederation of the Cantons, and is really no more than three villages joined together, with a small shopping centre, several museums and a penknife factory – the original Swiss army penknife factory. The museums all looked very interesting but unfortunately they were all closed on Mondays. There was a hiking shop where I could have got a waterproof cover for my rucksack, but that was closed on Mondays too. We headed off towards Flüelen: the walk should be pretty flat today, according to the guidebook, mostly along the lakeside. On the way out of the rural sprawl of Schwyz we spied a cobbler's shop and made a beeline for it as Angela's boots had once again started to come unstitched, after having been resoled and temporarily mended in the Odenwald. The cobbler, who said he could sew them on the spot, was a member of the Syrian Orthodox (Aramaic) Church, although he can't have had many fellow adherents in the neighbourhood, and as he worked he talked, firstly about a subject dear to all Swiss people. Angela asked him about how people in Schwyz buy their milk. He explained how he buys large quantities at a time to make yoghurt. "The Swiss government have been making laws recently to make it illegal to milk your own cows and sell unpasteurised milk," he told us. "They want all milk to be produced in large co-operative dairies 'for hygiene reasons', so that those farmers who don't want their cows to be fed on silage can do nothing about their milk being mixed in with everyone else's." We asked him whether the farmers had made their voices heard in some way. "Oh yes," he said as he tapped away with a miniature hammer. "They had a demonstration recently and tipped thousands of litres of milk into the main street, but it has changed nothing. The trouble is there are so many different bodies making such laws: the canton, the federal government, the European Union..." He charged Angela a minimal amount for his labour, perhaps because she had initiated the conversation about milk, and sent us off with good wishes for crossing the mountain pass further south.

We walked uphill to the left near a grotto or shrine placed at the edge of the wild forest where pilgrims could pause to pray for their safety before continuing above the lake, and made our way along a narrow lane which gradually dwindled into a mule-track. Near Morschach the path was signposted to go off to the right although it looked as if the village was just ahead of us. We followed the sign to avoid having to walk on a main road and found ourselves being led a long way round past a golf course. Outside the clubhouse was a banner saying:

BMW – FREUDE AM FAHREN!

("the joys of driving!"), and three brand new models of BMW, possibly waiting as prizes for the winners of some prestigious tournament. For us it felt like a kick in the teeth to have been diverted from our path only to be shown how much more quickly we could be travelling if we had a fast car...

From Morschach we wandered downhill gradually to Sisikon, passing signs which announced that we were crossing the North-South divide for flowing water: the rivers rising beyond this point would all be flowing southwards towards the Mediterranean. At Sisikon we were on a beautiful lakeside footpath. The misty drizzle we'd encountered earlier had been burnt off and the sun shone fitfully between white clouds as we strode along through the woods. Often we had to zigzag down and up again to cross a stream bubbling down from the hillside to the left, whence we could occasionally make out the sound of traffic on the road or the railway line above. Sometimes the path went along a cliff-face and once or twice beside a waterfall. This was a dedicated hikers' path created in 1983 which even has a couple of tunnels blasted through the rock specifically for the use of walkers and cyclists. At one such point we met a group of three German cyclists who had dismounted, spellbound, to admire the spectacular view across the lake to the mountains beyond. We passed the Tells-kapelle, which is a strange shrine to Swiss nationalism with frescoes depicting scenes of heroism and confederacy (including of course the famous William Tell!), and the nearby ferry-stop, where a ferry arrived just as we did: the skipper asked us if we wanted to go on the boat to Flüelen, but we turned the offer down as we were tired but enjoying the walk. Just above the little jetty was a giant glockenspiel in a field, with a notice saying it had been donated to the Swiss people by the chocolate industry. If you were there on the hour you could press a button to choose a tune and it would play it for you. Arriving in Flüelen we approached a man who was standing outside the first house on the left and asked him for directions to the B&B. "It's here!" he said, pointing over his shoulder with his thumb. "It's my house!" And he chuckled as if he played this joke on everyone who came to stay. He showed us where the Hotel Tourist was, just down the road, and after dropping off our bags we went there for a beer and a bite to eat. Unfortunately we arrived just behind a coachload of Chinese tourists who had apparently landed expecting a slap-up Swiss meal without actually having ordered it in advance. The staff were all run off their feet and starting to get shirty with the tour rep, so it took quite some time for us to be served. We tried to use the tablet to Skype with a friend, but it wouldn't work. We never found out if it was to do with a lack of reception due to the surrounding mountains or some other reason. At any rate we were also unable to get onto the Internet to find somewhere else to stay the next night, although it was notoriously unreliable for that purpose as it only showed us the places which had advertised themselves online. There are plenty of B&Bs, farmhouses and so on, which just have a sign outside the gate saying that they offer beds for the night.

DAY 97 FLÜELEN – GURTNELLEN
27 km; cloudy, sunny intervals; 20°C

"The most distant places seem accessible once one is on the road."

The morning was bright and breezy. Stepping out of the B&B (well, it should have just been called B, as the old man didn't actually offer breakfast) to go for breakfast at the Hotel Tourist we were met by a bracing wind, a scattering of rain and a truly magnificent rainbow over the choppy grey lake. The Chinese had left early, but walking down through the village, with the lake on our right being whipped up by the north wind, we came across a couple of small groups of Chinese people in plastic macs taking photographs of things we take for granted but they obviously found strange and remarkable, such as particular plants, rooftops or lamp-posts. Angela remembered having once seen a Japanese man crouching in the middle of a busy road taking a photo of a cat's-eye. Presumably he'd never seen one before.

It was a strange day's walk after the last few days of dramatic ascents and descents. We had decided that we had no idea where we would be staying so we would just go as far as Amsteg, which seemed to be at the top of the valley, and see where we could stay when we got there. It looked on the map as though there would be fewer and fewer possibilities for lodgings from here on as far as the St Gotthard Pass, another two and a half days' walk away. From the lake we followed the river Reuss, which rises near the pass and flows into the southern end of the lake. There was an imperceptible rise in altitude at this point; it felt as though we were walking on absolutely flat ground but the mountains were getting higher and higher all the time on either side, so that by the time we arrived at Amsteg it was becoming quite claustrophobic and there seemed to be no way out. We had been joined by a man and his dog for the first portion of this leg. He pointed us in the right direction amid a jumble of busy motorway junctions and road bridges, then accompanied us along the fiercely flowing river at the bottom of this wide glacial valley and spoke of the catastrophic flood they had had there in the 1960s before the conversation turned to the next favourite topic among Swiss people, after milk: that of immigration. We were hearing much from both sides of the fence, but mostly this version, which runs along the lines of: "Blooming foreigners, they come here and take our work and sponge off the state etc., etc.," although in this case the gripe was more to do with Germans coming to live in Schwyz canton where they could earn more doing building work than they could at home and had a better chance of getting the work than say Turks or Spaniards because they could already speak the language (well, a version of it!) and had a reputation as good workers.

Near Erstfeld we passed a spot near the modern railway where a very old rail system had stood in the 18th century operated by pulleys and winches and pumps driven by horse power to ferry iron ore from the mines to the smelting works and foundries in the valley. Erstfeld has a big military barracks and as we sat beside the river eating our sandwiches we were passed by platoons of soldiers jogging off in formation up towards the forest The flood had devastated the town and surroundings so most of the buildings were new. We had to cross the river and walk along the railway line for a while then go uphill onto a little footpath that runs along the side of a sheer mountainside, going through another pedestrian tunnel, this one older and festooned with angels of all sorts and sizes. Just before arriving at Amsteg we passed the 2,000- kilometre mark, which felt like a major breakthrough, and very timely as it was so close to the natural boundary of the St Gotthard Pass, as well being right next to a big warehouse with the name WALKER on it in large letters!

The countryside continued to amaze us with majestic views around every corner, but this is a wild and dangerous beauty of bare rock and soaring cliff-faces. To celebrate our milestone we stopped at Amsteg for coffee and cake, and telephoned a *gasthaus* in Gurtnellen to book a room, as it was still quite early and there was nowhere to stay in Amsteg as the only hotel was closed that day. "It's about four o'clock now," said the lady who answered the phone. "When do you think you'll arrive?" "Well, we're on foot. It's about five kilometres, isn't it? How long do you think it will take?" I answered. "Oh, it's more than five kilometres. It'll take a while; it's uphill all the way and steep. We'll see you at about seven or eight. Be careful!" Someone in the bakery said they weren't sure the road would be open because of the rockfall, but maybe the footpath would be OK. We set off with some trepidation and found a rough path which led steeply uphill for about an hour and a half, sometimes on the verge of petering out, sometimes very overgrown. When we arrived at the *gasthaus* the owners were amazed that we had got there so quickly, and it felt as though we had somehow magically gained (or lost) an hour. They were clustered around their TV set with a couple of grim-looking customers. News was breaking of a rockfall which had evidently happened earlier in the day just across the valley – you could see the spot from the front door (*Fig. 28). A massive avalanche of rocks and slate had slipped onto the main railway line, where some men had happened to be working at the time. One was killed and two seriously injured. The valley is breathtakingly steep and the peaks on either side are all up to 2,000 m high. On our way up we had passed two memorial stones – one to a family – killed in unspecified accidents in 1917 and 1958. An 'expert' on the TV was saying it was a result of the erosion of the permafrost due to climate change, and this was repeated independently to us in person by a knowledgeable alpinist the next day. There were warnings of further rockfalls and bad weather tomorrow, and the railway, which goes over – and under – the main mountain barrier to Ticino and towards Italy, would be closed for at least a week. The overall impression of our ascent to Gurtnellen had been of a landscape of savage beauty which man has tamed with feats of dramatic engineering, with tunnels, motorways, railways and high bridges, but which is able to strike back at any moment. We wondered whether we would even be able to make it to the top, if the weather was going to get much worse…

DAY 98   GURTNELLEN – HOSPENTAL
22 km; cloudy, drizzle; 16°C

The morning dawned cloudy and cool, and the thermometer struggled to rise above 16° all day, but then the temperature in London was 13°, so we weren't missing much. We walked out of the village and down the hill past meadows of spring flowers. We had been told by a local goat farmer that this year everything was about four weeks later than usual, and up here it definitely still felt like spring although we were already a week into June. The further downhill we went the cooler it became, as the bottom of the valley gets so little sunlight, and the noisier it became as we descended towards the rush and whine of motorway traffic making for the great St Gotthard Tunnel, 30 km long underneath the mountain. Just outside Wiler we noticed a lithe but elderly man leaping over a dangerous gorge with a large log on one shoulder. He carried it to the house nearby and we stopped to chat. He invited us to stop for a cup of coffee (which later included a drop of schnapps for the road) and told us how he had grown up in this house with nine siblings. When his parents died the remaining heirs had agreed to look after and use the house although none wanted to live there full time. This one, Martin, who was now about 65, cared for the house the most as he was the most interested in outdoor pursuits. He lived for walking, climbing, skiing, cycling in the country he loved. He had contacts among many clubs, groups and fraternities therefore, and gave us a tip for a good place to stay that night: "Not in Andermatt – it's too expensive – but a few kilometres along the valley in Hospental is a new hostel for such as us. I know the owner. Tell him Martin from Wiler sent you." When we asked him about the weather forecast and the danger of continuing, he laughed it off, saying maybe there'd be a little bit of rain and mist, but there could be a rockfall any time, or not; there was no more likelihood of it now than any other time.

We wandered on past the Pfaffensprung, a violent waterfall harnessed for hydro-electric power where we stood and marvelled with a bunch of Saxon bikers; past a sunny spot where newts played in a large puddle on the path; over ancient stone bridges; past a swarm of black butterflies; over the glacier-like remains of winter snow lying across our path; past more old smelting equipment and railway sidings full of rolling stock from the Matterhorn-Gotthard railway. After Göschenen the country became wilder still: huge rock-faces, mighty waterfalls, roads and railways in tunnels or galleries to protect them from falling boulders or avalanches. We stopped for a moment to chat to an elderly couple who were puffing up the serpentine road on heavily-laden cycles; but the climbing was easier up to the gorge of Teufelbrücke (another Devil's Bridge!), where there was a spectacular view down into the gorge from the old pack-horse bridge – an incredible architectural feat! Past there it was a doddle to get to Andermatt, as expected a posh and pricey ski resort recovering from the winter season. From there it was easy flat walking to Hospental across the plateau. It was calm and warm enough, but we could imagine on a cold windy day it would be a different story. When we got there we had to help chase two cows out of the middle of the village, where they had strayed down an alleyway. We found the hostel: it turned out it had only opened that Monday and we were the very first guests! Mike and Beat, a couple of snowboarding and climbing enthusiasts, were the first young people to move into the village for twenty years and were very keen to please. They had taken on a former army barrack-house and done it up smartly with some financial backing from a local businessman. Since it was virtually next door to a Youth Hostel (from which the elderly cyclists came that evening to pay us a visit) and there were a couple of hotels in the village they'll have plenty of competition in the winter months but they were full of optimism, expecting it to be the coming place for young extreme winter-sports fans. They assured us that the weather would be good the next day for our final ascent to the pass, and we went to bed feeling positive that we had overcome the hardest part of our journey – little did we know then...

DAY 99   HOSPENTAL – AIROLO
23 km; variable; 10-20°C

We wound our way through the ancient village street, lined with heavy grey granite houses with thick walls and roofs of heavy slate slabs, to the church, which had a legend carved above the doorway saying (roughly translated): "O wanderer rest awhile, whether you are going to Cologne or Rome or the Frankish lands".

We crossed the road and started to tread the mountain path, soon seeing our first clump of gentian, followed by another type with large bells. All along the way were odd patches of colour in the shape of Alpine flowers and shrubs like a huge rock garden, including a couple of different types of orchid. As we climbed gradually up the rocky footpath it clouded over and began to be chilly (*Fig. 29). After an hour and a half we declined the opportunity of elevenses at a roadside café, put on another layer of clothes, and pressed on. Above 1,850 m. we stopped to add anoraks as the wind got up. Struggling along the old path, laid out with flat slabs of stone on the wide valley floor, surrounded by those sheer granite cliffs, we said we were feeling as tiny and vulnerable as insects. Just then we almost trod on a line of centipedes migrating across the path, a seemingly endless string unravelling from a writhing knot to march purposefully towards somewhere or other. Up above that valley was another, wider and flatter and dotted with massive stones half-covered in snow. We scrambled over this, negotiating streams by stepping-stones at first, then finding our own way across; splashing up the roughly cobbled path until it met huge drifts of snow, several feet deep, which had spilt down the mountainside or been left behind by lack of sunlight (*Fig. 30).

Often these drifts covered unseen rushing brooks, and we had to be careful where to step. The wind was once again howling into our faces and the cloud was coming down fast, so that it was becoming harder to see the red and white markers painted onto rocks to delineate the path, the same path used since time immemorial by monks and merchants, shepherds and soldiers. At the very top as the land flattened out, the path gave up trying to force a way through the immense boulders and suddenly decanted us onto the main road. We had spotted it occasionally in and out of the mist as we plodded through this hostile terrain like Arctic explorers or travellers from a bygone age with our hazel sticks, but it was still a shock to see people clad in T-shirts staring at us from their warm dry cars. We met a couple of students at the sign saying

GOTTHARD PASS 2106 m.

and asked them to take the obligatory photo of us standing next to it (*Fig. 31), then went to the tourist centre to drink mugs of Ovaltine and thaw out and buy a postcard to send to Angela's hip surgeon. When we came out the drizzly mist had turned into a steady fine rain, and the mountains were invisible. We had long harboured fantasies of arriving at the top to be able to look southwards and see the snowy peaks gradually diminishing as they rolled towards Rome in the sunshine against the deep azure of the sky…

From the pass there are two roads leading south: the new main road which was laden with traffic, mostly cars and coaches full of day-trippers or holiday-makers; and the old cobbled road, known as the Via Tremola or trembling road. We'd been expecting it to be so called because of the effect on your knees as you descend steeply almost a kilometre in altitude to Airolo, but came to the conclusion it was more to do with the rattling effect of the cobbles on carts and carriages in the days before rubber tyres. There is of course a motorway as well, carrying fast traffic and freight, and on this day the number of trucks on the road would be massive due to the closure of the railway after the rockfall. But the motorway was well out of sight and sound over half a mile beneath our feet in the tunnel which it entered back at Göschenen.

We took the Via Tremola. We would have done so anyway – it was marked as part of the E1 – but since it was blocked in several places near the top by heavy snowdrifts it was still closed to traffic, so it was a wet but wonderfully undisturbed walk down. We passed a few hardy cyclists straining upwards but no hikers, and only one car, which was a police car. It stopped, and the window rolled down for a policeman to ask us whether we'd seen anyone drive up the road as we came down. It was hard to know what they might have been looking for: car thieves, lost tourists, illegal immigrants? They were giving nothing away, and the window rolled shut to keep out the driving rain after wishing us a good day. The rain continued to intensify as we descended, and after another two hours or so we arrived soaked to the skin in Airolo. Mike from Hospental had given us an address in Airolo of a similar kind of backpackers' hostel, but I couldn't find the scrap of paper – perhaps it had melted in the rain – so we went to an old-fashioned bar/pensione where we found a room for the same price and booked it for two nights so we could dry out and bask in the achievement of having actually crossed the Alps.

Suddenly we were in a different land: still Switzerland but so different. Everything was in Italian and no-one spoke – or tried to speak – English. The glitter and fancy clothes-shops of Andermatt were a distant memory here, where the rain poured down relentlessly all night and all the next day. The houses were grey and thick-walled and smelt of damp wood-smoke, and the few streets were joined by alleys with wide steps and poor lighting. Down below in the valley the railway stock stood indecisively: some trains were going through the tunnel but only as far as Göschenen. A small crowd lingered on the platform waiting for a train which might never come. People meandered about the small town looking lost We spent our day off trying to find an Internet connection, buying food to eat in our hotel room, walking to and fro past the supermarket, the yoghurt factory, the bank and the cemetery. We met a German couple at the hotel whose car had broken down on the way to Corsica. The bar in the hotel had only three other customers all evening and the owners bemoaned their fate with: "Ever since the motorway was built…", all the while throwing their hands in the air in resignation.

DAY 100 AIROLO
0 km; rain; 14°C

Our one hundredth day! We went to the Tourist Information Office as soon as it opened at 9 o'clock and emailed a report to everyone on our address list who wanted to be kept informed of our progress. Then we needed to contact 'Bluebells' from Hospitality Club and Anne who was organising a fund-raising concert for Soundsphere (Angela's four-woman a capella group who sing quirky, funny and beautiful songs from around the world) near Montreux at the end of June. We had to tell her that by then we would probably be somewhere near Milan and would have to come back by train to fulfil the commitment. Plans would have to be made over the next fortnight or so about where we could stay when we got there, for how long, etc.

9th June 2012

Dear Friends far and wide,

We have done it! We are over the big Gotthard Pass, and down the other side. It is Saturday morning, we have just left behind another rather over-priced hostelry (a bit of a theme here in Switzerland) and are shortly heading off towards the Strada Alta which will take us in the direction of Bellinzona and the meeting with family members who will join us for sections of the walk. This will be wonderful, even if it brings organizational complications.

Switzerland, the land of cows ringing clangy bells with every move, the land of water moving mostly in various degrees of roaring, the land of unrivalled engineering feats availing – much and noisy – traffic to be somewhere nearby at most times, that is traffic of road and rail, plane and helicopter, all in all gives the impression of a very crowded and noisy place! I had a deep and well-loved soul impression of this country from the time twenty-odd years ago when I was up a mountain for many weeks working on an 'alp', making butter and cheese, milking and mucking out stables, and in between sitting quietly and listening to the brooks gurgling and babbling, and the cows ringing at a peaceful distance on some slanted meadow where we had taken them. Then the farmers, who in some co-operative fashion had organised themselves to send their cows up there, spent the summer months making hay for the same cows to feed on in the long winter.

This Switzerland now is a very different place, pressured by its own compulsion to be well-off, regulated by governments who seem to favour the rule of Mammon over all; I doubt if their members have ever walked the length and breadth of their own beautiful land. Rich in the treasures Nature has to offer, in its most dramatic guise. We, Nick and I, continue to delight in the small, marvel at the grand, tackle the slithering across snow and wet root, clamber rocks, and suck the air between our teeth when paying for the next cup of coffee. We continue to sing our little repertoire to each other, and will be glad when we get an opportunity to share some of it with someone again.

The people here are very interested in exchanging their thoughts on their own country, which is exciting, as one doesn't have to hold back on one's own observations. The individuals we meet are, as they have been everywhere, most warmly welcoming, but here they have a sort of soberness and practical no-nonsense feel to their way, which is great.

Dear friends, I wonder whether you would mind if this once only I ask you to mention the fundraising aspect of all this walking to one friend of your own, someone new whom we don't know? It would be so very good if that side of things grew along a little too, and I am certainly not asking you all to give more, as you have already been so very generous! People on the continent do not seem to understand the idea of 'sponsorship' in the same way as it works in GB, and we have not really picked up much more support for Medecins Sans Frontieres whilst on the walk (here and there of course but not ongoingly). Anyway, enough of that...

It continues to give us great joy to hear from you, and many of you have been sharing this thought or that anecdote with us, giving us the sense of not missing out on things rally, which is lovely of you! Please continue.

Much love to you all until the next time I have access to a computer with a full compliment of functions, probably from Italy! Behind me the language is being spoken already (double speed now!). Not a chance to understand anything any more... now the roles will switch and Nick will be spokesperson.

We hold you in our thoughts,

Angela and Nick XX

DAY 101 AIROLO – OSCO
21 km; sunny intervals; 19°C

"We can take a walk which is a sampling of different airs: the invigorating air of the heights; the filtered air of a pine forest; the rich air over ploughed earth..."

We left Airolo on a misty morning. The rain had stopped, but there was a heavy cloud cover sticking to the tops of the mountains across the valley. We went off to look for the Strada Alta, which leads along the left hand side of the Ticino valley. While we had followed the Reuss for two and a half days from the point near Flüelen where it poured into the lake all the way up to the St Gotthard Pass, we would now be following the Ticino off and on for about a fortnight until it flowed into the Po. The Strada Alta links a series of villages which until about forty years ago would have had no other direct road down to the valley. Many of them would have had no connection to the outside world except on foot or mule along the path we were to follow now. It turned out to be a mixture of old cobbled roads, tarmacked lanes and footpaths leading up and down through meadows and mixed forest The air became warmer but was trapped beneath the cloud cover in the deep valley, and we made our way along muddy paths with slippery wet stones and tree-roots underfoot with stunning views at every turn (*Fig. 32). To our left a towering precipice cleft by tumbling streams and waterfalls, to our right a wooded mountainside so steep that a slip would have meant sliding ever faster down 500 metres to the bottom. As our path wound its way at a more or less even height, the valley floor below us was gradually sloping, so that from Airolo to Biasca (about 40 km by road along the river) the height above sea level goes from 1141 m to 293 m, while our path went steadily at around 1100 m all the way to a point above Biasca which we would reach at the end of the following day. The views across the valley were doubly impressive. At the beginning, near Airolo, we could see back up to the pass we had crossed and the peaks surrounding it, while looking west were layer upon layer of mountain tops and ranges, peaks and saddles folding and unfolding, over the Italian border and on towards France. The wall of rock on the opposite side of the valley was just over

2000 m high, but beyond were many peaks in excess of 3000 m, whose crests were entirely covered in snow, and would remain so throughout the summer. We stopped halfway along at the entrance to a village where we found a bench and were sitting eating our lunch (the usual bread and cheese) when we met Hans, who had been so hospitable to us in Schonach. What an extraordinary coincidence! We walked on together with him and his companions, who were from their local Alpine Walking Club, as far as Osco, where we all stayed the night at the municipal bunkhouse and ate at the village hostelry, where they were obviously unused to vegetarians – the only option was a lump of cheese and some mashed potato. Afterwards most of us saw Holland, Germany's great rivals at football and hot favourites to at least reach the final of the European Championship, beaten 1-0 by Denmark. We slept unsoundly six or eight to a bed (they were very wide beds, but still…), not before Angela saw a marten rooting about under a car in the village street on her way back to the bunkhouse.

DAY 102 OSCO – BIASCA
30 km; cloudy, sunny intervals; 18°C

"Storm clouds, rain, hail, when we have survived these we seem to have taken on some of the solidity of rocks and trees."

Some of the hikers started making a racket at about 6 o'clock, so we didn't feel greatly refreshed when we got up for breakfast We let the Alpinists get off first as they'd been setting a cracking pace the day before and doubtless would be again as they had to cover 30 kilometres before driving home to Schonach and Furtwangen that evening. We'd actually kept up with them for quite a few kilometres, which was gratifying as they were obviously experienced and regular mountain hikers and had much smaller packs than us, but we didn't really want to walk that fast. We felt we'd much rather wander than yomp, so we bade Hans a warm farewell again and girt our loins for a long trek. In turns we clambered one moment up, one moment down; through forests rich with beech, oak, holly, chestnut, box and birch, pine and hazel; through meadowlands full of grass and flowers or soft-eyed chocolate-brown cows. At times the path descends steeply to a stream which has come rolling and tumbling down the hillside towards the wide glacial valley below, crosses over by a log or some boulders, and climbs again so sharply that you have to pull yourself up by holding on to tree roots or pushing yourself up with your stout hazel stick. We passed through several idyllic villages, peeping into tiny medieval churches and marvelling at the old wooden houses, often with intricate carvings around the doors. It was a slow journey in parts as there were some places which were dangerous unless one moved with extreme caution, especially one with artificial hips! We stopped in the early afternoon at the Grotto Por Bell, which was a sublimely beautiful spot on a sunny afternoon in early June: a little family-run restaurant in the middle of a grove of 500-year-old chestnut trees, surrounded by great blocks and chunks of granite which had metamorphosed over millennia into huge mossy lumps in the landscape.

Having decided not to stay the night at the last available *albergo* on the Strada Alta but to press on to somewhere in or near Biasca in the valley bottom, we began to regret the decision when the rain started again at about four o'clock and we were still at the top of the mountain having no illusions about how difficult it would be to get down, especially if the rain kept up and the path became more slippery. Now I know going downhill 2,000 feet or so, even at the end of a long day's walk, even with a 10-kilo pack, even in the pouring rain, can be a doddle, but this was **seriously steep**. I would just like to note that when we got to the bottom and looked at each other and one of us said: "Well, that was a walk in the park!" there was a certain amount of irony involved, not to mention a lot of knee-ache. We stumbled off to look for the nearest bed, at the pizzeria off the motorway, where we ate a very decent pizza served by a heavily tattooed lady to a Country & Western soundtrack in a huge dining-room shared with two truck-drivers. We retired to our room, which was festooned with dripping garments, and snoozed through the football (England 1, France 1).

DAY 103 BIASCA – BELLINZONA
31 km; cloudy, sunny intervals; 20°C

"Looking, singing, resting, breathing, are all complementary to walking."

We had arranged to meet Michael later in the day in Bellinzona, so we faced another long walk, but at least it should be fairly flat. First we went into Biasca, where we had been advised to visit the church, which was certainly worth seeing. Climbing up a set of well-worn steps we entered to find that the floor is on a pronounced slant and the back wall is built into the rock behind. The inner walls are covered in early medieval frescoes, some dating back well over a thousand years, including some very similar to Celtic patterns. We walked out of town, stopping at a supermarket for supplies. Outside the entrance stood an Ecuadorean woman playing the charango with a bowler-hat on her head and a baby wrapped up on her back. We chatted in Spanish while Angela was shopping and she told me her husband was out looking for work. They didn't have papers to stay beyond the period covered by a temporary visa, so he couldn't find work, and because he had no work they couldn't find a place to live, and because they had no fixed address they couldn't get a more permanent residence permit – the usual Catch 22. So they had been living in a car for a year, getting odd days' work here and there; but she was not bitter about it, and her toddler was plump and cheerful. We gave them a franc and wished them well. Continuing southwards we walked on huge slabs of stone beside the teeming river, narrowly avoiding the many lizards which scampered across them, although one did find its way into Angela's rucksack when we stopped to eat. The mountains to our right were heavily forested and about once an hour we were startled by massive explosions as the granite quarries were dynamited above us. The path wandered quietly otherwise through leafy glades full of robinia and nightingales and although a busy motorway was just the other side of the river the noise was drowned by the sound of the rushing steel-grey water, which cleared the air enough to let us appreciate each breath.

Arriving in Bellinzona to meet Michael at the Youth Hostel we were caught in a sudden heavy rainstorm which didn't stop play, however, at an impromptu cricket match being played on a basketball court between two groups of young Indian or Sri Lankan men.

When we got to the Youth Hostel we were delighted to find that Michael had secretly arranged for his son Vincent (27) to join us for a few days having just finished his studies in Germany to become a master carpenter. What a lovely surprise – we would be able to explore our cross-country route to the Italian border as a foursome, and have the perspective of a young person to mix in with ours.

DAY 104 BELLINZONA – ISONE
18 km; rain, then sunny; 20°C

"There are walks on which we tread in the footsteps of others, walks on which we strike out entirely for ourselves."

Waking up in the Youth Hostel we found it was still pouring with rain. A charming lady at the TIO printed off some maps for us and gave us advice on how to get to Isone, which included phoning a man who lived at the top of the mountain and would then drive down to operate a cable-car. We decided that Michael would travel up with him and all the bags – there was nothing in our contract to say that we had to be carrying our rucksacks all the way, after all – and we walked up with Vincent on a very steep narrow footpath to a spot about 500 m higher, where we all met up again. It was obviously seldom used: we had to ford a stream to get onto the path at all, near the cable-car terminus, and there were several points at which the path was blocked by fallen trees. The woods it passed through were extremely quiet, apart from the scurrying of lizards through last autumn's dead leaves. At the top of the cable-car's ascent stood a single house: a footpath led across a meadow into more forest and a climb of another 250 m in altitude to the highest point, which had fantastic views down to the valley from which we had ascended, with Lake Maggiore to our left. Later we followed a small path through a military training ground full of signs saying something in Italian which looked like it probably meant

KEEP OUT! TRESPASSERS WILL BE SHOT!

We decided none of us understood them, we were just ignorant foreigners and we'd have to go all the way back to the bottom of the cable-car journey if we didn't push on, so we wandered on until we came to a little guard-house where we saw some soldiers standing around looking bored. When we approached them for directions they said "Well, you shouldn't be here really, but go that way and you'll be out of the military zone and you should get to Isone." We followed a series of small lanes without signposts and luckily found our way there without getting lost It had been a steep but short introduction for Vincent. We asked around the village, which was even smaller than it looked on the map, for a place to stay, and were told there's only one hotel. The owner looked us up and down and said it was full. It would have been too expensive anyway, but it was already seven o'clock and the next town was about four hours' walk away. We were standing outside the hotel wondering what to do when the boss came out again and said: "I'll tell you what. I've got a pizzeria as well, just up the road. You could sleep there, I suppose. I'll show you – jump in," and he held his car door open. We politely refused, as we'd passed it a minute earlier and we knew we'd get there quicker on foot than unloading and packing all the luggage in the boot. He ended up letting us have two perfectly adequate twin rooms with bathrooms and the use of the coffee machine downstairs for 200 Swiss Francs including breakfast at the hotel in the morning, which was a good price.

DAY 105 ISONE – COMANO
19 km; warm, sunny, cloudy patches; 24°C

"Wrong turnings, doubling back, pauses and digressions, all contribute to the dislocation of a persistent self-interest."

Before we set off Michael removed a tick from Angela's armpit. Vincent had had one the day before, so we'd been warned. It was that kind of country, where you'd find heather and scrub, with bushes and bracken sometimes encroaching onto the path, and signs of sheep or goats or foxes nearby. We started by going uphill to about 1000 m, where we paused for a long debate about whether to go this way or that; then came a measured descent through mixed deciduous forest with many beech trees, followed by a gradual slope down to Tesserete, which was being rattled by the noise of a helicopter flying to and fro carrying tree-trunks and large branches from what looked like a building site up into the forest We carried on along more civilized paths through a couple of villages, stopping more often than usual for extensive discussions about which way to go and at the same time revelling in the feeling that whichever way we went we would end up in Rome – we just had to keep on going southwards. On the way downhill to Comano we began to see glimpses of Lake Lugano in the distance, and at Comano we found an *osteria* with a few beds. It was very basic and expensive, but we managed to negotiate their 'best price' and they also knocked something off their pizzas, so we didn't grumble too much. We went out for an evening stroll in the part of the village off the main road and found a jumble of alleyways and steps and archways, which suddenly felt very Italian.

DAY 106 COMANO – MERIDE
25 km; mostly sunny; 24°C

In the morning we all walked down the hill on the road to Lugano through the suburbs. Lugano is very chic and expensive, on the shore of the lake. We came across an exhibition at the Art Museum of Giorgio Morandi's work – very simple, spare still- life paintings. We had to decide which way to go now as we were about to depart from the E1, which was in any case about to run out of steam according to our guidebook when it hit the Italian border at the end of the peninsula south of Lugano. At that point travellers following the E1 rigorously would take a ferry and presumably buy a new guidebook for the Italian section of the path, although when we went to look for one a few days later in Como we were told it didn't exist. Our guidebook (in German) only gave very sketchy indications of how to proceed in Italy, so we'd have to make up our own path again. In any case we had all been invited to stay with Vera in Morbio Inferiore, two days' walk to the south-east. We decided against walking the recommended E1 route, which would have involved a climb 600 m up to the top of San Salvatore. Instead we would take the road beside the lake to Melide, then cross the lake by the bridge. Unfortunately the lakeside walk was far from idyllic as the road became more and more busy and there was no provision for pedestrians. Next to the lake was a railway line, then a wall about twenty feet high. Between the wall and a sheer cliff was the road, so you had to either walk on the road itself or on the wall, which was about two feet wide: not quite wide enough to feel safe when carrying a heavy load on it for any distance as the cars and lorries sped by. We finally arrived at Melide an hour or so later feeling hot and bothered, and happy to find a quiet square to sit by a fountain where we could eat our provisions and recover our sense of balance. It was time to rethink: based on that experience, and looking at the amount of traffic going over the bridge and along a road on the other side of the lake, sandwiched between a railway and a motorway, maybe it wasn't such a good idea to go that way after all. We could catch a ferry, someone suggested. We looked at the timetable – yes, the last ferry called at the jetty in 20 minutes. When it arrived we embarked and the little boat cast off its moorings. We had to go to a small window with a sign saying Borsa, which I supposed was like Purser, where the ticket-collector said: "Where do you want to go? Brusino Arsizio? Ah, we don't stop there." "Well it says you do on the timetable at that jetty!" "Just a minute, I'll check with the skipper...Oh alright, we'll stop there for you." Of course when we got there five minutes later there was a gaggle of people waiting, including a group of schoolchildren, but in the meantime we'd haggled with the purser and got half-price tickets because one of us was over 60, so in the end everyone was happy. I'm sure many Italians (and I'll include these Italian-speaking Swiss in that category) like saying that sort of thing – "Ah, we don't stop there" – completely deadpan, just to create a reaction, a drama. It stirs things up and makes the day more interesting. Everything is more open-ended, like the price is fixed, but if you're prepared to question it and have a chat or an argument or a debate about it, then maybe it's not so fixed.

Once we had disembarked and waved goodbye to the purser we found a path signposted to Crocifisso, which was allegedly on the way to Meride and sounded like one of those crossroads with a crucifix and a shrine which we had already met often along the way. It was immediately apparent that this path was not used often, as we had only gone round one corner when we had to climb over a large fallen tree trunk. However we soon found notices saying we were in a 'Site of Special Interest' protected by UNESCO, and there were signs of much wildlife: we saw a herd of wild pigs rushing up the hill across the path just ahead through the ancient overhanging forest; Vincent and Angela saw a fox, and Vincent also found a large stag's antler. We also found a long snake lying on the path with no head. It had obviously been recently killed, but by what? The section from Crocifisso – where we took a wrong turning near a small chapel and had to double back – led through lighter, airier woods of beech, hornbeam, birch and holly on a path hewn out of the local slate. This small area must lie on a complex geological fault as it quickly changed from granite to different forms of limestone. When we arrived at Meride we found an enchanting well-preserved old village with one street, totally off the beaten track but surrounded by fertile land and vineyards. The street contained the town hall in an empty little piazza looking out over the fields, two old-fashioned guest-houses, a fancy-looking place where you could stay and do courses in painting or cooking, and a fossil museum. It was very quiet, and everything was closed, either because it was Thursday (one of the guest-houses) or because it had closed for good (the other one) or because it was too late (the Town Hall and the museum) or too early (the fancy place). However as we were standing outside the latter, a car drew up and drove into the courtyard. The driver, a distinguished-looking man in his fifties or sixties, got out and came over to us, saying: "Were you looking for a place to stay? I'm sorry but we're full... Just a minute, I'll ring a friend of mine down the road and see if she's taking guests at the moment. It's very early in the season, you see, and also usually she only takes people in for a week at a time. But we'll see… Yes, it sounds as though she may have rooms for you. Let's go down – it's just along here. She has a beautiful house . I think you'll like it. So where are you from? Where are you going? Ah, Roma!"

When we got there he knocked at an enormous oak door and we entered a shady courtyard where he introduced us as travellers to Rome and said there was nowhere else for us to stay the night, and whereas she had looked rather suspicious at first she soon thawed and let us have her holiday flat for 50 Swiss Francs – about £30 – each, which was still a lot for us but was great value for what it was, furnished with style and good taste including some beautiful antique pieces which had always belonged to the house (*Fig. 33). There were fantastic views over the valley which spread out between hills covered in chestnut trees and limestone crags (*Fig. 34). We went out to eat at a pizzeria just outside the village on the road and ate heartily and tastily, walking back in the dark, our way lit by myriads of fireflies, with the fields on either side alive with the croaking of frogs and the snuffling of wild pigs.

DAY 107 MERIDE – MORBIO INFERIORE
17 km; sunny, warm; 25°C

We took it easy in the morning: a leisurely breakfast on the balcony then a look at the Fossil Museum, which was tiny but well-presented and informed us that the nearby Monte San Giorgio, which we had passed the day before, is a geological freak: eight to ten million years' worth of oil is trapped in layers of bitumen between the limestone strata. People have tried to mine it to use as tar, but with little success. We also spoke to Daniella, our hostess, before leaving: she grew up in that house, moved away and then inherited it from her father. She had spent some time in Britain, notably at the Findhorn community in North East Scotland. We left the village with mixed feelings – it had been such a beautiful and nourishing place we could have stayed longer, but Vincent needed to get back to Bayreuth to wrap up his studies and move house, and we needed to get to Rome, so we set off again and walked down a cobbled country lane which at first was wide enough for a horse and cart then beyond the last farm in the parish became a mule-track. We felt lively and refreshed, the day was sunny and warm, and we wandered along singing a medieval French song in four parts. At Mendrisio we hit a major industrial estate and conurbation beside the *autostrada* and said goodbye to Vincent, who was going to hitch-hike north. It was only 7 or 8 kilometres further to Vera's house and she wouldn't be home until late, so we wandered through Castel San Pietro past vineyards – each row of vines decorated with a rose-bush, which we were told acts as an early warning system against mildew, to which both plants are susceptible. We went along paths littered with massive flat slabs of slate, past an abandoned cement works which had already been designated a historical site, and through a 'geological park', which took up a large section of the steep wooded valley and showed visitors the extraordinary shapes and colours of the rock formations to be found there. When we climbed up the other side to Morbio there was not a shop to be seen where we could buy a bite to eat, so we settled for a beer and a bag of crisps at the *osteria* on the main road. What had once been a thriving little town with a large church had become a shell with a busy road running through the middle and a hypermarket on the edge of town. Vera met us with her son Moise (13) and took us to her house, a large villa to which she had come back after living abroad for many years. The house was in good condition but felt as though it was somehow left over from another age; a picture of the neighbourhood from a century ago when the house was new would have told another story altogether. It would have stood alone in a large garden, surrounded by orchards and vineyards on the south-facing slope looking down over Chiasso, a market town on the Italian border which is now a hive of industrial activity, with high-rise flats, motorways, office blocks and garages; supermarkets and fast-food outlets; billboards and square new factories, all scattered about at random. Vera took us to a restaurant hidden away in Morbio run by an Englishman who had been there for twenty years and was "always experimenting", as with the savoury strawberry risotto we tried.

DAYS 108 & 109   MORBIO INFERIORE
0 km; hot!; 29°C

(There is of course a Morbio Superiore as well – it doesn't have anything to do with one being better than the other, although no doubt the locals would tell you different: it's just like Upper and Lower.)

We spent two fabulous days resting at Vera's: late breakfasts, washing clothes, visiting Como, hanging out in a hammock on the patio…We went to collect the key for the Chiessa Rossa, an old church which teeters on the edge of the cliff that had been quarried for the cement works and is full of beautiful wall-paintings from the 14th century and a double-sided inscription reusing an ancient 9th-century patterned block of stone. Vera has been writing a little book about the church, being something of an expert on ecclesiastic history and medieval art. She is also very interested in her Jewish heritage and was going to go to Israel to study Hebrew in the summer months: she told us stories about members of her family who had to flee Italy in the 1930s to escape from the Fascist dictatorship. Vera had spent a year in Germany in the 1970s as a teenaged au pair with Angela and Michael's family, which is how they know each other, although they had not seen each other for many years.

We also went for a longer walk in the geological park, venturing upstream to see some fantastical rock formations, and one evening walked down to Chiasso as we had heard there was to be a 'world music festival' in the town square, with tickets at a reasonable price. We arrived as it was getting dark at about 9.30, as a woman singer from what used to be called Spanish Sahara[7] was finishing her set and giving a description of living conditions in her country. During the ensuing break we wandered around looking for something to eat and drink. There were stalls set up all around the square with food cooked by Turks, Portuguese, Indonesians, Cambodians or Rwandans. In among them was a stall being operated by Daniella, from the holiday flat

---

7   It is still in contention whether this land exists as a separate state. It is currently being claimed by Morocco, which has occupied the country since 1975. Most of the small population have had a family member killed or mutilated in a pointless war which has flared off and on for forty years. A cease-fire was declared in 1991, arranged by the UN and subject to a referendum being held among the people, but that has still not taken place as no-one can decide who is eligible to vote. Meanwhile in recent years about 10% of the population of the self-proclaimed capital are living in an internal refugee camp.

in Meride, who was helping out to raise some money for refugees! Just then the sound of live music came banging out of the speakers and we went to investigate: there was a group of seven or eight African men on the stage, half of them in wheelchairs and another on crutches. It was a band from the Congo whose music I've heard on the radio and had been hoping to see for a long time. Called Staff Benda Bilili, they are made up of a collection of disabled musicians and homeless orphans from Kinshasa. Some of them have made their own instruments out of bicycle spokes or oildrum lids or electrical wire, and they ROCK!!

17th June 2012

Dear Friends, wherever you are,

I feel as though I owe another chapter to Switzerland since we have now spent several glorious days in the Ticino canton. Even though it rained probably more than with you for the first day or two we were over the pass (and we had expected a whiff of Mediterranean climate!), we could not but enjoy what we walked through. The River Ticino, broadly and steadily, rushed along our side, one moment on the left, one moment on the right as we kept crossing over it, and along its banks we walked on huge granite slabs, sometimes skipping to avoid one of the many lizards on the way. Once Nick leapt back as the curled-up dog mess he was just about to step over carefully stretched and slithered away! This part of our walk was accompanied frequently by the song of nightingales, who seemed to favour the river glades of the Ticino more than anywhere I have ever experienced. Now I know why so many texts of songs refer to the heart moving when hearing their song: I could not help but chuckle with joy.

Michael, my brother, joined us in Bellinzona, where he came whistling out of a side street just as we were about to squabble over the direction of the youth hostel. He had already found out and took us there – tension averted! Furthermore, to our great surprise, my gorgeous nephew Vincent came too, and so for the next three or four days we were a little family caravan roaming the beautiful countryside. When I say roaming I actually mean steeply climbing, clambering, sweating like a good 'un when struggling to the tops, and leaning heavily on our hazel sticks on the rock-strewn paths downwards, no less steep than those going up.

The woods on the mountain sides are mostly of sweet chestnut trees, which give a wonderful dark rich light, cavernous and protected, and the ground is crackling underfoot with the remains of last autumn's riches. But every so often the light changed and we felt ourselves among mainly birches, or oaks, or beeches again, this time shorter and stouter than those in the German forest Along the seam of the mountains we would find ourselves crossing roaring waters cascading just by our sides from many tens of meters high towards the rickety wooden bridge or the hardly detectable stepping-stones we were on. Once we heard a loud rustle in the woods below us, only to spot a herd of wild pigs crossing our path rushing away from us. Often we hear cuckoos, especially in the evenings.

An amazing thing happened last week up in one of those picturesque mountain villages of the Ticino, grouped around a core of dark wooden carved houses with red geraniums in the window boxes and huge roofs hanging over the edges to protect against the weight of the snow masses in the winter: Nick and I were sitting on a village bench having lunch, when a troupe of German walking club members wandered by and greeted us then one or two hung back mumbling something about one of their members being lost, and how they had to wait for him. Then one said: "There he comes, our doctor." Along came a figure, looking slightly bemused to see those waiting, and it was none other than the lovely chap whose house we had visited for a meal some weeks earlier in the Black Forest! By complete chance he had in the meantime accepted an invitation to take part in this weekend walking tour in the Ticino Valley, and lo and behold he found himself running into us again! It was a joyous hello and we joined their party for the remains of the evening.

Well dear friends, I understand the weather has been no less than testing for you all in England; why, even in Germany I believe, so I will not taunt you with descriptions of how it is here now, but suffice to say, now it is what one would expect it to be in the middle of June in spitting distance of Italy. In fact we have been to Italy already as it is literally down the hill from where we are now, with a friend from many years ago who lives in a fantastic villa at the foot of a geological park, where a volcano many zillions of years ago turned every layer of sedimentary arrangements over and on their side, so that it has created the most stunning effects in the formations, even to those who haven't got a clue (ahem…). On the other side of the mountain is Lake Lugano, along and across which we travelled two days ago before succumbing to the invitation to have a break here. So we went to an exhibition of works by Morandi, to another –permanent – one on the cultures of the South Sea Islands, we wandered around the city of Como and marvelled at how Italian it was! We enjoyed our first icecream in Italy, even though we haven't actually walked there yet! But we will tomorrow. Then we wandered down to Chiasso in the evening to a music festival and were bowled over to see a band from Congo where four guys in wheelchairs, one on shoulder-high crutches and a couple more very lively wiry characters make the most funky and life-enhancing sound and impression.

Well, my brother is still with us for a couple of days then Jannah and Jean will meet with us; then we will have to 'interrupt' for a Soundsphere concert and workshop in Vevey. 'Interrupt', because again we are too far to make it fit without some sidestepping of the route. But the concert is also fundraising for Medecins Sans Frontieres, so in a way it is totally part of the walk.

On the subject: thank you from the bottom of our hearts for the lovely response to our last email, and the appeal bit in particular. You are all just so lovely!

Looking forward to our replies again, which as ever we treasure greatly.

Lots of love from us both,

Angela and Nick XXX

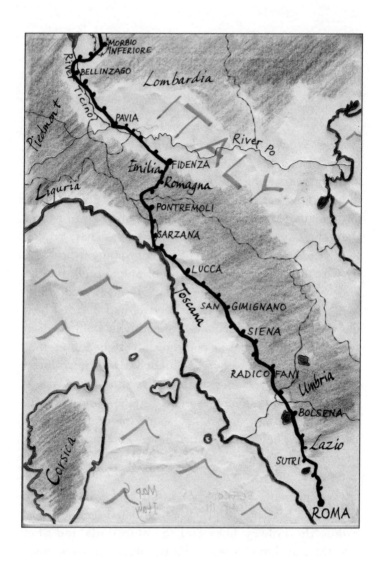

MORBIO
INFERIORE
River Ticino
BELLINZAGO
Lombardia
Piedmont
PAVIA
River Po
ITALY
Emilia
FIDENZA
Romagna
Liguria
PONTREMOLI
SARZANA
LUCCA
Toscana
SAN GIMIGNANO
SIENA
RADICO FANI
Umbria
BOLSENA
Lazio
SUTRI
Corsica
ROMA

THE ITALIAN JOB

DAY 110 MORBIO – TRADATE
31km; hotter!; 32°C

Before we left Vera's house we had a tricky problem to resolve. We were about 60 km north-east of Bellinzago, where 'Bluebells' had invited the two of us to stay and was expecting us on or about this date, but she didn't know yet, because we hadn't been able to send any emails for days, that we'd also arranged to meet Jannah, our daughter (26), and Jean – her French boyfriend – at Bellinzago. They were coming from Lyon by Covoiturage, which is a kind of online hitch-hiking, and we had had to arrange a place to meet them on or near the E1. On top of that Michael had decided he'd like to stay on in Morbio and meet us in Bellinzago in two days' time so that he could walk with us for another day. We managed to email 'Bluebells', who introduced herself as Laura, and explained the situation. "Would we able to find somewhere else for the other three to stay in Bellinzago?" "No, no," came the reply. "It's not necessary. They can all stay here. You must all stay together as a family, no? Now, is there anything you can't eat?"

We left with Michael, who said he'd walk down to the Italian border with us. We negotiated the industrial estate, the railway lines and the autostrada and after less than an hour crossed the border at an unmanned frontier-post surrounded by weeds. Michael left us at the first village to find another way back and we took a signposted footpath which quickly became utterly overgrown. After a short while we retreated, scratched and sweating, and walked round on the road. We followed it for a few hours through several villages, mostly on cracked and crumbling pavements, stopping at Fignolo for a long break where we sat outside the village shop/bar and drank a couple of litres of water each. It had been hot in Morbio, pushing 30°, but now in the middle of the day the heat was overwhelming. Walking off down the road we found that the pavement ran out, the traffic was fast, and there was no way into the Parco Regionale to go south to Tradate, so we had to double back to Fignolo. When we finally found the path it was a good one but the woods became increasingly boggy, hot and mosquito-infested, so we took to a road again which led straight and fast through the forest and had a pedestrian/cycle path alongside it at least some of the time. Outside a place called Castelnuovo Bozzente, which actually had quite an old castle, we passed a girl waiting at a non-existent bus-stop, or at least there was no sign for one. Shortly after we saw another girl on the other side of the road, just as a young man came running towards us, pulling his sweatshirt up to cover his face. Since our greetings were not returned and we were merely stared at by the girls, we soon guessed they were not waiting for a bus. This was confirmed when we saw three or four more further along, all black, all about 18 years old, all dressed quite provocatively. Waiting for Berlusconi?

Turning off the road as soon as possible to avoid the traffic onto a footpath we soon became hopelessly lost, with no sense of direction. Standing in a patch of scrubland scratching our heads we were beginning to think we would have to go back to the road again when we spotted a small boy playing alone on the hillside ahead. We approached him and he told us he was called Lucca and he was five years old and his granny was at the top of the hill. We told him we were from England and we were lost, so he took us to his granny. She knew exactly how to get to Tradate, where she said there were a few hotels, and took us a little way along a path which then meandered through the woods very distinctly for a couple of miles until it came to a main road and soon afterwards to Tradate. We found a welcome at a little hotel where we collapsed exhausted.

DAY 111 TRADATE – BELLINZAGO
18 km; hot; 32°C

We had to pause and figure out how to proceed: we were about halfway to Bellinzago from Morbio but looking again at our map and going by yesterday's experience it was going to be very tough indeed to find a way to get there directly while avoiding main roads and without crossing Milan airport runways. We decided to make a sideways shift by train and rejoin the E1 at Somma Lombardo. From there we could follow the footpath alongside the canal as far as the next river bridge, the Ponte di Oleggio, cross over and walk to Oleggio to meet Jean and Jannah. We found our way out of Somma Lombardo with some difficulty and it took a long time just to get to the canal, passing through Maddalena, a village in mourning where the whole population was out in the street waiting for the funeral to begin. When we got to the canal we had to climb about thirty feet down a narrow perpendicular ladder attached to the bridge, then walk between two canals for about 10 km. It was extremely hot, and we hadn't topped up our water-bottles in Maddalena as planned as the café was packed with mourners. We trekked on stoically, occasionally waving at a cyclist or fisherman on the other bank, and finally arrived at the road bridge from which we had another eight kilometres to go to get to Oleggio, where we had arranged by phone to meet Jannah.

It was immediately obvious that it would be impossible: the road was a straight flat two-lane highway packed with traffic. It had no pedestrian access, not even a gutter, and apart from slowing down to cross the bridge the cars and trucks were rattling along at 60 mph. There was no grass verge either, as the road was only separated from a thorny hedge by a continuous crash barrier. We went back to the lay-by where we had stocked up on liquid next to the river and asked advice at the kiosk. "There's nothing to be done," chuckled the fat hot-dog salesman. "There are no buses to Oleggio either. Well, not from here anyway. You could go up the hill a few kilometres to the village and see if there's any more buses from there." "We'll just have to hitch a lift then," said Angela. "Oh, no-one will stop for you here," sneered the only customer, who had previously been trying to tell us his repertoire of dirty jokes, judging by his gestures. "People round here only stop for pretty young girls." I have to admit I tended to agree with him, having hitched through Italy before, albeit forty years earlier. "No-one will stop," I said to Angela as we positioned ourselves at the edge of the lay-by. "Look, they're all families. Or single women, and they never stop in Italy." "Well, let's give it ten minutes," she said. About eight minutes later a car stopped for us, driven by a single woman.

She said she never normally goes this way, and never picks up hitch-hikers, but she saw us and something made her stop, so she took us to the town square in

Oleggio and we rang Jannah, who came running round the corner to greet us. She said she had walked there from Bellinzago with Jean, who was feeling the heat. He is used to spending time in the sun in the South of France but is red-haired and light-skinned: the temperature had evidently got to him, which did not bode well for the next week. Shortly afterwards we met Laura, who had driven over to offer us a lift to her house, which we gratefully accepted – in for a penny... We were excited to meet each other after such a long period of anticipation since Christmas, and when we got to the house we met the rest of her family, who were waiting with Michael: husband Piero and offspring Patricio (21), Maria (19) and Susanna (15). Maria is severely disabled and needs almost constant attention but both the men of the house look after her whenever they are at home. Piero had been made redundant three or four years before but had recently found a job working at a wine company which also produces grappa on a large scale, while Patricio was about to go to university in Germany.

Laura sat us all down and produced a wonderful meal of several courses followed by sweet wine and then grappa, and we conversed at length about all and everything in English with scraps of Italian and German. She had prepared beds or mattresses on the floor for everyone, and at the end of the evening insisted that we should all stay another day and night to ensure that Jean was well prepared for the rigours of the journey ahead.

DAY 112 BELLINZAGO
(several km); still very hot; 32°C

We walked. We had decided we needed to catch up the kilometres we'd skipped by getting lifts the day before so we walked down to the river on a path with Michael and

Jannah and Jean, who said he felt better and wanted to get some practice. Patricio said he'd drive down and give us a lift back. When we got there we found it was a popular spot despite the fact that the river was very shallow, and many people were sunning themselves on large flat stones on the banks. Returning to the house we found Laura had washed our clothes and hung them out to dry and phoned a friend of theirs who does a lot of walking, so he came round with a pile of maps of the region, some of which he gave us to take away. We planned our route as far as Pavia, where the Ticino joins the Po, and Piero let us print off the <u>relevant</u> pages of the Italian Servas address list (it had 389 pages in total!). We helped prepare another huge meal then listened to Susanna play the piano – yet another prodigious teenage musician we had encountered on our travels. What a wonderfully hospitable family, whom we would never have met if we had not laid ourselves open to whatever might come our way.

DAY 113 BELLINZAGO – ALBAIRATE
28 km; hot; 30°C

We left our new friends in the woods near the river and went along a pleasant woodland path as far as a bridge where we could cross the Ticino and get to the canal again. Along the way we phoned Arabella, a Servas member in Abbiategrasso, who had said she could put us up for the night. She told us to meet her at the yoghurt shop next to the castle. Most of the way we could walk with the water on our left and shady trees and bushes on our right.

At each bridge there was a little collection of houses, and sometimes an inn or even a market square. This was the canal known as the Naviglio Grande, which cuts across country from just south of Lago Maggiore to Milan, having been excavated by the Milanese in the 12th century and widened later, partly to carry marble for building the cathedral, although we were informed knowledgeably that it was designed by da Vinci. All the way along it was dotted with crumbling villas and *palazze* (***Fig. 35**), and the imposing castle at Abbiategrasso, at the confluence of this and the Naviglio di Bereguardo, which was built in 1470 to ship salt from the Venetian lagoon, was constructed to house an official with the splendid title of Il Guardiano delle Acque (The Guardian of the Waters). At Bernate we stopped for an ice cream at a little shop and fell into conversation with the local police chief who thought it was hilarious that we should want to walk to Rome. At Boffalora we stopped for a moment to watch the local teenagers diving into the canal from the bridge. We'd got as far as Ponte Vecchio when we realised we'd already walked 28 kilometres; it was getting late; we, especially the newcomers, were feeling exhausted and dehydrated; and there were no buses any longer. Jannah and Jean stopped and said they'd had enough; they would try and get a lift. About a kilometre down the road Arabella rang up and said: "We'll come and pick you up, it's not far at all by car," so we agreed, although had it just been the two of us we would probably have said no thanks. While we waited on a street corner some people came out of a cycle shop for a chat and pressed some more local maps on us. Arabella turned up with her husband Alessandro and son Roberto (7) and squeezed the three of us with our bags into their tiny car. They took us to a pub which did a cheap buffet deal then to the yoghurt shop they run. They said they had come to an arrangement with some friends who run an 'agriturismo ecologico' for us two to stay there while Michael, Jean and Jannah could stay with them. We said goodbye to Michael once again in the farmyard and agreed to meet the others in the morning, and met the farmer's wife, who seemed rather grumpy, but maybe she'd been asleep.

DAY 114 ALBAIRATE – BESATE
21 km; very hot indeed; 36°C

"Walking is egalitarian and democratic: we do not become experts at walking and one side of the road is as good as another."

In the morning we met the farmer, who made breakfast for us. His wife was much more good-tempered and saw us off armed with a new map to walk back to Abbiategrasso. It took us about an hour along a straight chalky track between fields of beans and corn with the western and southern Alps spread out far away in the distance to our right, glistening in the sunshine. We met Jannah and Jean at the yoghurt shop and took some flowers to Arabella then set off to the Bereguardo canal, which we walked along for a couple of hours as the sun blazed inexorably. We had to stop for an early lunch – great thick slabs of pizza from a shop on the way out of town – and a paddle in the canal before carrying on to the fortified abbey of Morimondo, which had obviously been a very important place 'back in the day' as it had supported an entire walled village, where we found a bar to shelter from the relentless heat for a while and drink lemonade. It became clear after some time that it was not going to get any cooler until about 7 o'clock so we thought we may as well walk on and hope to find plenty of shade on the way. The map showed a chunk of green which signified a forest next to the lane, but we must have taken a wrong turning as we never found much shade. We walked past a rice-field for the first time (*Fig. 36) and marvelled at the amount of water involved compared to the dry and dusty road alongside. After coming to a dead end at a farmyard we followed an unmarked footpath which came out near a large complex of farm buildings, old and new, clustered around a courtyard. Going in to ask directions I found a farrier shoeing a horse. A swarthy young man who was overseeing the operation pointed the way down a path behind a collection of farm workers' cottages, so we all traipsed along past an old blind man sitting on his front porch, past a collection of astonished mothers and children who were out in their back garden playing in a paddling pool. There was something timeless in the scenes: not that any one of them could have been painted 300 years ago, but that somehow the history of the place was jumbled. The original farmhouse probably dated from the 16th century, with enormous thick walls and a walled enclosure like a fortification around the whole farm, while barns and smaller houses had been added in more recent times. There was still an air of the feudal past hanging over the place, while the plastic pool gave a hint of material comfort, and the whole scene was somehow preserved by the stillness of the baking hot day with its interplay of light and shadow and the rhythmic tapping of the farrier's hammer, while the old man sat oblivious to our passage, watching the past.

We eventually arrived at Besate, which felt like far enough for a day's walk, but the only place to stay was being refurbished. We stopped at a café/shop where a kind assistant tried phoning a few contacts with no luck. We thought of catching a bus to the next town then coming back in the morning, but the last bus had already gone. The only option was to go back to the agriturismo farm/conference centre we had passed a couple of kilometres down the dusty lane. The lady in the bar rang them and they had an empty room, so we walked back as the sun began to sink and asked if Jean could pitch a tent in the garden. It was going to be relatively expensive for us to have a room, but at least it would be cheap to camp. Jean and Jannah slept there, we slept in a converted pigsty which was better than it sounds, and we all watched football in our room (Germany 4, Greece 2) while eating the remains of our pizza from the morning.

DAY 115 BESATE – BEREGUARDO
11 km; hotter; 37°C

In the morning things looked brighter as the manager took to the philanthropic side of our venture: he gave us a good rate on the room and the best breakfast we'd had for weeks, as well as charging nothing for the tent. Thus fortified, we walked back to Besate and turned down to the river to rejoin the E1. When we found the footpath we also found signs saying it was temporarily out of use. In other words, completely overgrown with nettles and brambles. There seemed to be nothing for it but to return to Besate and walk along the road, but coming upon a crowd of people preparing for a canoe club outing, complete with barbecue, we asked their advice and a stocky woman with glasses said she was driving back to Motta Visconti and could give us a lift. After looking at our map we decided we wouldn't be losing any walking miles by accepting, and shortly afterwards we were in the town centre, where I found a charming young woman in a travel agency who was only too pleased to help find us somewhere to stay the night – she was obviously underwhelmed by the number of other customers she had had that morning. She spent half an hour ringing around local hostels, farm B&Bs and the like, without luck. Finally she phoned her dad who said there was a place in Bereguardo but nothing else this side of Pavia, 20 km further on, unless you went on the motorway bridge to the other side of the river. She rang Bereguardo and booked a room for us, and we walked along the canal to get there, stopping for lunch at an abandoned hunters' clubhouse which had some tattered rusty chairs outside. We sat in the shade of some willows and had a long conversation about holidays. What is a good holiday? What is a holiday?

The town of Bereguardo sits at the end of the eponymous canal and consists of a massive 14th-century castle surrounded by five or six streets. A couple of bars, a shop, a post office, a hairdresser's, a bakery and a takeaway pizzeria: that was about it. Our hotel was the only one in town and the clientele were seemingly travelling salesmen and a group of men who looked like they'd been outdoors all day digging a trench and were now shovelling in vast amounts of pasta. The owner, head chef and waiter was a comedian with only one tooth. His assistant in the kitchen and bar, to whom he referred as "my cousin" or "the boy", was a slow-moving fellow with a wandering eye. After partaking of a meagre feast – they weren't used to dealing with vegetarians – Angela retired to our room while the rest of us went up to the castle grounds where a midsummer *festa* was going on. This was a strangely disturbing experience as the six-piece band were mostly miming while the townsfolk trance-danced the waltz, tango and foxtrot. A sort of 'Strictly Come Dancing' on sleeping-pills. Jannah and Jean pitched their tent in the back yard of the hotel on a slab of concrete under a roof of corrugated iron but managed to get a fair night's sleep.

DAY 116 BEREGUARDO – PAVIA
20 km; some cloud; 35°C

First thing in the morning 'the boy' let us in to the bar and gave us a hot drink and a banana. The Italians seem to be averse to having a filling breakfast: maybe their digestive systems are still working on the pasta from the night before. Having got up early to get some kilometres under our belts before it became too hot we then wasted the advantage by walking out of town in every direction but the right one. Eventually we found the right and proper road – a straight flat old country road with little traffic – and followed it for ten kilometres or so until Jean spotted a sign to a campsite/ restaurant/swimming-pool off to the left, where we rested for a couple of hours, ate our picnic, and went swimming. What a relief to get our sweaty shirts off – by this time of the morning they were already wringing wet – and have a cool dip! The place was run by a woman from Sheffield with her (local) husband, and she was happy to let us in for nothing, despite us being very hot and sticky. The locals who had driven out from Pavia to loll about at the pool-side being impossibly fashionable looked at us askance as we tramped in and out with our heavy packs, but what did we care? Walking on towards Pavia our paths diverged at a point where Jean and Jannah went east to find their Couchsurfing host in one part of town while we took to a footpath along the riverside as far as the old bridge, which we crossed to get to the street we were looking for, where our Servas hosts lived. We hadn't walked all that far, but the last mile or so seemed endless along this cobbled street which turned out to be longer and longer as it straggled out of town before coming to an abrupt stop at the edge of the National Park. A young professional couple, Roberto and Caterina, showed us proudly around their gleaming flat then asked us: "Do you want to have a quiet meal with Roberto's sister, or would you rather go to the flat next door with a bunch of mates and watch the football?" "Dunno, who's playing?" "Italy versus England!" It seemed fairly clear what they wanted to do. A group of 9 or 10 thirty-somethings were gathered in Sebastian's flat next door and produced a sumptuous buffet, at which we were guests of honour, then we settled down to watch the match, which became increasingly exciting as it went down to extra time and a penalty shoot-out, which Italy won. Our hosts were very generous in victory, but the scene was not as raucous as it might have been in a bar in town and also we – especially Angela – were not really bona fide English despite living there, and there was quite a lot of friendly banter going on between the sexes along the lines of "well you women don't understand the offside rule anyway" and "you blokes just sit on the sofa while we do the washing up".

DAY 117 PAVIA – BELGIOIOSO
26 km; some cloud, but extremely hot; 37°C

We had arranged to meet Jannah and Jean near where they stayed, which took about an hour to get to as we went slowly through the Renaissance town centre, astonished by the crumbling walls of the cathedral: one of our first glimpses of the miserable state in which so many great Italian buildings are languishing, along with the magnificent villas beside the Naviglio Grande. The trouble is there's just so much of it – how can they possibly maintain all the great historical architecture in

Italy without emptying the public purse? Perhaps the answer is "Gamble! Vote for Berlusconi!" or "It's all a joke – vote for the Five Star Party!"

By the time we all met up and hit the road it was about 9.30, the temperature was already in the 30s, and we vowed never to start so late again. This was the fifth day out of Bellinzago and the temperature had been above 35° every day, which somewhat slowed down our progress, and since we had no idea what conditions would be like in the next weeks we had an urge to start getting up and out early to beat the heat. For one thing it was extremely hard on our visitors, who had thrown themselves into the hardest conditions we'd met so far with gusto but were understandably struggling at times. We had finally found ourselves on the Via Francigena, which had come over the Alps from the west on its way from the south of France to Rome. This is an ancient pilgrims' way which is maintained by various organizations, some state-funded and some run by volunteers. There are numerous hostels and resting-places along the way where we could stay using our pilgrims' passports, and we were hoping to find the first one in Belgioioso. The route led along roads of varying widths, often without shade for miles, through fields of rice and maize which are flooded by intricate irrigation systems, but we passed through a village at least a kilometre from the river Po which had been flooded by natural causes several times in recent years, as had the street we stayed on in Pavia. We went off the road into some woods for a picnic lunch as I thought we could reach the riverbank, but we got as far as a shady clearing and flopped down exhausted to gorge ourselves on melon and beat off the horseflies. We found mosquitoes no great challenge on the whole except in a few localised spots, mostly in the Ticino valley a few days earlier, but the locals in Pavia told us they all hear their neighbours clapping and slapping themselves at night, and I think they meant it was because of the mosquitoes...

We walked into Belgioioso in dribs and drabs as Jean and I had both stopped in the shade to read or study maps. Both he and Jannah had brought hefty novels which they had found impossible to leave behind and dipped into whenever we had a long break, whereas we had decided not to carry any books from the outset to save on weight, and were missing a good read. Belgioioso was the sort of town which had spilt out from the centre over the centuries but only in one direction, which happened to be the direction we were coming from, so it seemed to take hours to get to the middle of what was not in fact a big town. Stopping at the first available bar, we slumped for the time it took to drink a glass of lemonade each and share a couple of large bottles of fizzy water, before Jannah and I regained enough energy to go looking for a place to stay. We went to the somnolent hotel across the street first and were quoted a price of €70 each, so we said we'd pass. We found a massive castle around the corner, like a chateau but with enormously thick walls, which was the centre-piece of the town. Behind it were extensive gardens which we tried to enter but found our way barred by a pair of huge locked gates. A young head gardener came to our aid and told us the rear portion of the castle was being refurbished privately to offer classical concerts, and that the best place to look for pilgrims' lodgings was in the old friary down the road. We went to investigate but the relevant door was locked and the cobbled courtyard next to the old building had a frankly creepy atmosphere: a cottage at one end had a collection of old photographs – going back to the 20s or 30s – on a table outside, all covered in cobwebs and next to some guttering candles. We had the feeling that although nobody had answered our knock at the locked door, someone was watching us, so we retreated and went back past the castle until we came to the Locanda della Pesa – the Weighing Station Inn – where we got offered a decent price for two rooms with a discount of 15% as pilgrims. Since we were all actually walking on the way towards Rome we felt OK about presenting ourselves as pilgrims despite the fact that the other two were not going all the way, but we weren't going out of our way to describe ourselves like that; people just assumed that's what we were if we said we were walking to Rome. It happened quite a few times once we had hit the Via Francigena that in the course of the usual conversation – "Where are you going?" "To Rome" – people would then declare: "Oh, you're pilgrims," and it wasn't a question, it was a statement of fact. So we went back from the inn to fetch the others and had a very welcome cold shower before going out to paint the town red, which was not easy as the few restaurants there were seemed to be closed. We ended up in a take-away *pizzeria* with a couple of tables and a fridge full of beer eating a wonderful pizza looking out at a full moon above the castle walls, followed by a fantastic organic ice-cream at the *gelateria*. It was still so hot even after 10 o'clock that we had to go and have another cold shower before going to bed.

DAY 118 BELGIOIOSO – ORIO LITTA
25 km; hotter still; 38°C

The last day we would be walking with Jannah and Jean, and it was going to be a brute. We got up early but

Jannah had to go to the Post Office and it didn't officially open until 8.35 (and for some reason closed at 4.25!) by which time a large queue had built up and we didn't get off until well after nine o'clock. The countryside was still flat, the path straight and shimmering in the heat. The sweetcorn was high, already as tall as us, and along the path were channels of water which had been diverted from the Po. Many farmers have pumps attached to their tractors to get the water up and sprayed onto the fields, so the path was occasionally squelchy with red mud. In the distance on our right hand side the brown mountains of the Apennines were closing in. At a village on the main road we stopped at a street market to buy cheese and bread, tomatoes and melon, then in Santa Cristina e Bissone we found a couple of benches in a playground and flopped down for lunch and a siesta. When we went into a bar nearby to round it off with an espresso we got some strange looks from the local men who were hanging around outside. Not surprisingly: we were hot and dusty, loaded with rucksacks and speaking English. The barmaid asked where we were going and seemed surprised, as though they have very few foot-travellers passing through, but the young men, who looked like former soldiers, just sniggered in a thick dialect behind our backs.

We had to stop and rest again in the afternoon at a hamlet where a very old church offered some shade, and later, after following a small road lined with alder trees, we called in at an old-fashioned inn in a village next to the bridge across the Lambro. The landlady sympathised with our state of heat-induced exhaustion and offered us a bowl of fresh apricots to go with our lemonade. We crossed the bridge and after a few more miles off-road across a wide grassy plain near the course of the Po we came into Orio Litta, where we had arranged to stay the night at a pilgrims' hostel. Although a very small town it has a dynamic mayor who has had an extension built onto the castle in the middle of town which houses municipal activities – council meetings, local clubs and societies and so on – and has turned one of the castle towers into a small hostel for pilgrims. The mayor met us himself and had his photograph taken with us for the local paper, then showed us our beds in the medieval tower, which had space for six or eight sleepers, and introduced us to the only other guest, a Dutchman called Harry in his sixties who had walked all the way from Pavia that day and was suffering from over-heating. Harry told Angela he had worked all over the world and that this plain reminded him most of Vietnam, with its heat, humidity and rice-fields. The mayor recommended a restaurant where he said we could get a good meal. Harry said he'd been there and given up because they didn't have any food, but we thought he'd probably just gone too early. We had discovered that we had rarely been able to find a decent meal before 8 o'clock in Italy. So it transpired: we were received by very friendly folk who greeted us like long-lost friends and brought us one course after another of delicious food accompanied by excellent local wine and followed by coffee and complimentary grappa, all for a very reasonable price. We sat outside in the courtyard next to the boules pitch, where a local derby was being played to raucous accompaniment. The mayor had also pointed out a telephone number before he left, saying: "You'll be wanting to get the ferry across the river tomorrow. Here's the number to ring this evening to book it." Our map didn't say you had to get a ferry; it had two alternative routes and Harry said he wasn't catching a ferry, but looking more closely it did make sense not to go the long way round down to the bridge near Piacenza, and it sounded quite romantic to cross the river in a rowing-boat with a wise ferryman or maybe even in a gondola, perhaps with a hooded monk... So before we ate I rang the number and spoke to someone who said: "You want to cross in the morning – what time? 8 o'clock? Make it 8.15. See you there."

DAY 119 ORIO LITTA – PIACENZA
20 km; exceedingly hot; 37°C

"Twenty years from now you will be more disappointed by the things you didn't do than the ones you did do, so throw off the bowlines. Sail away from the safe harbour. Catch the trade winds in your sails. Explore. Dream. Discover." (Mark Twain)

Actually the ferryman was a grumpy old man in a speedboat who grumbled all the way across about the falling number of pilgrims, the council's lack of efficiency in maintaining the jetty, the cost of fuel, the weather, and anything else he had time for in the ten minutes it took to speed to a mooring downstream on the other bank. The other thing he had to complain about was our lack of punctuality as we had taken a wrong turning on the way and arrived at 8.30, which caused an outburst of operatic proportions. He did make up for it when we reached the other side and he took us to his house, where he showed us his official pilgrims' ferryboat book, an enormous embossed tome which had been signed by all the passengers from the last ten years or so. He stamped our pilgrims' passports and told us about the pilgrimage he was going to go on later in the summer, which sounded more like a guided tour of the vineyards of Tuscany.

We had been up early to have breakfast with Jean and Jannah, as arranged the evening before, and were knocking on the door of the *ristorante* at seven o'clock since the boss had apparently forgotten the arrangement. A small girl appeared in the street and went off to get him out of bed. We four had a quick bite to eat together then the two of us were on the road alone again, after an emotional farewell. They had been such splendid companions and were now going off to prepare for a brass band festival they were playing in together in Brittany.

Once we left the ferryman's house we fell into an argument about which way to go – perhaps the grumpy mood had been catching, and we were feeling a bit fragile anyway about losing our companions – but by the time we got to the next village it had dissipated and we stopped for elevenses (aka a proper breakfast). We had just passed a very old house with various signs carved on the stone front and some lettering which indicated that it had been a resting-place for pilgrims at some point, set up by the Knights Templar, when we came upon the modern equivalent: a café/hostel run, surprisingly, by an Anglo-Italian family from Preston, Lancashire. Later we were trudging along beside a high brick wall, behind which spread a vast tract of Ministry of Defence land, on the road into Piacenza. We were beginning to fade fast in the extreme heat, and had to stop again to drink before we got to the main square where we needed to sit down somewhere cool for a good long rest then find a place to stay the night. No luck with our Servas contact in Piacenza whose phone would not reply, and no pilgrim hostel to be found, so we booked into the Youth Hostel then sat down in a shady spot for an excellent salad. When it was time to walk off to the hostel on the edge of town we felt the heat immediately beating down: as soon as we stood up and strapped on our bags we already felt the sweat running down our necks. When we got there we had the first of three cold showers that evening before bed-time.

DAY 120 PIACENZA – VEVEY

The time had come for us to make our way back to Switzerland, this time to the French-speaking part on the shores of Lake Geneva, so we had to get a train over the border to Brig. The Italian train system, as we had discovered earlier, is very cheap and efficient compared to the British and German versions, and a very helpful clerk at the ticket office made sure we got the cheapest tickets possible by selling us singles to Domodossola (about 200 kilometres, but still in Italy) for €13 each, while it cost the same again to go from there to Brig on a Swiss train, which was only one stop and took half an hour, mostly through a tunnel. We were picked up in Brig by JC, a French-speaking Swiss man who had accidentally found himself hosting a houseful of people on behalf of his wife Anne, who is from Yorkshire. We had got to know her sister Helen through various singing activities, notably a concert she organised for a local charity a few years ago which brought together several choirs and a capella groups to sing in York Minster. So when Anne was in York for a visit a few months before we set off walking, she innocently said to Soundsphere: "Oh, if you ever fancy singing in Switzerland let me know. I could organise a concert in our local church," which to be honest didn't sound very exciting to me, but they all jumped up and down and Paula said: "Ah, great, we can do it when the Montreux Jazz Festival is on!" Sarah said: "Yes, there'll be good music on <u>and</u>

there'll be loads of interesting stalls there!" Judith said: "And it'll be hot and sunny with beautiful snow-capped mountains all around," and Angela said: "Hmmm, we'll be in Switzerland at the end of June, won't we, Nick?" Nick said: "Yes, we'll be near Lake Geneva at the end of June," because he was being very cautious before we set off about how quickly we'd walk and didn't want to tie us down to dates which we would have to rush to meet. Anyway things turned out differently. One of the group – who are well known on the folk circuit and have supported some big acts over the years – had been unavoidably detained in England, and another had walked way too far. But the concert had been booked and the show had to go on! Anne had kindly said we could all sleep at her house, which would mean a total of six women and me staying as guests for two or three days. JC was understandably full of trepidation at the idea, but was extremely generous in picking us up from Brig and driving us to their house in the hills near Vevey – where Charlie Chaplin used to live, on the shores of the lake close to Montreux. It was a shock to the system to suddenly be plucked out of the baking heat of Piacenza and dropped into the cool mountain air of Switzerland. As Angela summed it up in her journal: "Weird to be back in Switzerland. Wonderful meal on terrace. Cowbells in distance. Football later. Germany out, beat 1-2 by Italy. Headache."

DAYS 121-124 **VEVEY – PIACENZA**
0 km; hot, 30° – cool, 16° –
thundery, 23° –hot, 36°C

In the morning we had to deal with paperwork and start telephoning banks in England to finalise details of maturing insurance policies and mortgage arrangements.

Finally we could go out with Anne and JC to visit the church where the concert would be the following day. It was still surprisingly hot: when we went for a jaunt up to Gruyere and the sun came out it was bright and clear and around the 30° mark, which they said was a heat wave. Gruyere is a very photogenic old town with a little castle on top of a hill looking out over fields and vineyards with a view of the high mountains in the distance. JC gave us a running commentary all the way in his eccentric version of English, telling us much about the local history, geography, politics, etc. Since he was brought up in the region he knows it intimately and made it come alive. They took us out to a big supermarket for lunch, which was unusual but very sensible: if you want to go out for a meal in Switzerland without paying an arm and a leg, this is the way to do it. When we went back to their house we met their son Christian (20), who suffers from autism and is very sweet and full of good will but was obviously somewhat thrown by having strangers in the house, which became clearer as more and more people arrived during the course of the evening.

The following day Soundsphere (Sounds4) – well actually Soundsdry (Sounds3) to continue the German/ English wordplay, but that doesn't have the same ring to it – put on a singing workshop at the church, which was very well attended and enjoyable, followed by the performance in the evening, where two local choirs appeared first and someone organised a barbecue in the car park during the interval. These activities raised a total of over £400 for MSF, which was fantastic. We had a day to spare to take in something of the world-renowned Montreux Jazz Festival. Unfortunately the weather had changed drastically overnight and the lake was swathed in cloud. We wandered about in the rain among stalls selling CDs, musical instruments, food, hats, ponchos and umbrellas then went for a cup of tea in a café with a Moorish theme which sold sweetmeats, mint tea and Turkish coffee and had at least one table full of heavily veiled women speaking Arabic. We had a hilarious evening which somehow included the European Championship final (Spain 4, Italy 0), which we were glad we hadn't watched in Italy. In the morning Angela wrote a report to send off by email and also sent a message to Harry Gration from BBC's Look North, who had shown an interest in our venture, letting him know of our progress...

July 2nd 2012

Heat, Sweat and Bites...

Dear friends wherever you are,

Since the last epistle to you, Nick and I seem to have hardly been on our own. Family members have walked with us, have stood on crossroads discussing with us, have endured the searing heat of Northern Italy with us, have found various accommodations with us and generally experienced the reality of these extraordinary walking days with us. As soon as we crossed the border into Italy, a fairly unsung event due to a flat battery on the tablet – so no photo – and not so much as one customs officer between the Swiss and the Italians, we realised that finding footpaths did not mean you could actually walk them. As we hadn't brought a machete we were obliged to beat a retreat after battling our way in for about 30 metres or so with our beautiful and very useful walking sticks. These thirty metres were enough to receive battle marks for the next ten days! Legs scratched and blistered from some plant juice reaction, arms, face and neck bitten by attacking horseflies and mosquitoes, we were forced to rethink our route and try to learn the lay of the land with urgency.

We came down into the flat lands of the Po plains, a humid expanse gridded with irrigation canals and large contributory rivers, where people divert the flow of water with pumping attachments on their tractors to simply flood a field for a while. Rice is grown here in swampy fields which croak with myriads of frogs, and we searched for shady fringes among maize fields and poplar plantations. One of the few other walkers (was he the only one in this hot place?) knew the world and said that this part of Italy most reminded him of Vietnam, where had spent much of his working life! Debating the route was still necessary before our change to the Via Francigena, a long-distance path which has been plotted from France to Rome, and for which we found a fantastic set of maps in a bookshop in Como whilst frustratedly searching for any walking maps at all for Italy. Consequently we resolved to follow this, but not coming from France but from the E1, the trusted route we had followed through Germany and Switzerland, we had to describe a long arc around Milan, an extended exposure to the hot climes of Lombardy, and this is where Jannah and Jean joined us. The two of them really did jump in at the deep end, but admirably took the heat, the debating which way to turn at one or the other junction, the not knowing where we would stay the night, the absence of shade to sit and have a stale-bread-and-sweating-cheese picnic, in their stride despite lugging weights on their backs which included a thousand-page volume of some fantasy novel each! They helped us two old fogies with some extensions on our technology use, downloading hugely useful lists of accommodation on this Via Francigena, which is an acknowledged pilgrim route and, it transpires, thus has *pilgrims' hostelries which offer the walking traveller beds for the night for donation only in many cases. All four of us stayed in a medieval tower the other night and it was a matter of great pride for the town mayor himself to administrate the welcome of pilgrims! The nearby spaghetteria equally offered a fantastic many-course spread for the 'pelegrino' at remarkably generous rates. But when we stalk alongside some small road in the midday heat people whizz by gawping at us as they might on suddenly seeing a dinosaur... The landscape is humming, buzzing, croaking with insects, and now with myriads of cicadas, the noisiest creature on the planet. But in the midst of moments of extremely sticky, sweaty, itchy midday searches for the right turning, we also get an airy lift in our hearts from the song of yet another nightingale. In this land, which I vowed never to enter until its songbird-hunting customs had stopped (when I was 12), there are more nightingales than I ever imagined. They obviously feel very at home in the proximity of rivers and in humid lands. Another striking thing is the number of fairytale castles and fantastical architectural piles from the 17th and 18th centuries, quietly crumbling away and falling into disrepair for lack of state money and lack of clear inheritance agreements, so we are told. Sometimes it looks as though someone still lives in and cares for one wing of it, but mostly they are a vision of grandeur from an era which knew splendour, nobility, duels, great dukes and artists, poets and musicians, passion and wealth. Another time I will tell you of the comical sound of the church bells here, and of the prostitutes in the forests (took me a while to realise what was going on – duh), but I would not want to conclude this report without mentioning the incredible and generous hospitality we have experienced here in Italy, where at one point we were a walking troupe of five people, but could not have been made more welcome if we'd been royalty! Such warmth and joy to give and share, and truly foster friendship, is truly special and somewhat beyond the power of words to describe!*

This computer is actually in the house of our hosts in Switzerland, to which we returned for a brief interruption and a whole new whirl, meeting with Soundsphere to sing in Vevey, and to be with and meet a whole other bunch of incredible people, an amazing family of singing and fun-loving English-French-Swiss, who made something possible to enhance the fundraising for Medecins Sans Frontieres. We are just brimming over with thanks! And learning so much...

We think of you all fondly, and as we today will return to Piacenza, south of Milan, we will for another month or so traverse this fascinating country of Italy – our sixth one (!) – before arriving in Rome. We are definitely earlier than we had anticipated, but we will be back in York some time in September, an idea which seems slightly scary in that I can't imagine not walking for most of the day any more!

But seeing you all will be delightful, so thank you for all the messages and good wishes! It is as ever lovely to hear from you.

Much love,

Angela and Nick XX

After a buffet lunch we all got ready to depart. JC said he'd happily give us a lift back to Brig with Angela's mother, who was going to a village in the mountains further east, which was incredibly generous of him. His trepidation had gradually evaporated over those few days and he had thoroughly enjoyed the experience of having his house invaded and occupied by a crowd of singing strangers – what a funny and charming man! The Swiss train was held up due to a Customs control as we crossed the border so we got to Domodossola too late for our connection. We waited with Annemarie, Angela's mum, for her train to Centovalli in a café across the road in the middle of a tumultuous thunderstorm, saw her off, then got the next train to Piacenza via Milan, and caught a little minibus back to the same Youth Hostel where we'd been before. We arrived at 9 pm feeling hot and sticky again but glad to be back after that dreamlike sequence of events, and were welcomed by the Moroccan warden who was surprised and pleased to see us again.

DAY 125 PIACENZA – FIORENZUOLO
28 km; hot and dry; 35°C

At breakfast there were a few families with young children and an older woman with cropped hair who looked interesting. We set off early to walk through the middle of Piacenza again then headed out on what seemed to be the Via Francigena, by which time it was already getting hot.

They say that when Captain Cook first anchored off the coast of Australia near Botany Bay there was a group of aboriginal hunters who didn't appear to notice the huge sailing ship moored only a few hundred yards away, and kept on doing what they were doing on the beach. When asked about it later they said they had never noticed it, despite often looking in that direction. There is apparently something in the human brain which will not allow us to see what we have never imagined before, even when it is staring us in the face. On the way out of town we helped a middle-aged transsexual who had stumbled out of a shop in front of us and dropped her groceries all over the pavement, and asked if s/he knew the way to the E1. Blank looks. "Via Francigena?" " No idea." Mention of the next village on the road brought some flicker of recognition, but she insisted on trying to put us on a bus. Perhaps a hangover was clouding her judgement, but we did come across a large number of people along the way who simply could not accept the fact that we were making the journey on foot; who just assumed that if we were asking the way to somewhere we must want to know how to get there by car, even though the plain fact of us standing before them in walking boots, carrying all our possessions, obviously contradicted that idea.

Down the road we met the older woman with the cropped hair again, and we walked together all day. She was a retired civil servant from Sardinia called Auxilia who was walking the length of the Via Francigena from the French border to Rome. The weather was not as humid as it had been before our break, but still extremely hot. We walked for long stretches along dusty lanes and gravel tracks between fields of maize, tomatoes, peppers and green leafy crops we could not identify, with hardly a tree in sight. We stopped under a small group of trees beside a little stream for our picnic then continued through the early afternoon heat past dilapidated farms and isolated industrial estates to arrive at Fiorenzuola at 4.30, where we found ourselves in an office in an old house next to the church in the town square, filling in forms as *bona fide* pilgrims and paying €5 each to stay in the bunk-rooms which the church operated in another house down an alley which also offered a laundry service for paupers. We went and sat in the piazza after dropping off our bags and having a shower and soaked up the small-town provincial atmosphere which reminded me of the Jacques Tati film *Jour de Fête*. It was such a quiet square, occasionally crossed by someone: a small group of joking boys with a football; a couple of nuns; a man cycling along very slowly carrying a plank, with his back wheel squeaking rhythmically. About once every quarter of an hour a Fiat 500 or a 2CV would come into the square, slowly drive round in a circle and go back out. A couple of old men sat at the café reading the newspaper and for a while two young mothers stopped and chatted on the bench, their voices echoing off the church wall. Back at the bunkhouse we met Frank from Kaiserslautern and Angela from Australia, who were also walking to Rome. Frank said half-jokingly that he was hoping to get a job at the Vatican when he got there. We were all going off to find something to eat so we decided to go together, along with Auxilia, who said she would translate the menus for us if necessary. After poking about the town centre and finding everything CLOSED or CLOSED ON TUESDAYS we came back to the one place which we had originally disdained, and it was actually very good. We had a merry time exchanging travellers' tales and trying out our Italian with Auxilia, who spoke hardly any English (or German).

DAY 126 FIORENZUOLO – FIDENZA
18 km; Very hot indeed; 38°C

We had intended to be up and out very early but by the time we had fiddled around packing bags and having breakfast at the café in the square, it was already getting on for 8 o'clock. The Via Francigena took the main road out of town, as was becoming habitual; gradually the lanes became smaller and we were led into something more like proper countryside again –

no longer the monoculture of rice-field after rice-field that we'd passed through so often since Pavia. The terrain was still flat but the mountain chain on our right was beginning to loom large. There were fields of sunflowers now, more hedgerows and trees, and more birdsong. We only realized the land had been getting gradually so birdless during the past week when we were woken at 6 o'clock by a combination of Auxilia's alarm-clock and the screeching of the swallows circling the church tower. We stopped halfway to Fidenza at another Castelnuovo (Newcastle) which also had an ancient castle, where we were accosted by a man who said his wife was from Glasgow. He asked us which way we'd come, and when we told him we'd come over the river Po on the ferry he said: "Ah, then you've met my good friend Daniele. I've known him for years; we're like this!" and he folded his fingers into a fist apart from the index and middle fingers, which were him and Daniele. "I know he's a grumpy old bugger, but he's a good mate." Round the corner the local pensioners were sitting outside a wooden shed next to a little play-ground. We asked a man painting the window-frames of an old-style coaching inn if it was open. "No." "Is there another bar in the village?" "No, but you can go to the pensioners' clubhouse; they won't mind. No, they'll be glad to see you." Many of the old men were glad to meet someone new and chat about distant places. One of them said he had been a chef on liners and cruise ships. He had been to various ports in England, and had also been on pilgrimages, albeit by coach, to Lourdes and to Medjugorje in Croatia.[8] He leant over and confided to

8   This was something we were noticing more and more in
    Italy: the number of people who had been on a pilgrimage
    themselves or knew someone who had, so that it was a much

us that a couple of these old fellows were very rich and owned large herds of cattle, which was surprising as we hadn't seen a cow for weeks. In fact now we came to think of it we hadn't seen a sheep either, or a goat or a water-buffalo. Where did all that famous cheese come from? I'd been expecting to see a lot of water-buffalo wading about in the paddy-fields, but no: maybe they send them up to the mountains for the summer or keep them indoors... Another man came into the clubhouse, scruffily dressed with his hair sticking out from under his cap like a scarecrow's, holding a basket of yellow plums which he passed around for general inspection and approval. "He's one of the richest farmers around here," whispered our informant.

Carrying on towards Fidenza we realized why the castle had been there: it was on a hill! Only about 150 feet high, but from there you could see for miles across the plain.

We arrived at Fidenza at lunch-time after 18 kilometres and decided to stop if we could find somewhere to stay the night here as it was so hot and we both felt we had not had enough sleep the night before. There was a Tourist Information Office next to the cathedral which had just closed, but it opened again at 3 o'clock, allegedly, and it looked as though it specialized in pilgrims' lodgings. We did have a couple of addresses already, but decided against ringing them during siesta hours, so we lolled on a bench in the square eating bread and tomatoes until it reopened. The helpful young woman at the office recommended the Franciscans and phoned them on our behalf, and that of

more normal enterprise to most people than it had been further north, especially in England where the notion of pilgrimage has been all but forgotten.

Angela the Australian and Frank. We all trooped down to the monastery on the edge of town and knocked on the door. A very grumpy young monk opened up, giving the impression that he'd been rudely awakened from his prayers by another bunch of dirty ignorant travellers, but he did his duty and led us to a wing where we were given a little room each. We had been looking forward to finding a swimming-pool, but settled for a nap, and strolled into town later for a good pizza. It began to feel thundery, and at 7 p.m. the temperature was still showing as 35° on the digital thermometers you see outside every pharmacy in Italy. We had noticed that we were developing a pronounced pilgrim's tan, which is similar to a farmer's: Angela, who had been wearing shorts more often, had a gradual shifting tan-line on her legs, but both of us had a definite T-shirt line and a very white torso.

DAY 127 FIDENZA – MEDESANO
28 km; hot, breezy; 36°C

We got up early and were out on the road by 7.30 but had to go back as we'd forgotten to leave a donation for the monks. We soon got to Costamezzana where we were served breakfast by a Templar at his café. I knew, because there was a notice on the wall advertising some cultural event being put on by a local society of the Order of Knights Templar, who were of course big in these parts about 600 years ago. I asked the café-owner about it and he said he was indeed a member of the society and if we were interested there was a Templar church nearby. We continued along a lane below the castle, where we met an old wood-cutter who greeted us with a sympathetic mopping of the brow, a heartfelt exhalation and a rolling of the eyes: who needs Esperanto when such an easily communicable international language – Italian – already exists? Near here we heard more orioles, and then passed our first olive trees. Enjoying the patterns and structures of the hillside country we were beginning to be bombarded by the noise of cicadas, who also love this dry sunny landscape. We followed the signs to a church, partly to see if it was the Templar church, partly to find a source of water which was marked on our map, but the church was closed and the tap didn't work, so we went back to the path, which soon came to a T junction at the top of a rise between wheat- and corn-fields. The map pointed left; the signpost pointed right.

We followed the little man on the sign, the hooded pilgrim with his staff and backpack, and soon came to a fork in the road with no signpost: looking down to our left we could see a valley but it didn't correspond with the contour-lines or directions on the map. To our left at the side of the road was a big old farmhouse with its rendering peeling off in chunks and a farmyard full of scrap metal and weeds. There did seem to be signs of life so we went and knocked on the door, disturbing two farm workers who were sitting down to some bread and ham with a penknife in a dim and dusty kitchen. They were surprised to be roused out of the stupor of the midday heat by these strange wanderers, and directed us with few words towards Medesano: "Down the track on your left to the bottom of the hill then turn left and follow the road." I had the impression that they spoke Italian rather slowly not because they could tell it was a foreign language to us but because they didn't speak it as well or as often as they spoke their local dialect. Down on the main road we were hungry and stopped at a dusty roadside shrine for a snack. Further on there was a village with no name, or at least no sign on the road at the entrance to the village, and when we asked someone where we were they told us a name which was not on our map. We spotted a restaurant where we could get a lemon soda and chatted to the owner/chef who spoke good English and directed us over the hill, as he said that would avoid having to walk on the busy road. "You see that Calvary? That cross on the hill? You go up to there and turn left then follow the path straight on." It was a steep climb and at the top we could see a small town which always seemed to be just behind the next hill. It is peculiar how it always seems to take longer to get to somewhere when you know it must be close but you can't actually see it. We finally walked into Medesano, which was a nondescript place, another casualty of Second World War bombing as it had great chunks missing or filled with ugly post-war buildings. We had been given a list of pilgrims' hostels which we could find online, including telephone numbers, and had tried to phone ahead to a place connected to the church in Medesano with no response. When we found the church, there was a building next to it with a sign on the door saying:

PILGRIMS' HOSTEL
CLOSED DURING JULY AND AUGUST

The old woman who ran the bar next door said: "I'm sure I've seen the priest today. He hasn't answered the door? Does his notice say he's gone away? You could wait here for a while and try again." But there was still no sign of life the next time we tried so she asked around for anyone who could put us up. There was no immediate response, so I went off to look for an *albergo* and found one in the main square where we could sleep and eat a proper meal for €80 for both of us, which was pricey by our new Italian standards, but was actually very good value. Opposite the hotel was a massive new town hall/arts centre, which advertised forthcoming cultural events (not many!) and also had copious notices stuck up to advertise Italy's semi-final match, to have been shown on a large screen in the square. Funnily enough there was no similar notice mentioning the final, which must have been shown the following week and subsequently deleted from the collective memory.

DAY 128 MEDESANO – CASSIO
33km; some cloud, heavy; 30°C

We resolved that today we would definitely get up early and be out on the road to tread some miles before the heat overcame us, so we were up at 5.30 and on the road within an hour. The first three hours were then relatively cool and we managed to put some miles under our belts, but it was not the most picturesque landscape, as the path ran alongside a motorway much of the way. At one point we saw a small turtle in a rather grubby pond; at another we stopped at a café outside a large factory, which had originally been the main source of Campbell's tomato soup. A customer saw us come in and offered to buy us a drink, and the woman behind the bar started chatting in English – it turned out she had lived in Highgate in the 70s working in an Italian restaurant for a few years. Beyond the industrial zone we crossed a dry river on a long bridge, after which the road began to climb substantially up a long straight stretch. It was here, after emerging from the village at the end of the bridge and taking the first steep hill we'd seen for weeks, that we stumbled upon a group of four or five black women, surely Africans, engaged in some kind of ecstatic ritual beside a large cross just off the path. Their singing was so evocative it made us want to join them but it felt like a private ceremony, so we never found out what their story was; where they had come from and how they had arrived there; what exactly was the song they were singing, and why? Trekking up the long stretch we could look down to our right and see Parma in the distance to one side and Fidenza to the other, with miles of open plain between and beyond. We were at long last penetrating the mountains we had been approaching for such a long time, and the road was more and more surrounded by rocks and pine forest At about lunchtime we got to a village called Sivizzano, where we knew there was a pilgrims' lodging-house of some kind. By that time the weather had turned hot and muggy and everyone was having a siesta apart from a young woman in a bar who was just about to close and have a nap herself. We decided to carry on for another 12 kilometres to Cassio, but I was feeling exhausted and just wanted to have a little rest first. If only I could lie down somewhere for an hour or two… maybe I could ask at the hostel! The woman in the bar said she would try and rouse the caretaker, but he was rather deaf and wouldn't necessarily hear her knocking. She managed to get his attention and he came downstairs and showed us around the sleeping quarters and washroom. I thought he said: "Yes, by all means lie down and sleep on this bed for a while. You look tired, you poor fellow, after all the walking you've done this morning. Here, take this bed for a little rest." But he went away and came back a few minutes later just as I was dropping off and said: "No, I'm sorry. You'll have to go outside. You can sit on this bench in the courtyard where it's very peaceful." He was most concerned that the misunderstanding should not be construed as being unwelcoming or impolite but if we used the beds we would have to pay the price of a night's stay. Fair enough, but no thanks; the bench was fine! He said that he had met Alison Raju, the compiler of the new English guide to the Via Francigena[9], and that his *ostale* would be mentioned in it. After a light snooze we continued: beside the little church round the corner was a stone carving of a pilgrim with the legend Romam peregrinantibus (*Fig. 37), which we took to mean: "We will journey to Rome," so we strapped on our bags and resumed the journey. In the next village there was another old church carved out of the local stone. If you went to a nearby house and asked for the key you could admire some astonishing 10th-century carvings on the altar for the price of an espresso. Although it had been 30° earlier and the clouds had even succeeded in squeezing out a few drops of rain as we rested in Sivizzano, by the time we had walked on a few kilometres we were up to 800 m and it was suddenly quite fresh, cool enough to think about putting on another layer. We phoned ahead to the hostel in Cassio and said we'd be there within the hour. The countryside became increasingly mountainous and less populated and we passed some extraordinary rock formations called "The Devil's Leaps", which stuck vertically out from the hillside like a row of shark's teeth [down into the valley]. On the path near here we saw a tortoise swimming in a pool of water, and an unusual blue butterfly. The *ostale* in Cassio was run by Andrea, a bearded man of about forty who had been a pilgrim himself and was obviously a man of good taste: the house was scrupulously clean and tidy and the solid oak

9   From Canterbury to Rome: Part 2, Great San Bernardino Pass to Rome : Cicerone Press, (presently due for release in November 2013).

table in the dining-room was decorated with simple but graceful ornaments, and a bowl of fruit and some bottles of good wine and grappa awaited the traveller. "Help yourselves," Andrea smiled as he waved us through to the kitchen. "There's a bowl here for donations if you can afford to give anything." The kitchen had tea and coffee and cakes ready for breakfast, and Andrea explained, as he stamped our pilgrims' passes, that we could get an evening meal at the *ristorante* up the hill: if we told them that Andrea had sent us we would get a discount. So we did, and paid €14 each for a fantastic three course meal with wine, sitting outside on the terrace looking out over the woods and valleys as the sun was setting over the mountains, and all was well with the world (*Fig. 38). We got talking to some of our fellow diners: one elderly couple said they come out there every weekend from Parma just to soak up the atmosphere of being out in the countryside. Another couple, who were rather drunk and unconventionally dressed, were eating next to us with their teenaged son, who was extremely friendly and polite. They lived nearby and were regular customers; they told us all about the area, their neighbours and their lives...When we got back to the hostel we found Frank again: we had been walking at the same speed as each other for a few days, but there is an unspoken agreement among pilgrims, we discovered, that people travelling alone or in pairs or small groups have chosen to travel like this with good reason. If someone prefers to walk alone then they may indeed fall in with a companion for half a day or an hour or three days, but people walk at their own pace. So we would bump into Frank or Auxilia or Angela or Isabelle at a café or a hostel; sometimes they wanted to walk with us and sometimes not. Perhaps it is also a bit daunting for some people to walk with a couple, and in some cases that's with good reason – "Two's company, three's a crowd" – but sometimes it just feels right. Frank was an interesting guy and we were quite happy to walk with him. He went at the same pace as us; but he had obviously set off to make this journey on his own with some interior purpose, and we had to respect that.

DAY 129 CASSIO – BERCETO
15 km; fresher, breezy; 25°C

We woke to a cooler morning and felt no guilt in setting off later as Berceto, where we had arranged to meet Anch again, was not very far away. It was a treat to be joined twice (albeit briefly) by Anch, who works as a sub-editor for a large magazine at their London office. He's a keen cyclist and often spends his holidays cycling around Belgium or France, but this time had left his bike behind and flown to Milan, where he had hired a car for a few days. The plan was, we would meet him in Berceto and stay the night there then he would drive to Pontremoli and walk back to meet us. We could then walk into Pontremoli together and on the following day to somewhere from where he could catch a train back to pick up his car and take it back to Milan.

The way to Berceto was lovely, it was beautiful and full of proper footpaths. We walked much through woods along hollow ways, and then through villages on gravel paths and country lanes. At the outskirts of Berceto the path suddenly dipped down and became an ancient cobbled way down into the town, which sat like a jewel in a wooded valley full of sweet chestnut and oak. We checked into a little hotel in the main street and went to explore. Berceto is very small

– the population is only about 2,500 – yet it boasts a Romanesque cathedral, a small but rather cavernous barn-like structure which has a certain charm just by being so primitive, relatively untouched and free of too many baubles. Near the Duomo a narrow street went off to one side and we saw people putting tables and chairs outside a pizzeria so that a motorbike would have trouble getting through, let alone a car. There were no street signs anywhere saying "NO TRAFFIC AFTER 1800 HRS", so the local people must have just reached an agreement. Since it was a Saturday there were quite a few visitors strolling about eating *gelati* and the biggest café-bar was full of people listening to a poet/song-writer being interviewed by a panel of pundits for a local radio station broadcast We went to the Tourist Information Office where a smart young man very helpfully gave me a pilgrim's passport for Anch. I bumped into him again later in a piazza at the other end of the main street when he was off duty and hanging out with his mates. I went and asked them if there were any buses from Pontremoli, as I was thinking maybe Anch could drive here, walk with us to Pontremoli the next day then get a bus back to pick up his car, but they said there were hardly any buses. One young guy sounded foreign (i.e. not Italian), and I asked him in my rudimentary Italian where he was from. "Croydon," he replied. "I've been here for three years doing up a house – I'm a roofer by trade – but to tell you the truth I'm getting fed up. There's no money about, no work, and everything costs too much." We were hearing the same story everywhere we went in Italy; not surprisingly, as their economy was on the point of collapsing and all the talk was of whether they would be the next to be on the verge of bailing out of the euro.

When Anch arrived we went out to that *pizzeria* and he said let's stick to Plan A: he'd drive to Pontremoli in the morning and walk back on a forest path. We could keep in touch by text and decide where to meet and how to get from there to Pontremoli. One advantage of this plan was that we could put most of our luggage in his car, and he was happy to spend half a day walking alone to shake the London air out of his clothes.

DAY 130 BERCETO – PONTREMOLI
31 km; fresh but warmer; 28°C

In the morning we rose early and the two of us took the old cobbled way out in the other direction up onto the hillside. It soon came out onto the main road leading up to the pass over the Apennines – Il Passo della Cisa – and we walked along the roadside, sometimes in the gutter or on the verge but often just on the road. Being early on a Sunday morning there was not much traffic at first, and most of what traffic there was was made up of motorbikes, cyclists and runners. We called in at the Ostello, where we would have stayed if we hadn't been meeting Anch in Berceto, and had some coffee and cake then continued to the pass, which at 1040 m was quite fresh, although definitely not chilly. At that point our path truly diverged from the E1, which goes off at a tangent along the top of the Apennine ridge for a couple of hundred kilometres, ending up at Perugia, while the Via Francigena leads down the other side of the ridge to Pontremoli and then on to the sea. We took a side road off to the left and followed it down past a stone memorial in a field to two British soldiers who were shot there for helping the Resistance fighters during the war. The narrow lane continued for miles, tranquil and breezy, serpentining down the densely wooded hillside, until it arrived breathless at a meeting with two equally narrow lanes outside a tiny village. There we found Anch sitting outside an *osteria* which served food and drink with a new acquaintance called Isabelle who was also walking to Rome. She had just started walking after having come by train from her job as a financial adviser in Paris, and looked like an elongated version of Michelle Pfeiffer. We all ate together in the pub garden – simple but delicious food including a local delicacy called *tarta all'erbe* – then continued for another few hours down to Pontremoli, taking a different route than the one on which Anch had chosen to walk on his way up.

We entered the old town of Pontremoli via a cobbled medieval single-span bridge – which now bizarrely crosses a railway line – and a large stone archway, and followed the footpath signs up a very narrow street, wide enough for a pack-horse, to the castle, where we arrived just in time to check in for the night. The warden was just about to lock up and leave, but let us in and explained that a small section of the castle had been set aside in which pilgrims could stay, thanks to the town council and the Ministry of Ancient Monuments. He led us through gateways and courtyards then up some stone steps to a gallery where we found two bedrooms with a shower room/toilet between them. In Bedroom 1 we discovered Auxilia, who had just arrived after having taken a day off to visit her cousin near Parma, and we three shared the other one. The warden went off wishing us a good night and telling us that Auxilia had the key for the front gate, so after a shower we all went into town to look for something to eat, and immediately bumped into Frank, who was browsing in a second-hand bookshop. The town had a bit of a thing about books: it was dotted with benches painted with lettering spelling out literary quotations and proverbs or sayings about the advantages of reading. Apart from that the town as a whole seemed remarkably unchanged since at least two centuries ago, aside from a few Fiats and Lambrettas in the spacious main square. The tables at the restaurant in the square were all full, so we were shown inside to an exceedingly ornate dining-room where we felt seriously underdressed. It was stuffed with rococo mirrors, chandeliers, and mock Renaissance frescoes, and sold expensive food and drink, but we did manage to find something fresh and reasonably cheap and very good.

DAY 131 PONTREMOLI – AULLA
30 km; hot, still; 30°C

Leaving the castle we had to accompany Auxilia as she had the key, so we arranged to leave at 7 o'clock and went down to a café in the quiet piazza for coffee and brioches. We left by a wide street with tall rich houses on either side, each one entered by a huge arched doorway, big enough for a horse and carriage, into a courtyard. Further down the street were some smaller older houses between which stood narrow alleyways and little cobbled squares. Someone had made an effort to brighten the place up with pots of red carnations, but many of the houses were run down and most were in need of a good lick of paint. Somehow we managed to miss the ancient labyrinth in the church of St Peter. We went past a very old church which was closed but that can't have been it because Frank told us later that he had stayed somewhere else in Pontremoli and been to see the labyrinth on the way out of town. It is a medieval carving in the same pattern as the one in Chartres Cathedral but built into the wall.

We walked out along the main road for a few kilometres with Anch and Auxilia before a signpost directed us to turn off to the left and go round the back of an abbey past some barns and outbuildings full of old carts. Just past here we hit a serious obstacle in the shape of a large locked gate blocking the path and too high to climb. Just as we were pondering what to do a man dressed in a fluorescent yellow jacket came along and unlocked it for us muttering something about a quarrelsome landowner who didn't agree with the footpath crossing his land. We made our way back to the road and tried another signposted footpath which led us to a pretty walled village called Filattiera. From there a cobbled cart-track led steeply uphill through some overhanging trees and out into open country where we stopped for a snack in a hayfield while Auxilia pressed on. We lounged there for a good while, appreciating the sounds and smells until Anch decided he had better get on and catch a train to make his way to Milan airport (the one near Bellinzago) via Berceto to catch his plane back to the hustle of the magazine office in London. We saw him off at Villafranca, where a group of men were playing cards at the station buffet so violently that Angela thought one player was about to pull out a knife until a man who was watching the game said: "It's always like this – they're Italian!" with a shrug.

The rest of the day's walk was long and hot as we followed a small road up and down along the side of the valley within hearing distance of a motorway at first, but then as we went higher it became more and more wild. After Lusuolo, where we managed to fill our water-bottles after becoming quite dehydrated, we stopped at a tiny hamlet below a castle which sat on top of a rock looking south. The only street was a mixture of habitations, barns and abandoned buildings; we crashed out on a set of stone steps leading to an old doorway on the shady side of the street and dozed for a while in the somnolent afternoon heat, when it seemed the only moving beings were lizards and cicadas, and imagined ourselves in a spaghetti Western (*Fig. 39). Finally biting the bullet we dragged ourselves up and off again and struggled along a tiny stone-paved track along the side of the hill, through scrub and lush undergrowth punctuated by wild fig-trees and olives: by the time we got to the next little town siesta-time was over and we could go and stock up on caffeine and sugar for the last leg of the day to Aulla, which was mostly downhill but involved walking along a very busy road at rush-hour with a wall hard up against the side of the road and drivers being very aggressive. It was the clearest example yet of a town council being very proud of being on the Via Francigena but apparently expecting all pilgrims to be either travelling by car or risking life and limb by stupidly walking. There are too often no concessions made for pedestrians at all, and they are too often made to feel grateful if they can walk in the gutter with the rubbish.

Getting off the road as soon as possible we ended up in an industrial estate then an out-of-town shopping mall. After walking interminably along the river and through the soulless city centre we finally arrived at the church, where we had been told we could stay the night. Pushing open the front door of the building next door to the church we were greeted by a priest who offered us biscuits and lemonade then showed us around the room we were in, which we discovered was a museum of pilgrimage, complete with pictures of people dressed like us, which felt decidedly odd. I saw someone look twice at us as we arrived as though we were moving articulate models or waxworks. We had once again arrived with minutes to spare before closing-time. When we were shown to our rooms, we found Frank in the men's dorm and Auxilia and Isabelle in the women's, so we all went out for a pizza together at a good unpretentious eating-house across the river. We found out that Aulla – which must have been a beautiful town once, nestling in a deep valley with mountain peaks all around – had been so severely bombed during the war that it was almost entirely destroyed, leaving only the church (or most of it) and a few houses next to it. Subsequently there had been terrible flooding one year which had washed away or irreparably damaged most of the new buildings so they had to start again, and the latest incarnation, built on an American model, is the ugliest yet.

Auxilia told us: "You're going to stop at Sarzana tomorrow? I'm going to press on further – I need to be in Rome for the 25th, so that I can be back in Sardinia for my sister's birthday, and today is already the 9th." We were thinking we probably had another twenty days' walking to do, plus a couple of days' break, and actually come to think of it we hadn't had a break since we left Switzerland for Piacenza, seven days ago. We probably wouldn't be in Rome before the end of the month then. We also thought we would keep on running into Frank and Isabelle but in fact we would only run into one of them again, and that in about a week.

DAY 132 AULLA – SARZANA
17 km; hotter; 32°C

We had said we would get up early the next morning, but it was not as early as the others, who started rattling about at 5 o'clock. We were the last to leave at 7, stopping for a quick coffee and brioche – really, how can you walk all morning on a brioche?! – then taking to the high road. We didn't have too far to go to Sarzana, but the first eight kilometres took almost four hours, as most of the terrain was on a steep mountainside, and we climbed on single-track footpaths littered with loose stones. It was hard sweaty work but every time we stopped for a moment there were beautiful sights to be seen as we climbed relentlessly from the valley bottom through oak, chestnut and robinia glades. The first village we came to had a little castle and a fantastic view back across all the hills we had crossed since Il Passo della Cima. We arrived at Ponzano Superiore as the church bells struck twelve and promptly lost each other in a maze. The town is built on top of a rock, in such a way that it seems as though the rock itself has been hollowed out first then houses put on top in layers (*Fig. 40). We disagreed about which way to go to find something to drink so went in different directions, which was a bad move, as we each began to wander through this labyrinth of tiny alleyways and tunnels, archways and steps, like the inside of a giant snail-shell leading to the church at the top. Without mobile phones we might have spent the rest of the day missing each other, but as it was we found a shop in the nick of time before they closed for the afternoon and bought some fizzy water and bread and cheese, tomatoes and apricots. We took them round the corner to some benches big enough to stretch out on, with a view south across vineyards and olive groves. After an hour's siesta it was time to rouse ourselves, which was difficult. It was so still and the air was shimmering in a haze of heat. We had an espresso to wake ourselves up in a little bar at the end of the alley, which seemed to be a kind of working men's club but nobody asked us for membership cards. On the wall was a notice which said:

DUE TO THE RECENT EARTHQUAKE THERE
WILL BE NO DELIVERIES OF PARMESAN
UNTIL FURTHER NOTICE

We left in the blistering afternoon heat, but we were going downhill now and skipping along a mule-track in between vineyards and small south-facing orchards of plums, apricots and figs. In the morning we had even seen a tree laden with hands of small but perfectly formed bananas. Shortly afterwards we caught our first glimpse of the sea, which was cause for celebration (*Fig. 41) – what an amazing feeling to have set out from our house on a March morning and got as far as the Mediterranean! At the same time the path became trickier as it went down more steeply over loose stones and scree, where Angela slid and fell over, near a ruined early medieval castle where the path almost petered out. I remember thinking: "This would not be a good place for either of us to have an accident." We arrived in Sarzana not knowing what to expect. We had an address for a pilgrims' hostel which I phoned in advance. Someone answered and said: "Come to the church," but when we arrived there was a mass going on with four in the congregation. I went in and was greeted by an elderly parishioner who took me down a corridor and showed me a cleaning cupboard which was just big enough to lay a couple of sleeping-bags on the floor but full of mops and buckets with boxes of cleaning-fluid piled high on all sides. I didn't think Angela would be happy if I agreed without discussion and I was right. We decided that as cleaning cupboards go it was not

very clean, and politely declined. That meant we had
to find somewhere else to stay, though, which proved
difficult. We trailed into the town centre and procured
a list of B&Bs, guest-houses, etc., and after weighing
up the pros and cons settled for the nearest place, up a
steep flight of stairs above a shop in the town square,
which was run by a Turkish woman who told us to help
ourselves to whatever was in the kitchen; she was going
out. It cost us €60 but it was a very comfortable bed!
This was something we hadn't counted on before we
left home: we thought that although we hadn't brought
a tent we would be likely to sleep rough in mountain
cabins or hay-barns or bus-shelters along the way once
the nights became warm enough, but we didn't: partly
because there are very few hay-barns in existence
these days; and then we came across several cabins or
mountain refuges but it was always in the middle of the
day and we didn't want to stop for the night yet. The
other thing was that we realised as we travelled further
– and developed a sense of how far we were going on
any given day and how far we had to go in total – that
we really did need to get a good night's sleep with a long
day's walk ahead of us!

DAY 133 SARZANA – AVENZA
13 km; hot; 34°C

The forecast for the next few days was for equally hot
weather, so we determined to get up and out earlier
and were out on the road at 6.45, although today's walk
was to be a short one. The main road was already quite
busy, and we plodded along on cracked and broken
pavements and occasional overgrown pedestrian lanes
for a couple of hours before the path went off to Luni,
a huge archaeological dig at the site of a Roman town.

At the entrance to the dig was a little museum with a reception desk at which you had to present yourself to pay a small fee to look around. The door was still locked although it was after 9 o'clock, but there were a couple of men standing around in uniform who refused to let us in through the open exit door. Eventually we managed to convince them that they had forgotten to unlock the entrance door so we had no alternative.

Wandering around the site admiring the mosaics and columns we could see a flock of sheep being tended by a shepherd on the other side of the fence, and heard their bells echoing timelessly. Continuing along narrow winding country lanes past abandoned glasshouses we arrived at Avenza, a suburb now of Massa but formerly a village clustered around an ancient fortress. It was early, still only lunchtime, but we decided to take the afternoon off, so we checked into a little guest-house. They sometimes advertise themselves by the English term Bed and Breakfast but usually don't actually offer breakfast, although sometimes, as in this case, the owner has cut a deal with the nearest café or bar and they will give you something in the morning there as part of the arrangement. Then we got a bus down to the beach. All the towns here seem to be strung together around the marble works and connected industries, and each little town centre has a bus connection to its own strip of beach, about 2 miles away. Presumably Massa with its cathedral, and its castle on the hill behind the town, was built inland on the river for defensive reasons. It must have been a significant port in the Middle Ages, shipping marble from the quarries of Carrara all over the Mediterranean world. So we got the bus to Avenza Marina, and most of the local population were there too. We had a swim then a sunbathe then a swim and another swim, at which point I retired to have an ice-cream in the shade, while Angela stayed to perfect her Neapolitan look (chocolate, vanilla and strawberry). On the way back we had a better view of the Carrara marble quarries, great white gashes looking like snow on the side of the Apuan Alps which run parallel to the coast. In Avenza I managed to buy a pair of flip-flops, which I needed badly, having no other footwear than my walking boots and a pair of slippers I'd been given at a hotel in Istanbul years before – great for indoors and very lightweight, but no good for outdoors wear. What a relief it would be to be able to take my boots off after a hot day's walk and go out without them in the evening! As a further indication of the thoughtlessness of the officials of the Ministry of Tourism who publicise the Via Francigena without making a footpath available for pilgrims, we saw a notice giving loads of information useful for walkers including a map, but it was placed on a narrow ramp leading to a 'footbridge' which was also for cyclists and motorbikes, so you couldn't actually stand and read it without being in the way or in danger of being run over. There were also several notices put up in the square next to the castle in Avenza boasting about the town's position on the Via Francigena, the pilgrims' route to Rome blabla, but we didn't see any pedestrian signs for the VF pointing that way, so your average walking pilgrim would miss out on all that interesting information. Of course this kind of oversight did not exclusively affect pilgrims: there was a similar information board at the excavation site at Luni which looked really interesting but it was too far from the path to be able to actually read it, and behind a fence, as I pointed out vigorously in a Grumpy Old Manner...

DAY 134 AVENZA – PIETRASANTA
27 km; fresher; 29°C

We got up early again and were in the cafe on the corner at 6.30 for breakfast. The young man serving us, Gianluca – instead of the usual "Say hello to Il Papa!" – asked: "Will you please light a candle for me in St Peter's?", and gave us a bottle of water each and €5 to buy candles. The stretch between Avenza and the other side of Massa was one of the ugliest of the whole journey. We were directed alongside old railway sidings, through filthy industrial estates and along rubbish-strewn roads leading to nowhere and then on a big ring road past car dealerships and furniture warehouses. It was noticeable how the pavements in the town centres in the region, and even the floors of the guesthouse, are all made of marble; whereas the pavements – where they exist at all – between the towns are outrageously bad, and this seems to be true all over Italy. It would be impossible to travel any distance at all in a wheelchair in the Italy we saw, and in fact we only saw two or three all the time we were there.

As we travelled on round the outskirts of Massa it was fascinating how many stonemasons' yards we passed, where we could observe massive blocks of marble being winched on and off lorries or trimmed to shape. One of the factories we passed was for the manufacture of diamond cutting-tools, which epitomised the service industries which have sprung up around the marble quarries. We stopped for a coffee at a cheerful workmen's café heaving with van-drivers and factory workers and car salesmen which hinted that it might double as a 'hostess club' at night. Another thing that happened was that, having given some change to a homeless Romanian as we were leaving Avenza, I found a euro lying in the mud beside the road on the way out of town – instant karma!

Turning left at Prato we meandered up the hill where there was a series of lanes and paths running parallel to the main road leading across the plain near the coast. Just past the castle at the top of the hill above Prato we found a suitable bench where we could stop for a snack with a gorgeous view looking down over the coastal plain and the long strand, with a 'compass panorama' etched into a metal disc next to the bench. The horizon was hazy, but according to this map you would be able to see Corsica on a very clear day. As it was we could see for at least 20 miles in either direction along the coast Afterwards we walked along a quiet country road, exhilarated by the smells of hot pine and wild plums and blackberries. We stopped at a run-down bar in a run-down village where a foursome were playing cards noisily inside in the shade, and sat down on a couple of rickety stools outside the open front door which was protected by a fly-curtain of brightly coloured plastic strips. We would not have expected this, that we always wanted to sit outside at these breaks now, rather than indoors in the shade. We must have just got used to the open-air life! After a while a scrawny middle-aged woman hobbled towards us using a crutch, plonked her bag on our table and the crutch behind my chair, and squatted on the floor to smoke a cigarette. When I offered her a seat she shook her head and muttered something, and soon went inside to join the card-players, who welcomed her. She then began to clear tables, seemingly driven to prove that her crippled state did not render her useless. It was a jumbled landscape from where we sat: there was an imposing old chateau within sight while across the road stood some neglected cottages surrounded by broken farming implements, rusting car bodies and large empty plastic sacks.

When we arrived at Pietrasanta we were in yet another world – the world of the smart set, full of art galleries and well-dressed holiday-makers who looked as if they were probably staying in Tuscan villas or on yachts moored at a nearby marina.

There was an exhibition taking place in the town hall which spilt out into the square outside the church so that it was full of huge rounded sculptures by the Spanish artist Botero: bulls, horses, people, all larger than life-size – and larger than life in the same way as a Beryl Cook picture. We knocked on the door of a convent up some steps behind the town hall and were welcomed by Sor Cecilia, who showed us to a little cabin in the garden with enough room for four bunks, where we washed our clothes and hung them out to dry in the garden. We found the best hostels on the Via Francigena were the ones like this which recognised the most important things for their guests on arrival, in order of urgency: a shower; somewhere to wash and dry their walking clothes (principally socks and T-shirts); somewhere nearby to drink and eat; a place to sleep. Being able to leave very early in the morning was also important, and in some cases crucial. We went out to eat and found Pietrasanta full of restaurants and pizzerias of varying quality but all pretty expensive. There were a couple of streets leading out of the square which had a restaurant in virtually every other house: some were very exclusive, serving truffles with everything; while some looked like they **were** someone's house – someone who had put a couple of pots on in the kitchen, a couple of chairs out in the street and a blackboard with a menu on the front door. When we got back we found a Russian in our room who said he was walking from Rome to Santiago, but didn't have a map. We gave him all the used pages of our loose-leaf guide to the Via Francigena, for which he was grateful. It had been very useful, consisting of about thirty folded maps, printed on both sides, in a see-through plastic envelope with notes, directions and indications of altitude.

DAY 135 PIETRASANTA – LUCCA
34 km; warm, sunny intervals; 27°C

In the morning we were off at 6, and glad of it, as it felt cool, and we were able to stride out and cover some distance, knowing that we had at least 30 kilometres to go in order to reach the next stop in Lucca. The path led up a steep and stony track to a spot where it seemed to run out in someone's garden, but in the far corner it disappeared, unmarked, between two hedges, and came out on a little road, at which point we were well and truly lost, with no idea which way to go, when a little black dog appeared and walked ahead of us, turning around every so often and cocking its head as if to say: "Well, are you coming?" For lack of any better ideas we followed, and the dog led us along the road, down a footpath off to the right; along another road, left at a T-junction, around a bend then off on another footpath... It must have been at least two kilometres, and we kept wondering when the dog would stop and leave us to our fate. We went past a crumbling villa with a plaque on the wall saying it was the birthplace of Zita, the last Empress of Austria. By this point we realised that we had mistakenly given our map and set of instructions to the Russian, so we relied upon the little black dog to be our guide. For its own part the dog behaved as though this was something it did every day, and acting with a caring and dutiful air it stopped every time we had to go off the road or take a turning, waited for us, then set off again, tail erect and wagging. Finally we reached an open road where it was obvious that we just had to carry straight on, and the dog stopped; waited for us to carry on; turned round and went back; stopped at a bend in the road, and watched us disappear.

An easy stroll along the river followed, as far as Camaiore, where we could (finally!) have some breakfast at 8.45 and go steeply uphill to a little village with another brilliant view over the coastal plain, with the sea twinkling in the distance. At Valpromaro there was supposed to be a pilgrims' hostel. It was too early in the day to think about stopping there for the night, but we were looking out for it out of curiosity when a couple of women chatting in the street hailed us and said they ran the hostel and did we want to stop and have a drink? Loridana and her niece Valentina took us into their courtyard and gave us tea and biscuits. Loridana had walked to Santiago herself, twice, and then decided to live on the Via Francigena so that she could be of service to fellow pilgrims. Her cousin's son was also there, visiting from Rapperswil – it surprised him greatly that we had walked through his town a few weeks previously. After they waved us goodbye we went as far as the village shop and stocked up on excellent bread, cheese and fruit for our lunch at a very cheap rate. Half an hour later we stopped at a shady spot to eat. We were generally beginning to find that having little or nothing to eat for breakfast and then stopping for a bread-and-cheese type of picnic lunch just was not enough to keep us going all day and we were often arriving in the late afternoon or evening feeling tired or grumpy, but this was a tasty and substantial pack-up and we stretched out on a bench for half an hour before continuing to Lucca via a 'sports club', which was actually a large marquee containing sixteen old men who were members of the *balli*, or bowls, club but were all playing cards in fours, very loudly.

We entered the city of Lucca through an arch in the city wall, which is the thickest we had ever seen, wide enough for a two-lane highway on top. The city within is larger than York, but compact, and there is not much overspill outside the walls. Most of the buildings are 16th- or 17th-century, with some older medieval houses near the main churches, and the Youth Hostel, where we had arranged to stay for two nights, was in a large and impressive villa, or townhouse, actually more like a palazzo, next to the church of San Lorenzo, which has beautiful frescoes painted on the façade. After eating in the little square in front of the church, surrounded by a group of Sri Lankan youths on mopeds, we came across an exhibition of Chagall's etchings, mostly Biblical illustrations, in a little church hall. It was inspiring to see the evidence of his spiritual journey and how one man had grappled with the conflicts of his cultural heritage.

DAY 136 LUCCA
0 km; warm; 27°C

We made the most of our first day off for a long time to be tourists, and wandered about very slowly looking at churches and shops, houses and people. We were also trying to get online to book accommodation for the next few days and also to sort out the mess the bank were creating over the finalisation of our mortgage arrangements. All very confusing and difficult to deal with when you're away from home and don't have access to your papers…and to cap it all we couldn't get Internet

291

access at any of the libraries or WiFi hubs we found, so had to get over the frustration and forget about it for the time being. During the course of our wanderings we ran into Frank, who was outside the amazing marble cathedral which looks like a giant wedding-cake, and invited him for a drink next to a busy flea-market full of people selling all sorts of stuff: antique furniture, paintings, African sculptures, pianos – all piled up higgledy-piggledy in a small piazza. When Frank bid us farewell to go to a concert in the nearby church we found he had paid the bill! Sadly we did not cross paths again so we could not return the favour.

DAY 137 LUCCA – PONTE DE' MEDICI
32 km; warm, cloudy; 26°C

We didn't get out of town very early the next day, but by about 8.30 we had walked along the wall to the Porta Santa Elena and were out on the main road, glad it was Sunday morning with not much traffic about. A side road took us off onto the Via Vecchia, or old road, which was abandoned when the new main road was built under Mussolini but has been kept as a 'historical artefact'. After some distance we arrived in Altopascio, where there was a pilgrims' reception centre, although it was closed, and at a restaurant in the square there was a merry crew of revellers who were dressed in medieval garb and seemed to be either film extras or members of a re-enactment society. Outside the square, which along with a couple of narrow streets and a small fort had a gated wall around it, stood a church with an open space next to the wall which was covered with children's pastel drawings, copies of famous paintings, which had been laid out for all to see. Just after this little town we met Luciano, a Roman citizen of about fifty who was walking in the opposite direction to us on his way to Santiago de Compostela, which he was hoping to reach in November. That sounded quite ambitious. Although he looked fit and sprightly, on the map it looked about the same distance as we had so far covered in four and a half months, and we were already into the second week of July. We wished each other "¡Buen camino!" and soon afterwards took a turning off the road onto a sandy path which led through heathland over a low hill towards the valley of the Arno. By now we were beginning to flag, and the last five kilometres or so were very hard going; we ran out of water and although the temperature had dropped to about 26° it felt hotter and it was difficult to appreciate the unusual landscape fully. Although by this time we were a long way from the sea, inland from Pisa, we were walking through sand-dunes dotted with scrub, and it felt thoroughly coastal. In addition to the usual interminable cicadas there were many butterflies here, different bird-sounds, and as we went down to the river, more mosquitoes than we had seen for a long while.

Having arrived at Altopascio so early we had missed the opportunity of staying the night there as recommended by our guide map, so we weren't sure where to stop. We arrived at a small village with a square and a pizzeria, where we were directed to the hostel on the bridge, which we hadn't noticed. To be fair the sign advertising the hostel was very small and stood next to a very large sign informing passers-by of the detailed history of this covered bridge – Il Ponte a Cappiano – which had fortified towers at either end and was more like a barbican in construction and purpose, having been rebuilt in its present form in the early 16th century by order of Cosimo de Medici to protect the new border of the Florentine fiefdom. The village on the north side of the river was variously called Cappiano or Ponte de' Medici and is a sleepy little place with a large concentration of Arabs and people from the Far East When we tracked down the official in charge of the hostel, who had to come from some distance away to stamp our cards and take our money, she led us across the road to a large building, on the riverbank but still in between the two gate-towers. We went upstairs and through a large room occupied by a Moroccan family, including a 5-day-old baby suckling at the breast, to our dormitory, which we had to ourselves. Having walked a long way, we fell asleep soon after agreeing that we had just eaten one of the best pizzas we'd ever had, at the only eating-house in the village.

DAY 138 PONTE DE' MEDICI – CASTELFIORENTINO
35 km; hot, clear; 32°C

Up early, we were out on the road leading south out of the village as marked on our map, past a long row of leather factories making shoes and handbags – the main source of labour for the immigrant population – many with well-known names such as Prada and Sax. We were diverted by a signpost after crossing the Arno and led around the houses for no apparent reason, other than perhaps someone thought it would be more picturesque to walk along the river, but since the path led mostly through a building-site this was unlikely. Eventually arriving at San Miniato we suddenly found ourselves in another world, surrounded by health-food shops, Brazilian coffee-bars and glamorous models with poodles. Perhaps this was where the Inter and AC Milan players lived. Although we were expecting to avoid the old village at the top of the hill, the signposts led us there anyway, not before Angela found a cicada nestling in her rucksack, and after being directed by an old friar from the church of San Francesco we made our way to the village of that name and stopped for lunch in a shady square with benches, next to the town hall. It was hot and getting hotter, and we had no idea where we would spend the night, but according to the map there was a village called Coiano a suitable distance away. Following a small road for about five kilometres we turned off onto a wide sandy track, walking a long way in blazing sunshine over dun-coloured hillocks with few trees to be seen. Everything was as dry as a bone and we ran out of water, but the views were splendid – we were beginning to see the famous Tuscan landscape colours: the umber, burnt siena and ochre all a result of the parched fields, the sandy or chalky soil and the bright bright light. (***Fig. 42**) We plodded on through an exhaustion break and got to Coiano at about 4 o'clock to find that there was nothing there apart from a church, one farm and a couple of cottages. There **was** a specially designated drinking fountain for walkers/pilgrims behind the church, and the farm **did** have guest rooms, but the owner told us that unfortunately they were all full, and she was ever so sorry but we'd have to go to Castelfiorentino, about seven kilometres away, where we would find a youth hostel.

This was well out of our way, but there was no alternative as the next place with beds on the Via – Gambassi Terme – was even further away, about 12 kilometres. So we trudged through the heat along the side of a country road, not very big but fast, with enough traffic to make it uncomfortable, especially at bends. You may imagine that the hottest time of day is around lunchtime when the sun is at its highest point and then it gets cooler, but it didn't seem to work like that. It became gradually hotter through the morning until about 2 o'clock and then stayed at that temperature until about 7 or 8. Finally arriving at Castelfiorentino we found the Youth Hostel, large but almost empty, apart from a family from Calabria who were staying there while the husband was working in the area, and a couple who were studying and doing summer work nearby. They all invited us to join them in a glass of wine and we tried to find out why anyone would vote for Berlusconi, but they just threw their hands in the air and said: "They're all as bad as each other. It doesn't matter who you vote for, the poor folk end up at the bottom." When we first got to the outskirts of the town and came across the first bar we had seen in about 20 kilometres we stopped for a lemon soda (*Fig. 43) and got precise directions to the youth hostel from an old customer in a wheelchair who was sitting chatting to a young man with special needs and a profound speech impediment – perhaps he had had a stroke, or had been born with brain damage. The old man was being very patient with him and we came across this matter-of-fact compassion towards people with disabilities a few times in Italy. In contrast we had stopped at a Tourist Information Office in San Miniato to ask directions and been attended by an unhelpful grumpy girl who was patently in the wrong line of work.

DAY 139 CASTELFIORENTINO – SAN GIMIGNANO
25 km; still hot; 32°C

After such a long haul we slept like logs and were up early again as the weather was set fair for at least the next couple of days. After putting on our dry clothes and repacking the length of agricultural twine which Angela had found on the path and ingeniously reused as a clothes-line, we stopped briefly at the same bar as the evening before for a quick breakfast then took a path along the river Elsa for a while. By 9.30 it was hot, and by 11.15 when we got to Gambassi Terme it was boiling. In the valley we saw a couple of hoopoes fly up just next to the path, much to Angela's delight as she had been wanting to see one all her life, and from there we climbed on white gravel tracks past fields of sunflowers and vineyards, olives, stunted oaks and oleander. Stopping for some shade in Gambassi Terme we found that it was a spa town with some hot springs, built on a rock above the valley. We met some English people who were on a tour of local vineyards, and one of them offered us €10 towards our MSF funds. Thereafter we went along more bright chalk paths and country lanes leading to remote vineyards and farms. We stopped at one farmhouse which had a shady corner in the courtyard and a water tap we could plunder, and a sign carved into the wall saying it had once been an abbey and resting-place for pilgrims, who were still welcome to stop and rest their weary feet. Going on through lovely terrain we were just beginning to wilt when we came within sight of San Gimignano, with its towers pointing to the sky like so many fingers. With a few kilometres still to go we had to stop and sit down somewhere: we spotted a health spa/ restaurant by the side of the road. It was a blessed relief to sit and drink a cool lemonade but agony to be beside the swimming-pool without being able to avail ourselves of it as it was for Members Only.

Arriving at San Gimignano at last at the end of another long hot day we passed through an arch in the city wall and took a narrow street to the left towards the church of San Agostino, where we had arranged to stay the night at the convent. A rather grumpy Italian-American monk showed us to our room, which had an amazing view out over the landscape we had just walked across. Angela had heard much about this town for about forty years since a friend of the family had gone to live there from Germany, and she had determined to find news of this old acquaintance, although after all this time all she knew was that she had a house in or near Castel San Gimignano. Because all the maps we had had were either of large parts of Italy and didn't show that name, or were very detailed and only covered thin strips of land beside the Via Francigena, we had not realised until the monk informed us that this was actually a separate town some 13 kilometres away, so we decided to go as far as Colle di Val d'Elsa the next day and make enquiries there.

San Gimignano is an extraordinary place with six tall thin towers poking up around the main piazza (*Fig. 44), although there were at one time more than fifty as rich burghers tried to keep up with the Joneses. The narrow streets around the square, connected to each other by alleys, passages or archways and surrounded by a wall, make up a kind of spider's web pattern perched on top of a hill. Being a great centre for the arts there is something going on in the open air on most summer evenings, and this particular evening being part of a festival of dance lasting for several days, a troupe of lissom young women was entrancing the large crowd gathered on the church steps as they moved gracefully upon the marble-paved stage. After looking for a place to eat in the middle of town we soon retreated from the teeming throng to the quiet square outside our lodgings, where we found one remaining table at the pizzeria and ate our fill. After another gentle stroll we made our way back to the convent. We had been given a key for the outer door, which opened onto a peaceful courtyard full of trees, reminiscent of the great houses of Cordoba, with a cloister around the sides. The charge for our room was €15 each, which we recognised gratefully as a bargain.

DAY 140 SAN GIMIGNANO – COLLE DI VAL D'ELSA
15km; hotter; 34°C

Waking in the morning to look out over the Tuscan countryside from our small window we resolved to set off at 7 o'clock. We crossed the square of towers and out through an old gateway onto the main road, easily imagining at that quiet hour what it would have been like for travellers passing that way centuries ago. Walking along lanes through a slightly greener landscape with splashes of sunflower yellow, the overriding impression was nevertheless of browns and creams and greys, with occasional stands of poplars breaking the horizon. San Gimignano receded gradually, with its finger-like towers remaining in sight for many miles. Within a few hours we were already arriving at Colle di Val d'Elsa – The Hills of the Elsa Valley – which is another fascinating town, but much less compact than San Gimignano. The town has two distinct parts: the older higher part is on a crest of rock jutting out into the valley, with the walled citadel at the tip, while a newer, mostly 17th- and 18th-century town, with many more recent additions, sits below, with a connection between the two by lift, which you access by means of a long tunnel cut into the rock. I went up to find the Tourist Information Office, which was open, to find a place to stay the night; they advised me to go to the former convent at the top of the hill or to a cheap hotel on our way out of town near the sports stadium, which we chose to do as it cost about the same after they had told us they would give us a special price as long-distance walkers. Angela went to the Post Office to see if she could find out anything about her old friend's whereabouts, who was already an older woman when they knew each other so must be getting on for 80 if she is still alive. A clerk at the Post Office phoned the local postman in Castel San Gimignano, but there was no record of her living there now, so she must have died or moved away. We decided to go for a swim, so took our bags to the hotel, which was an anonymous new building whose guests were often visiting sportsmen or performers as the stadium doubled as a concert venue. Walking back to the swimming-pool it was baking hot – apparently 34° but it felt more like 40° as it was so dry. By the time we got there we were longing for a cool dip, and spent an hour and a half in and out of the Olympic-size pool, then went up to the old citadel and strolled around the cliff-top walls, looking out over the plain with the hills of Tuscany in the distance.

Wednesday July 18th

Dear friends wherever you are, at home in England – reputedly very damp this year – or abroad on holiday or otherwise.

I had never really been to Italy before (What? I hear you cry. What about the two nights in Florence last year? Well, it was not enough to teach me about this place...)

What an amazing country! It is as though the 70s never happened here. The mutual attention given by the sexes is marked by coquetry and blatant up and down staring, all done with the charm of the unselfconscious. Nor have the 80s and 90s brought about the same cancerous spread of supermarkets at the edge of towns. There are lots of tiny shops crammed with everything the locals might need, and we of course frequent such places for our latest bit of cheese and the tomatoes for our lunch. This is taken as like as not in the shade offered by some roadside wall or on church steps, or sitting astride the long-suffering rucksacks, sheltering by some tiny bush. Shade cools us down by many degrees; it has most days been in the mid-90s or even over 100° Fahrenheit (35-40 Celsius). I imagine you sighing "if only!" Please imagine in return doing 8-12 hours walking with a 12 kg. pack on your back!

Italy then, with its complete dedication to the automobile, to the point of mostly omitting pavements altogether, with its warm-hearted and tactile people, full of operatic gestures and talking eyes, people who seem to love noise and love their children, who seem to integrate the disadvantaged with genuine warmth yet pick a fight in the middle of a traffic junction, who get involved with everything they pass, who stare. Call out, love to be generous, love to swagger; this Italy we pass through is dry, hot, scented of herbs and pine sap one moment, and of the sulphur they sprayed on the vines the next. Its colours are olive green and ochre and beige, its skies are cloudless, its fields are mown, its olives and grapes are ripening. We have feasted on wayside apricots, plums, figs, and the first early apples and blackberries.

We pass our long hours of sweaty walking with geeky games – here is a taste of our letter searches: Italy summed up with O's = Olives; oleander; orioles; oaks; operatic (behaviour); old towns; ostelle; osterie; O such love of life…Please feel free to continue the list *if such games appeal to you. We are now coming up to Siena, having been through places where the streets are paved with marble; others where there are entire town walls fifteen meters thick; others again where there are extremely high medieval towers seemingly without purpose, or perhaps as status symbols, but I know little; and we are often passing things without knowing why they are there, or even sometimes that they are there. We have become pellegrini, pilgrims who walk to Rome, part of a troupe of mad people who walk instead of driving in an air-conditioned car but who will then often find a bed in a pilgrims' hostel for free or very little.*

One more friend has announced his company, which is lovely, as indeed it was very lovely to have one of Nick's brothers come out for a weekend's walking.

This, dear friends, is the penultimate letter to you, since we are only about 275 km from Rome. It has been a great joy to communicate with you over these last few extraordinary months and to receive your emails, lovely glimpses of your many worlds, of home, of your thoughts and warmth, and all that well-wishing. Thank you again, and thank you for any you may yet send us. We continue to gain great support from them.

So, until Rome then, we remain your intrepid walkers, with much love to you all,

Angela and Nick XX

DAY 141 COLLE DI VAL D'ELSA – SIENA
29km; clear, very hot; 36°C

It was hot and promised to be even hotter so we were up very early the next morning and left the hotel at 6.15 to cut across country to rejoin the Via Francigena. At that point we paused for breakfast at a roadside café then found a country lane as far as Abbadia Isola, which was a rundown place as its name suggests. *Isola* usually means 'island', but in this case 'isolated' would be more appropriate. The abbey was miles from the nearest village and looked as though it been abandoned centuries ago, leaving only the shell of its defensive fortifications. From there a sandy track led between fields of maize and sunflowers (*Fig. 45) towards Monteriggioni, another fortress town built upon a hill, and we found ourselves overtaken by four Italians hiking to Rome in stages. They gave us the address and phone number of the convent where they were going to stay in Siena. I already had it, along with several other possibilities, but hadn't phoned any of them yet. By now I knew how to start this phone conversation about accommodation – although I couldn't necessarily sustain it for very long at least I usually understood the response to this opening gambit: "Buon giorno. Siamo due pellegrini inglese. E posibile dormire quá aquesta notte?" It seemed to be comprehensible, and it worked this time as a pleasant voice replied: "Si, si. Inglese? You have the address?" Yes, we had the address, the hikers had just given it to us and it corresponded to the address we had on our list

We got lost shortly afterwards trying to negotiate a thicket which had numerous unmarked paths going through it, one of which led past Monteriggioni in the direction of Siena – but which one? Angela worked it out and we found ourselves going up a steep hill on a small path until we came out at the outskirts of a village. Spotting an elderly man loading some gas bottles onto a trailer outside the first house, we asked him where we were. "Mandorlo," he replied; and after the usual questions and answers, "This is my house, yes. It is a very very old house. It was built in about the year 980, so it is a thousand years old! It has been many things: a nunnery, a hospital; a hostel for pilgrims; an inn with stables – here, you see, behind the house. Also it was a meeting-place for local partisans during the War, and for Communist Party members after it. It is old, older than any house in Monteriggioni, and there are many ancient buildings there, inside the walls." He was a retired art college lecturer from Siena who was doing the house up himself to live there full time, and generously gave us a bottle of fizzy water – our favourite thirst-quencher on the road – and some plastic cups. Passing through old groves of oak and chestnut and beech with their welcoming shade we came into some ancient villages of sandy-coloured brick and stone with the ubiquitous red tiles; organic huddles on top of hills surrounded by dense forest cover. The tracks became dusty white gravel again, glaring in the sunshine and standing out sharply against the red earth. In one hamlet a woman offered us some water, as there was no public tap. She went off into her flat, which was in an old castle built around a courtyard, and came back with another bottle of water for us straight from the fridge. It became more difficult thereafter: although we were going gradually downhill on a country lane at first, it led us straight across a military exercise ground, where we stared at them staring at us – strangely dressed people walking about carrying rucksacks! – as we followed the path which led across their field. We then had to go uphill and onto the main road from Florence to Siena. We had to stop to cool down for a while at a *gelateria,* which was a big air-conditioned space full of people eating ice-cream – so refreshing after the roasting heat outside which had gone up to about 95°F – then carried on to arrive through the Triumphal Arch at the old city of Siena. We stopped to buy a town map to find the convent we were making for, but coming out of the shop bumped into the four hikers we had met earlier. They said they knew where the hostel was, so we followed them as they went charging off ahead until we got to the address we had been given, just behind the Duomo. Funnily enough it was not there; it definitely did not exist in that street, despite the fact that it should have according to our new city map as well. They bought us a beer in the nearest bar and made some enquiries. It turned out that there were two streets with the same name, except that one was Something street and the other was Something Alley, and the map had put them the wrong way round. However when we finally found it, we were greeted by a welcoming party of nuns who smiled and shook us all by the hand and showed us to a dormitory full of bunks. Sor Gianetta, the Mother Superior, obviously ran a tight ship but it was dedicated, at least at this time of year, to the service of pilgrims. When I asked her whether we could possibly stay another night as we were tired and needed a break, she put her forefinger to her mouth in a gesture of secrecy and led us down the corridor to another room with a single bed and a camp-bed and said we could stay there for two nights. This room even had its own shower attached so we felt doubly privileged!

DAY 142 SIENA
0 km; very hot; 35°C

In the morning we were offered breakfast with an international group of pilgrims who were all setting off that morning, then went out to do some business and sightseeing. Angela had a haircut; we did some photocopying of our sponsorship leaflet and some emailing; we went to the chemist and the bank. Finally we could sit on the cobbles of the famous Piazza and imagine it being used as a horse-racing track (as it is one day every summer), and climb up the tower beside it, from which we could look down and see people clustering in its shadow to escape the fierce afternoon heat. (*Fig. 46) Visiting the Cathedral we were allowed in free with our pilgrims' passports through a special side door, and shown to the frescoes, the marble pillars and patterned floors. I was fascinated by a flock of nuns who fluttered about with their habits flapping. We finished our little stint as tourists by doing some window-shopping(*Fig. 47) and exploring the museum, in a grand *palazzo* next to the tower, where we admired the paintings, murals and furniture of this relic of the opulent Renaissance city. Looking out from a balcony we spotted a strange orange mist drawing in from the south, which must have been the *scirocco*, the wind which blows up from the Sahara full of sand-dust When we returned to our lodgings with a meagre bag of groceries to share in our bedroom, we were greeted by a jolly nun who said: "We're just serving some food. Will you join us?", and we found the dining-room full of a merry throng of about thirty pilgrims, mostly French, who were tucking into a large hot meal. We joined them and talked about our various routes: they said they had come this far by minibus and were going to walk from Siena to Rome, although the bus would take their luggage, which sounded like a good plan if you were travelling like them in a group. We had however returned to the convent during the afternoon for a little siesta and found Sor Gianetta having a rather heated discussion with a couple of French people about where they could park their minibus, then muttering something under her breath which sounded as if she were wishing that all pilgrims would travel on foot, full stop!

DAY 143 SIENA – PONTE D'ARBIA
26 km; hot, becoming overcast; 28°C

In the morning we got up early and packed then went down for breakfast, where we found the French people already there and a couple of their party bustling about officiously telling them when they should be ready and waiting outside. The wonderful Sor Gianetta gave us each a kiss on both cheeks and sent us on our way with instruction of how to get out of town and onto the track again through the Porta Romana, an enormous arch which makes the gateways in York's city wall look positively insignificant. We walked on footpaths and gravel tracks for most of the day. For the first three hours we could turn around and still see Siena in the distance, but from that side it looked very small, apart from the two enormous towers: the one we had climbed (400 steps) the day before and the tower of the Duomo, which stands close by. Soon we were in the bread basket of Italy as the rolling hills unfolded before us all covered in stubble: the fields of wheat, barley and oats had almost all been shaved now and the land looked curiously bare. The importance of the crop was brought home vividly at a little village called Grancia di Cuna (pop. About 100), where we stopped to sit on a bench in the shade next to a public drinking tap – the three prerequisites for a perfect lunch break – and gradually became aware that the massive castle next to the village square wasn't a castle but a fortified granary. Owned by the church, it had served the local abbeys and monasteries, and they in turn must have had a monopoly in the region for the milling and distribution of flour. Over the centuries, particularly in the late Middle Ages, the succession of wars between the city-states such as Florence and Siena, and the plagues and famines leading to a lack of bread would have demanded that any storehouses of grain should be fortified and heavily guarded, so this granary is a remarkable example of that period in the history of Southern Europe. After finishing our lunch we went to have a closer look and found a young couple measuring the walls for scaffolding to be erected. They explained that they were surveyors working on behalf of the nearest city council and the Regional Department of Culture and Monuments and the National Ministry of Something or Other to plan the refurbishment of what they described as a national treasure. They said if something wasn't done very soon it would fall down: there were already significant cracks in one wall and the roof was leaking badly. "But go and have a look!", they said. "You can go up to the second floor on the ramps (*Fig. 48) but the top floor is too dangerous." So we left our bags by the main gateway and went up a series of long stone ramps which zigzagged up four flights. Up these ramps cartloads of wheat used to be pulled by donkeys to be stored on the different floors. The walls were rendered with crumbling mortar, the corners were dark and the roof was full of swallows and bats. Occasionally there was a niche cut into the wall holding a statuette or a candle, or a carving in the stone, and there were several doors which looked quite new. It gradually dawned on us that there were people living here in flats or tenements. When we got back to the entrance we spoke to the young couple again and discovered that they were indeed a couple and that she was not climbing ladders because, she told us with a sweet blush, she was three months pregnant.

From the granary we left Grancia di Cuna by a little archway in the defensive wall on a sandy lane and walked on down the hill: through the middle of a field, over a fence and a railway line, all the while thinking: "This can't be right." We had been following a couple of signposts and hadn't noticed any others directing us off the path but the path was getting smaller and smaller. Coming down off the heath we had to cross the railway line then came upon a deserted station next to an abandoned quarry. After walking along the weedy platform the path miraculously reappeared and we came out on a road at an isolated bar whose owner looked surprised to see any new customers, let alone a couple of foreigners walking. However as we sat outside slaking our thirst another hiker appeared walking in the opposite direction, a young Spanish pilgrim who was walking from Rome to Santiago. We explained to him how to negotiate the last bit of path, which had been particularly tricky, and he told us he'd just come through a village but it had nothing in it apart from a bar and an expensive shop. Across the road we hit a broad sandy gravel path which followed another railway line which was in use, while on our right were sunflower fields whose flowers had already begun to wilt in the fierce heat. Along the way I began to notice what at first seemed to be large feathers but on closer inspection Angela pronounced them to be porcupine quills. I was sceptical – do porcupines really exist in Europe? Gathering the best ones up as we went, we ended up with about twenty (*Fig. 49). We were told later that there are many porcupines in the region, although it may be the last place they are still to be found in Europe, especially the larger species. Arriving in Ponte d'Arbia very hot and tired we found several of the French pilgrims from Siena sipping lemonade outside the bar in the square and looking perky. "Wait a minute, we definitely left before them and there was nowhere they could have passed us. How had they beaten us to it?" we asked each other silently. "You got here quickly!" one of us said out loud, to which the answer came: "Oh, we got a lift halfway in our minibus". "Is there anywhere to stay the night?" I asked. "No. I'm sorry, there's no more room at the hostel. We booked it in advance, you see, and there are no more beds." Actually I'm not sure that she did say she was sorry. She had a sort of wry smile when she said it as if to imply that she might feel sorry. "So that's what Joseph and Mary felt that night!" we thought to each other. At that moment a young lad of about 17 approached us, wearing a T-shirt that said "Fuck Google, ask me!" He said: "You are looking for a place to stay? You can have a room for €35 at the house over the bridge. First house on the right," and walked off. We went there and met his mum who said she would have charged us 40 but showed us to a pleasant room next to the river with a shower, gave us a key and said: "There's another bar just down there which does good food," so we took her advice and ate well indeed, with fresh pasta and local vegetables and a dish made out of spelt, the original ancient Roman grain.

While we'd been waiting in the café earlier, wondering whether to go to this B&B or walk on to the next town – not a very difficult decision as it was another eight kilometres with no guarantee of finding anywhere better – we were approached by a woman of about fifty who was walking alone. She was exhausted and thirsty, and spoke no Italian and little English. As it transpired she was German, so Angela told her what we had found out; she said she couldn't afford €35 for a room and she would go to the hostel and see if she could sleep on the floor if they had no mattresses left.

DAY 144 PONTE D'ARBIA – SAN QUIRICO D'ORCIA
25 km; cooler, cloudy; 25°C

Setting off early, we stopped at the next small town, Buonconvento, which was a place singularly lacking in charm with a busy Tourist Office in the town hall, to have a morning break on the veranda of a café in the main square. At the next table was a middle-aged English couple who were steadily working their way through the *Daily Mail*. We noticed the German woman again, who looked as if she was going in the wrong direction, so we hailed her and put her right. She introduced herself as Elke Elli, from Thuringia in Eastern Germany, and announced that she would walk with us for the rest of the day, which I have to say I found an imposition, as she only spoke German, and she talked a lot. Angela was happy to listen to her, however, and they walked along together chattering for hours. She had plainly not had a decent conversation with anyone for weeks and was someone who was certainly on an inner search and needed to talk about it. I wouldn't have had a problem with it if we had been in Germany, where I could have said to myself: "Why should you expect her to slow down when she's speaking German? You should learn to speak it better," but we had left German-speaking territory about a month ago and I was trying to understand and speak Italian now, so I didn't want to fall back into German again. As we walked on into the afternoon the weather turned cloudier, and cooler than it had been for about ten days. We studied the landscape with joy: vast expanses of mown fields creating complex geometrical patterns on the hillsides out of the stripes created by the combine harvesters in different shades of yellow, gold, sand and ochre, offset by graphic lines of cypresses and poplars, with the blue smudge of the Apennine range in the background. Increasingly heavy clouds were being blown across the scene as a blustery wind built up, creating sudden dramatic shifts of light and shade. It is empty country with few villages: we walked for about 15 kilometres without seeing a shop or a bar. The last couple of hours was an uphill slog into the wind on the winding road to San Quirico, where we were greeted by the bluff and hearty priest, a bearded man of about forty with the build of a rugby player, who was something of a showman. He instructed all the pilgrims who wanted to stay the night to attend his office at 7 o'clock, when he inspected everyone's documents and gave a pep talk in fairly slow Italian but not slow enough to be able to interpret into two other languages, which we tried to do: me from Italian to English then Angela into German for Elke. He was saying that the next day would be the toughest day's walk on the whole Via Francigena: we must ensure we have enough water and food as there is nowhere to stop all day until the hostel in Radicofani, 26 kilometres away. He then invited us into the church for a blessing, where he repeated his admiration for Elke's pilgrimage, saying that she was the only one who had a personal letter of introduction from a priest, and gave her a little picture of a pilgrim, a detail of a larger medieval painting hanging in the church. The church itself had two columns outside the main door which stood on stone lions and were carved in a slip-knot pattern which gave them a Celtic air (***Fig. 50**). Our lodgings were in a house behind the church and although it was cramped we managed. Our fellow-hostellers were two Italian *alpinisti*, or mountain-walkers who were undertaking the entire Via Francigena from Canterbury to Rome through France; a Hungarian couple who had lived in Italy for many years and were now based in Ireland; and two Czech girls who were very tired and looked as if they had bitten off more than they could chew. We didn't sleep very well.

DAY 145 SAN QUIRICO D'ORCIA –
RADICOFANI
26 km; cool, overcast; 22°C

It was quite chilly when we set off early in the morning. After an hour or so walking downhill we came to a thriving spa resort built upon the original Roman spa, whose remnants you could still see in the form of water channels, underfloor heating ducts, pipes and pools, all situated on top of a bluff. The excess water fell down a sheer drop into a sulphurous pool which was the only place where we could bathe, but it was disappointingly cold, both in the water and out. There was a notice up beside the entrance to the spa saying (in English) that it was sponsored by the NHS. Perhaps they meant to say it was recognised as a suitable place for treatment.

Despite the priest's protestations we did actually find a bar/shop open in a hamlet on the main road, which we had to follow for a while, so we stopped for a coffee and a bun, and bought some bread for lunch. Elke was still with us and it was becoming clear that she had virtually no money and was relying on the kindness of strangers. We walked along together and she chattered away as on the previous day.

We got to Radicofani at about 4 o'clock after trekking uphill as we had the day before for the last hour or two – Radicofani was built on the top of a conical hill, like most of the towns in that area and stands at about 800 m – but this time the wind was stronger: remarkably the temperature had dropped by a good 10° since Siena and the landscape also seemed quite different, much less bare rounded hills and much more wooded steep slopes, with rocky mountains close at hand. We were getting back into the kind of country we had left behind near Pontremoli. The wind, although not cold in itself, had picked up and was blowing in our faces from the south carrying a hint of rain, so for the climb up to Radicofani, along a road with very little traffic, we were muffled in anoraks and tempted to walk backwards. We were expected at a small hostel near the church in the centre of the little town, where we had phoned ahead earlier in the day to make sure that they had room for us. There didn't seem to be many people on the road doing the same as us, and it was the end of July, so it didn't look as though it would be any more busy than this at any other time of year, although according to the ferryman on the Po the numbers of pilgrims to Rome are steadily mounting year by year.

The hostel here is run by members of the Confraternity of Hospitallers of St James, who maintain the pilgrims' routes to Santiago de Compostela, which has been one of the three most important sites of pilgrimage since the Middle Ages, along with Jerusalem and Rome. The members of this order are duty bound to serve pilgrims in every way possible and take turns to run their local hostel; the three people who were in charge of the house for this fortnight prepared a meal for those of us who were staying that night, and we were not allowed to help in any way. Along with the Hungarian couple and the *alpinisti* there was a young Italian student who was spending his summer vacation walking as far as he could from Rome towards Santiago. Before we ate we were asked to sit in a row on a bench against the wall and remove our socks (our boots were already on a special shelf near the front door). All three of the hospitallers then put on brown felt capes decorated with the cockle-shell of St Jacques/St James/Santiago, and washed our feet. It was a symbolic gesture, so only involved one foot, which in a way was more moving than if it had been a purely practical ablution. One of them read a prayer or blessing, one brought a bowl of water and one dried and kissed each washed foot. After this simple ceremony we ate a hearty supper including jugs of wine, with much animated conversation around the table, and it occurred to us how similar this might have been for pilgrims in Chaucer's day. We were shown a bowl where we were invited to leave a monetary contribution at some point, but no mention was made of it being obligatory. Angela and I decided to make a generous donation of €25 each; although we were starting to feel the pinch somewhat and were very grateful that we were generally paying less for accommodation since we had discovered the Via, and could have got away with giving a donation of much less, it wouldn't have felt right: we wanted to give a suitable recompense in gratitude for such good will being shown.

DAY 146 RADICOFANI – ACQUAPENDENTE
22km; warmer, overcast; 24°C

We were sent on our way with a hearty breakfast by these good and generous folk – they donned their capes again when we were prepared to leave and spoke a blessing upon us as we stood outside the door with our backpacks strapped on and our trusty hazel sticks at the ready. It was already 8 o'clock but that didn't feel too late as the weather was less windy but still cool, and we felt on top of the world as we surveyed the vast panorama from the hill-top. Elke Elli was still with us, and as the day wore on I had to accept the possibility that she might attach herself to us for the remainder of the trip. But I consoled myself with the thought that it would be good for me to cultivate my patience, while I contented myself with contemplating the wild and stony landscape. In Charles Dickens' *Pictures from Italy* he describes his journey over the pass between Radicofani and Acquapendente in 1845 thus:

"The wind was so terrific…this land-storm might have competed with an Atlantic gale…It was dark, awful, and solitary to the last degree; there were mountains above mountains, veiled in angry clouds; and there was such a wrathful, rapid, violent, tumultuous hurry everywhere as rendered the scene unspeakably exciting and grand." The wind had dropped and the scene was much calmer now (*Fig. 51), but remembering what it had been like the previous day I could imagine the place in Dickens' description. Radicofani Pass was known until quite recent times as a dangerous place because brigands took advantage of its remoteness from towns to assault pilgrims on their route to Rome.

We were going to meet Chris that evening in Acquapendente, and he would be walking the last week or so with us to Rome. Chris was the only person we knew from York who would come to walk with us apart from Judith on Day 2. He is also a musician – trumpeter, choirleader and singer – and music lecturer, and had been persuaded by Paula to forget about his former girlfriend and get a bit of fresh air and sunshine and exercise, so he'd been in touch to see if that would be OK, or did we want our triumphal entry into the Holy City to be a private affair? Nah.

So we wandered down the hill with Elke and along the flank of the range of hills, on one of which Radicofani sits like a hat. Looking back towards it, past the stubble fields and the hedgerows and bushes, our gaze was drawn towards the red-brown rock which was exposed in great swathes on the hillside, and looked for all the world as though an enormous mudslide had just happened. Who knows when, but there must have been volcanic eruptions or earthquakes there at some time. As we continued we found several of these ravines, covering many acres and hundreds of feet deep, around which the farmers had arranged their fields full of wheat or sheep. By the time we got to the bottom of the hill it was past 11 o'clock and time for a break at a café on the roadside at Ponte a Rigo, which we had expected to be a reasonably large place at a junction on a busy main road, but there was nothing there but a little chapel, a petrol station, a bar, an old farm and a couple of houses. We managed to find a footpath alongside the road, luckily, although the path did become quite overgrown at one point as we tramped along the edge of a sunflower field; then took the old Via Cassia, which was a wide cobbled road with a long history.

At the height of the Roman Empire it would have been possible to travel by paved or cobbled road most if not all of the way from Rome to York, and sections of the original road still remain. Other parts have been covered over with tarmac or re-cobbled or allowed to become overgrown, and this section was one of

those which was refurbished for motor traffic almost
a hundred years ago then superseded by a faster road
on flatter ground (which in turn has been partly taken
over by the *autostrada)*. We followed it for quite a few
miles up to the border between Umbria, in which region
we had been for a couple of days, and Lazio, where it
fizzled out at a village called Centeno. We went past a
house here which had a plaque on the wall saying:

"HERE GALILEO GALILEI WAS FORCED TO
SPEND 20 DAYS IN QUARANTINE TO KEEP
THE PLAGUE OUT OF LAZIO ON HIS WAY TO
TESTIFY AT THE INQUISITION IN ROME."

Quarantine should have been forty days so they must
have been in a hurry to get him there.

As we walked we talked, and I began to revise my
opinion of Elke Elli as she spoke interestingly, and
to both of us rather than only to Angela, about how
conditions have been in East Germany since the collapse
of the Wall. Western interests have exploited the people
just as badly in many cases as had the previous regime.
As an example, she told how her mother, who had been
manager of a factory in the old DDR, was relegated to
being a worker on the shop floor after 'reorganisation'
by capitalist interests from the West, who impose such
rigorous rules upon the staff that they are not even
allowed a toilet break.

We arrived in Acquapendente early, at about 3.30,
after going off the main road at a fruit stall in a lay-by
and climbing a steep hill, past a man standing outside
his smallholding who engaged us in a long conversation
about weather, crops, how things have changed, etc.,
which was good for our confidence as Italian-listeners

if not exactly Italian-speakers. We had to ask several people the way to find our temporary residence, next door to a church in the aptly named Via Roma, which was a long narrow street cutting through one side of the town and ending up at the cathedral. Just round the corner a little alley ran up the hill toward the castle. (*Fig. 52) A notice was stuck on the massive front door, which filled an entire archway and had a smaller door built into it, giving a phone number to ring for entry: I rang it, and got a voice telling me she'd be there in ten minutes, so we waited outside next to a bench until a short stout friendly woman of forty-odd arrived and showed us where everything was. She looked at our passes and Elke's letter and chatted about how she'd been to Germany once, to see her football team Fiorentina play Bayern Munich in a European Cup tie. She told us the house had previously been used for about 400 years as the priest's lodgings, and that there were four bedrooms with at least two beds in each so we would have plenty of room to spread out if we wanted as she wasn't expecting anyone else except us and Chris.

We got a call from Chris saying that his bus had got in and he was on his way, so we went outside to wait for him in the street and saw him coming from afar. He looked very pale and plump and we were both wondering whether he'd manage the rigours of walking so far every day for the next week? Did he have any idea how hot it was going to be? We spent a restless night being woken by every vehicle in the street, which echoed like a tunnel, making a Vespa sound like a plane taking off.

DAY 147 ACQUAPENDENTE – BOLSENA
22km; warm, cloudy intervals; 28°C

Our fears were immediately allayed as Chris strode out
with us past potato pickers sorting their treasure into
piles of different sizes, through vast fields of solar panels,
then up into the hills alongside Lake Bolsena where we
trod an older original section of the Via Cassia beside
orchards of hazel-nuts and apricots. After a while it
turned into a wide sandy path and we went past signs of
ancient volcanic activity in quarries near the path. From
time to time, as we had all along the way since Pavia,
we would see a sign saying VIA FRANCIGENA, or
with the hooded pilgrim symbol, but now there were
also one or two saying ROMA for the first time. We
were starting to get close! The lake – another result
of the volcanic eruptions so commonplace in this area
at one time, and the largest volcanic lake in Europe –
shimmered in the middle distance as a warm rain began
to fall. When we reached Bolsena itself we clambered
down endless steps (*Fig. 53) through the castle and its
gatehouses and barbicans into the Renaissance centre,
where we found a fold-out camp-bed to sleep on in a
hall connected to the nunnery of Santa Cristina. The
nunnery itself belonged to the church of Santa Cristina,
who was a young girl who had been martyred in the
3rd century. As with many such stories in the Roman
Catholic tradition there are a number of versions of the
legend[10], but the most common one is that she was buried
in Bolsena after having relinquished the paganism of
her father, a powerful man in the politics of the region,
who tried to kill her by various ghastly means, all of

10 One of these is that her skeleton is to be found in the cathedral
of Cleveland, Ohio, to which it was presented by Pope Pius
XI in 1928; another that she lived in Tyre in Lebanon.

which she survived, until she finally died aged 13 or 14. The nuns urged us to visit the church across the square to see her sarcophagus and the curious catacombs underground, which house a huge collection of graves, and also to pray at the site of the miraculous apparition of blood dripping from the host, which occurred when a priest from Prague was visiting on his way to Rome in 1263. There was a crowd of people in the church queuing to visit the site behind the altar, but it all felt rather too manufactured for our liking, especially with the obligatory gift-shop on the way out. However, the nuns who greeted us and showed us the way to our lodgings were most welcoming. Sor Stefania, who was given the task of looking after us, was a tiny woman in her seventies who led us through the garden to the hall. The garden contained an orchard of semi-tropical fruit-trees including persimmons, kiwis and guavas and was a haven of tranquillity in the middle of the town.

Going out to eat in the evening we were collared by a young Polish woman who invited us to a free concert by an extraordinary choir who performed a soundtrack to an animated film. After strolling through the bustling streets back to our camp-beds we slept like logs as usual.

DAY 148 BOLSENA
0 km; hot; 32°C

"When I spend a day talking I feel exhausted, when I spend it walking I am pleasantly tired."

We were up early and ready to go when Elke Elli announced that she couldn't find her passport and money. She rifled through her bags two or three more times with increasing desperation. "They were there. I know they were there! What am I going to do?" We decided to help her find them, so first of all we went back to the pizzeria and the church where the concert had been, looking at the ground all the way. No luck. I went to find Sor Stefania and told her what happened, saying that we would have to report the loss to the police. "I'll take you to the police station," she said, and off we all went on a circuitous route down some side-streets to a building in a suburban cul-de-sac (*Fig. 54). As we went along the little old woman graciously allowed cars to stop and let us cross the road, and greeted everyone we passed by name. Arriving at the station she told the tall police officer the details of the case and how he should proceed, but in a gentle manner as if she were talking to a child. We left with an official letter stating the loss of said items and decided we would like to stay an extra night as the morning was almost over by now and it was already getting hot. We asked whether we could and permission was granted readily, so we went to explore the old town, which is a fascinating mixture of the ancient, the medieval and the modern. It was an important centre for the Etruscans before the Romans became so powerful, and upon a wall of the castle which looks down upon the lake from a height (*Fig. 55) there are Etruscan statues from the period lying about or built into the wall. Having decided to go for a picnic and a swim at the lakeside, we went back to the nunnery to prepare our picnic. As Elke took out her packet of cheese, what should she find stuck to the bottom of it but the plastic envelope containing her passport and money! She wept with relief and frustration at the absurdity of it, and we laughed even though our plans had been thrown off kilter – we had calculated that it would take us another six days to get to Rome, and we had been anxious to bring the journey to a close now that the end was in sight, but this event had served to make us stop and appreciate this place slowly and recognize that there was no rush. After all, as your man Thomas Clark said:

"A journey implies a destination, so many miles to be consumed, while a walk is its own measure, complete at every point along the way."

And we had been trying to let it be a walk, not to be counting the miles ahead. Yes, we had a destination, but we had always wanted to be able to appreciate what was along the way, hadn't we? The message was reinforced, in case we hadn't quite got it, shortly afterwards. As Angela was putting the final touches to our picnic and cutting a *panforte* into slices with a borrowed penknife, it somehow twisted in her hand and sliced deeply into her finger. It obviously needed a couple of stitches so we found a doctor's surgery and Angela presented herself. "It will need a couple of stitches," said the doctor. "But I can't do it here. You'll have to go to the hospital at Acquapendente." "How can we get there?" "Without a car? I don't know, it's difficult. Probably you'd have to get a taxi. You could try to get an ambulance. You have to go to the ambulance station just the other side of Piazza Santa Cristina." So we went back to where we'd just come from, Angela holding on to her finger, which we had wrapped up in a cloth, and feeling faint. There was no ambulance available and nobody to ask. Finally we found someone – a cleaner – who said that the ambulance must be out on an emergency. There were buses, but they didn't get back to Bolsena that day. On top of that, we had virtually no cash left and there were only three cashpoints in town, none of which were working. We went back to a chemist's shop we had noticed near the surgery but found it closed for the day as a protest against some government pronouncement. Things were not going well. We returned to the nunnery, where Sor Stefania was prevailed upon to fetch the first aid box and bathe the offending digit with copious amounts of iodine and wrap it up in plasters and bandages. At least it had stopped bleeding as Angela had been alternately squeezing it and holding it up in the air, and she said it felt much better and were we going to the lake for this picnic or what? So the four of us wandered down a street lined with massive plane trees to the narrow beach and watched the sun set over the still waters and thought of how far we had come.

DAY 149 BOLSENA – MONTEFIASCONE
16 km; very hot; 35°C

"The most distant places seem accessible once one is on the road"

Leaving Bolsena with a heavy heart – we would miss Sor Stefania; the little nooks and crannies of its densely packed streets and squares; its lakeside beach, and above all its sense of drama – and a light heart, for we would remember it well, we strolled off through olive groves and plantations of walnut and hazel, with views of the lake on our right. We had determined to set off early and to take it slowly. We only had 16 kilometres to go to Montefiascone, at the other end of the lake, but it was going to be even hotter than yesterday, and Angela's finger was throbbing.

Part of the route lay on the old Roman road again, paved with large flat stones, and although it was so hot, it was a beautiful walk. Approaching Montefiascone we could see the dome of the cathedral from afar, at the top of the hill (*Fig. 56), and as we drew closer we had to follow the road round the side of that hill. Towards the top we stopped at a café – the first one we'd seen all day – for a well-earned drink and met a fellow customer, a very ordinary-looking middle-aged man who looked like a solicitor or a bookseller on a day off, who enquired about our destination and told us that he had walked to Santiago from the French border. Another customer was a stalwart of the Local History Society and had travelled all over Europe visiting similar societies. He offered to show us the way to our next destination, a former convent just outside the city walls. He took us most of the way giving us a potted history of the place as we went. Among other things he said the Duomo is the third biggest in Italy.

After checking in at the hostel, which looked unchanged since the monks had left about 30 years ago according to the framed photographs on the walls documenting the dwindling population, we had a siesta, followed by a stroll into town in search of a beer. Needing to stretch our legs we climbed to the castle, where a film festival was taking place. From the castle walls there were fantastic views down to the lake far below on one side and the cathedral dome on the other. We descended into the crypt beneath the cathedral anticipating a chapel dedicated to Santa Lucia Filippini, but nothing had prepared us for the bizarre spectacle of a partially desiccated, partially waxen corpse of a young-looking nun lying doll-like and empty in a glass sarcophagus in dark gloomy surroundings pierced by the last of the light streaming through some rather beautiful stained glass[11]. We ambled back down to the town square, which was small and perfectly formed and full of cyclists all milling

11 The saint was instrumental in promoting education for women and girls, and died here in 1732 aged 60.

around after finishing a big race. After a lot of random activity, which included each participant being given aq huge piece of watermelon, someone was declared the winner and stood on a podium to collect their medal, and we settled down to a delicious meal in the middle of it all and toasted Chris on another successful day's walk.

Somewhere just short of Montefiascone we had passed a place which was exactly a hundred kilometres from Rome by foot and was the closest point to Rome from which you could walk and call it a pilgrimage. Someone told us there was a similar place 200 km from Rome from which you could be a cycling pilgrim. It was another moment that made us pause for thought about who was eligible to call themselves a pilgrim: Chris had felt unsure about it when he joined us, for instance, but we were never asked at any point whether we were Catholics or Christians of any stripe, and after several days he began to feel happier about it, particularly when he heard about the 100 km limit. It is worth noting – for the benefit of any reader who is contemplating travelling on the Via Francigena – that the pilgrims' hostels are specifically designed for those with a pilgrim's passport, which are only meant to be given out to people who are travelling by foot or bike, and the people in charge of the hostels only expect people to ring them on the morning of the day they want to stay rather than weeks beforehand.

The other question – "Am I a bona fide pilgrim?" – you can only ask and answer yourself.

DAY 150 MONTEFIASCONE – VITERBO
18 km; even hotter; 39°C

We were glad to get an early start as it was boiling hot from about 7 a.m. At first the country was well wooded and we passed vineyards and orchards of apricots and figs along the old Roman road, now paved with large cobbles. There was enough shade to make progress bearable, we had spectacular views of the surrounding volcanic hills, and we were looking forward to seeing some thermal baths on the way, although there was no way of knowing whether we would be able to bathe in them. Coming down a slope we suddenly saw a huge plain stretching out ahead of us, with the blue mountains beyond Viterbo about 10 km away. For a moment it reminded me of a battleground – maybe the scene of some ancient conflict between Romans and Etruscans[12]. Past the railway line there was no longer any shade, and by the time we got to the thermal baths we were knackered. They stood in the open air by the side of the path, which was a dusty lane by this stage, behind a fence but with an open gate and no-one 'in charge'. Anyone could just turn up and avail themselves of the facilities, and several cars were parked nearby. We soaked ourselves for a good while in a small pool carved out of the limestone and let the warm sulphurous water bubble up around us; if not for the Audis in the car-park, two 'businessmen' in swimming-trunks and sunglasses speaking Russian and a couple of girls in bikinis, we could have been there two thousand years ago, lolling in the shade of the olive trees and eating grapes...

We eventually dragged ourselves out of the water and struggled on into Viterbo through searing heat: by the time we got to the outskirts of the town the chemists' thermometers were showing 40°+. We staggered blindly through the silent sun-drenched streets to the hostel,

---

12 Montefiascone is adjudged to have been the site of a shrine where representatives of the twelve main Etruscan settlements met to make collective decisions.

which was in a tower attached to the city wall, and arrived streaked with sweat and dust to be met by Lucio, who said he was in charge that day and would be cooking something with his wife later, but we might like to have a shower and then would we like to look around the town? He inspected our papers and showed us to a small room upstairs, and we made the most of being able to have a cold shower before meeting Domenico, who was the main man. He escorted us into the town centre and showed us all sorts of little corners we wouldn't have found by ourselves, and pointed out the unique architectural features of the city: the outdoor steps leading up to many front doors (*Fig. 57) and the unusual fountains in each little square. There were odd collections of stairs and houses tucked into the corners of alleyways which made us think this might have been the inspiration for some of the drawings of M.C. Escher (who incidentally was later dubbed a Knight of the Order of Orange-Nassau) in the 1930s, when he lived in Rome. At one point Domenico led us into a little shop where he chatted to the smiling woman in charge of what seemed to be a miniature museum dedicated to Santa Rosa, the patron saint of the town. They told us about the local custom of creating statues or sculptures of the saint which are carried around the streets every year on her saint's day on enormous floats up to thirty metres high. He took us into the cathedral too: a well-dressed couple, surrounded by family members, were preparing for a service to celebrate their wedding anniversary. Domenico said: "Give me a minute, I'll see you outside," and disappeared. When he emerged shortly afterwards he said the sexton didn't know where the key to the bell-tower was and he'd had to go and find it for him. He seemed to know everyone in town and have a finger in every pie, and at the same time he had spent a long time away travelling: he had walked six times to Santiago on different pilgrims' routes, and had come back to his home town to run the local branch of the Boy Scouts and look after the Via Francigena on either side of Viterbo. The tower he had found to use as a pilgrims' hostel had a history: one story was that Napoleon had briefly held Pope Pius VI captive there on his way from Rome to France in 1798. When we went back to the tower we sat outside in the courtyard and had our evening meal cooked by the two volunteers as the light faded, after which Domenico said: "You will be leaving early tomorrow, yes? This is a map for you – I show you the best way to go – not your map, a different one, a new way." He got out a pencil stub and a scrap of paper and started to draw: " OK, this is here. You follow the road so…it becomes a path. You see a stone with VF painted on in red paint and turn left. You climb over a fallen tree. It's OK. It's good, the correct path. You go up – here – then turn left at the – how do you call it? – the electric pole." "The pylon?" "Yes, maybe. You go up another 20, 30 minutes to the road and turn right. Then you see the lake. It's a beautiful walk – I hope you enjoy it!"

DAY 151 VITERBO – SUTRI
30 km; very hot; 35°C

Any doubts we had about the value of the scrawled map were laid to rest as we followed it faithfully through a steaming forest early in the morning. The path climbed relentlessly along with the temperature; after we turned left at the pylon onto an unmarked track our doubts resumed, but we figured we were going in a southerly direction so we couldn't go far wrong. The path eventually came out onto the rim of a volcanic crater about five miles across, and we saw the lake which fills the basin sparkling far below us. (*Fig. 58) Just over the road we saw and smelt smoke: a forest fire was smouldering on the pine-forest floor. Angela climbed down and tried to put it out, but without water it was impossible. We met a forest ranger who said it had been going on for a week and he was just hoping the wind didn't get up again to reignite the fire. We walked around the rim through dense beech and oak woods for about three hours before getting to Ronciglione, passing the 3,000 kilometre mark along the way, which would merit a beer later. (*Fig. 59) As we had been up since 5 o'clock it was still only early afternoon, and we loitered for a while in the shade of a roadside bar in Ronciglione before resuming the trek for the remaining six kilometres to Sutri.

In the main square we found an open Tourist Information Office where a helpful girl directed us to the Carmelite nunnery across the street. It was an unusual experience to present our documents across a revolving hatch covered by a grille to avoid any direct contact with the nun who served us. We understood that apart from this task they keep as mum as Trappist monks and shun contact with the world as much as possible. We each had our own room with shower in a separate house, very bare but clean and tidy, for €12 per person, and were most grateful for it. We all went out to eat together and I managed to negotiate a good price at a little restaurant run by a Spanish-speaking Italian on a terrace next to the public clothes-washing tub, looking over the hills as the sun set (*Fig. 60). The meal was probably the best we had in Italy: three courses lovingly prepared, with wine and coffee, for €15 each – an extravagance for us but a worthwhile one! We were beginning to get a bit giddy now that we were within three days of Rome, and wanted to soak in every drop of experience. I had imagined that once we got this close to the Eternal City we would already be in commuter-land, that the country would be full of Italian versions of Dorking and Milton Keynes, but far from it; each town has its own definite character and its own distinct landscape.

DAY 152 SUTRI – CAMPAGNANO DE ROMA
19 km; hotter again; 37°C

We were awakened at about 5.30 by someone shouting outside our window, so got up soon after and when everyone was ready we were off at 7.30 to have a quick breakfast and look at the Roman amphitheatre and Etruscan necropolis (*Fig. 61) on the way out of town, both hewn out of the local volcanic tufa. We were calculating that we would really only have two and a half days to go: one day to Campagnano, one to La Storta and a short dash to Rome the following morning: about 60 kilometres in all. So there was no hurry. We could pace ourselves, and the next couple of days should be easy, well signposted and with good paths made available for the large numbers of pilgrims who must surely undertake this section of the Way. Ha! At first we got off the main road (SS2) for a little while and walked through orchards of hazel-nuts, olives and almonds, but soon were back on the road, which we had to follow for about eight kilometres before we could get back onto a path alongside a gorge into the town. As practice for the last day – from what we heard – it was useful to appreciate the pitfalls of sharing the road with Italian drivers driving fast and with scant regard for pedestrians. It was generally OK apart from one bend where visibility was totally obscured by bushes hanging right over the narrow hard shoulder we were walking on, protected from the traffic by a yellow line. There was another spot where there was a footpath running parallel to the road – which was equivalent to the A1(M) at this point – but it suddenly petered out and we had to scramble up a bank and through undergrowth, only a barrier away from speeding cars and trucks. The other problem with being a walker in such places is the amount of plasticbagsdrinkcartonscondomsroadkillCDstinfoil cardboardbrokenglasstyrestissues you have to wade through.

We got to the uninspiring town of Campagnano all feeling tired, hot, thirsty and irritable and found a mattress each on the floor of a grubby parish hall/youth club/further education centre. We couldn't tell what it was, or what it had been originally. It had a table-tennis table downstairs and posters up advertising various courses, but was entirely empty apart from us, although there were a couple of big rooms full of mattresses. The janitor who showed us round the place had a shady air, but we saw him again the next day unloading a washing-machine for the priest at a remote abbey in the hills so maybe he was really all heart, just looked scruffy and had an offhand manner. We went into the town centre and looked in vain for a place to eat something until we finally found a take-away pizzeria with a couple of plastic chairs and tables outside. Chris was sitting comfortably one minute; the next he was on the floor surrounded by bits of plastic, which got us talking to the other customers. Chris also began a long conversation with Elke Elli, who had been rather avoiding him up to that point, and we ended up having a good evening out.

DAY 153 CAMPAGNANO – LA STORTA
24 km; extremely hot; 40°C

It was late by our recent standards – about 7.30 – by the time we strode out into the morning. It was daunting: it was going to be very hot, and we had a fair way to go today, but if we could make it to La Storta we would only be an early morning walk away from our goal. At the same time there was a part of both of us which had become so habituated to this way of life that we didn't want it to end, and wanted to savour every moment of each separate day's journey. For the first few hours we traversed a barren landscape on a dirt track for several hours. The first town we came to, Formello, was now only about 30 kilometres from the Vatican, but still felt more like an independent hilltop city-state. We entered by an archway into a little square, which was full of building-works, noise and dust, so we decided not to stop at the café, but to follow the Via Francigena signpost down a long narrow street. We expected to find some shops down there, or somewhere to stop and have a drink, but before we knew it we were already out of town. The street had meandered downhill becoming narrower until it suddenly stopped, and to continue we had to go down some steps, and cross a road. We had found a public tap but foolishly I had decided not to fill my bottle, thinking I still had enough to last until the next one. Across the road we went through bamboo groves and off our map entirely. On the ridge to our right among the last houses of Formello we spotted a London bus peeping out of the bushes in someone's garden. Across a cornfield, over a couple of streams and through a dense wood where it threatened to fizzle out altogether, the path then led down into a richly wooded gorge and up to the sanctuary – a church built upon the remains of a pre-medieval castle – where we saw the priest having his washing-machine delivered. By this time it was seriously hot, probably already 40°, and we were praying for more shade. There was some discussion soon afterwards about whether we were going in the right direction but we decide to strike off in what seemed to be southwards. After crossing the SS2 at a place we could locate on the map (but didn't know how we got there!) we were taken on a long detour: because having apparently been sent the wrong way at Formello we were now obliged to go through a wooded gorge with Isola Farnese up on our right, making a great loop past it.

We first saw the fire ahead of us after we came out of the forest and took a small road which led up and over the top of a bare broad-backed hill. We were running very low on water: everyone had donated some to me and now we were all almost down to empty. The soil was dry and cracked, and a wind sighed across the brow of the hill, stirring the dust It was siesta time. At a junction of paths stood a long low house divided into a few farm-workers' dwellings, and Angela and I volunteered to knock on a door to ask for water, which caused a cacophony of barking to shatter the silence. Standing next to a nearby barn to share the large bottle of mineral water we had been given we began to see dirty brown clouds drifting towards us. As we passed over the hilltop it became clear that this was the sign of a serious forest fire, and as the afternoon wore on we began to wonder – jokingly at first – whether Rome itself would be burning when we arrived, to correspond with our childhood pictures of Nero fiddling…

After crossing a stream on stepping-stones there followed a long steep climb up to the town, which was a large residential conglomeration spreading out from the old castle. By this time we were parched and in desperate need of another drink. Fortunately there was a public tap near the castle and we slumped on the roadside to recover the strength for the final push, drinking about two litres of water each. As we carried on through the quiet dormitory town we began to see great plumes of smoke approaching over the rooftops ahead followed by helicopters carrying containers of water. This was beginning to be worrying. Finding a bar at the sign announcing La Storta, we sat outside drinking Lemon Soda and mineral water next to a table full of pot-bellied locals as the cloud of smoke approached and intensified and a litter-bin caught fire spontaneously. I phoned the Convent of Poor Sisters for directions: it turned out to be just round the corner on the main SS2. When we arrived we were sympathetically welcomed by a nun who told us it was much hotter than normal: the fires had closed the railway and were on the national TV news programme. We were advised to go to a certain pizzeria down the road which would do a concession for pilgrims, and we sat outside as the sun went down watching helicopters and light planes flying past, loaded with pitifully small amounts of water. Fire engines zoomed up and down the road as we enjoyed a tasty meal and a bottle of good wine.

DAY 154 LA STORTA – ROMA
15 km; becoming hot; 20° – 36°C

Many people in the course of the last few days had assured us that the last day's walk into the centre of Rome was the most difficult or unpleasant of the whole trip as it involved walking along the main SS2 all the way. Even the guidebooks give dire warnings about not attempting this stage at rush hour, and apparently a couple of pilgrims have been killed in road accidents in recent years here. When we told the nun in charge that we would be setting off before sunrise she seemed quite unsurprised and said that way we would miss the worst of the heat, so we went to bed early and were up at 4.30. Walking along the edge of the highway in single file, those at the front and rear wearing reflective tabards, we had covered six or seven kilometres before the sun rose and it was late enough to stop for breakfast at Ottavia. At a big fork in the road we took a right towards the right bank of the Tiber, and the rush hour traffic began. Luckily for us most of the traffic was of course going into the city so as long as we stayed on the left hand side of the road it was OK. After another few kilometres we took a left fork towards the Vatican City and from there it felt as though we were in Rome, albeit on the outskirts. At Monte Mario there was an alternative footpath marked on our map which led through a large park spilling down the hillside to the river then along the Viale Angelico to St Peter's Square, which looked like a good plan, but just as we got to the park a car drew up and two policemen got out who quickly closed the gate and said: "No entry. Fire! Look!" And indeed now we could see the whole city spread out before us but it was very hazy, and clouds of smoke were beginning to drift towards us from the upper portion of the park. Surprisingly, despite the police officers' sharp words, they did nothing to stop someone else who had entered the park just before their arrival from walking their dog towards the inferno, and loitered about next to their car for a while inspecting their finger-nails before driving away. We came upon a few examples of this insouciance in the face of apparent disaster during these couple of days and were unable to decide whether it was all down to bravado or laziness.

Going back to the road we followed it down a steep zigzag then cut the corners with steps which led to a small back street, in which we found the church of San Lorenzo. Since we had purposely read nothing in guidebooks of what we would find on the way it was a surprise to find upon entering that it was considered to be a major part of the Pilgrimage from early medieval times (it was built in the early 12th century) as the penultimate stop before St Peter's Cathedral. This was also true for all the popes and emperors who were making a triumphal procession to the Vatican City, and from here they would all complete the journey to the Vatican City on foot. We were welcomed in by the priest who was painting the front door. He stopped his work to introduce himself and told us some of the history of the church, which is peaceful and without much ornament. Proceeding along the Via Trionfale we finally arrived at the gate leading into St Peter's Square (*Fig. 62) and the throng of people queuing for a hundred metres to get into the cathedral. Chris wanted to mark the occasion in some ceremonial fashion, but Angela and I were rather dazed and somehow unprepared for the moment of actually arriving. All along the queue were touts trying to sell cheap tickets to enter the Vatican, and we were surrounded by a babel of different tongues. After dithering a bit we decided to have our credentials stamped at once to receive our Testimonium. (*Fig. 63) We negotiated our way past two pairs of Swiss Guards (in their medieval costumes but equipped with mobile phones) to a police checkpoint in a Portakabin, where they were about to refuse us entry with our rucksacks: we would have to go to some other office to leave them first. Angela became so incensed at this that they backed down and said we could go into the Vatican compound in pairs, leaving our luggage all together. Greeting the Swiss Guards again and passing another police checkpoint we were directed to a pair of Kafkaesque bureaucrats in a round office who kept us waiting although there were no other customers then gave us receipts for our passports and pointed us to the office of the Sacristy to wait for a scribe to complete our documents while the other two stayed with all our bags before taking their turn. (*Fig. 64) From there we walked across the river in the midday heat to a pizzeria to celebrate our arrival with Elke Elli and Chris then out to the convent where we were staying off the Via Marmorata. On the way we walked past the National Anti-Mafia Bureau, and were eyed suspiciously by a man in a black suit and sunglasses with a mobile phone earpiece and a miniature microphone clasped to his lapel. By the time we got to the end of the street he probably knew we had just come from the Vatican and had our passport numbers and shoe sizes.

Inside the convent the Confraternity of St James operates a pilgrims' hostel where those who have just completed the journey may stay for two nights for the cost of a donation. In charge were a local man and an Italian woman who lives in London. They were as generous as those we had met in Radicofani, and made our arrival feel like a homecoming, although funnily enough Elke Elli was not seen as being sufficiently well accredited at first and it needed Angela to swear she was a genuine pilgrim for her to be accepted. In the end though, we felt we would have been happy to go straight there and skip St Peter's and the Vatican experience altogether. I suppose it was the formal part of the pilgrimage that needed to be done: it had just been overwhelming to suddenly find ourselves in the middle of such hustle and bustle, and part of the anticlimax was the sense that we didn't really want it to finish.

Aug 7th 2012

Dear friends far and wide, new and of long duration, and family,

We have done it! We arrived in Rome on Wednesday the 1st of August at 10 o'clock in the morning. Having set off at 4.30 with Nick as our leader donning a reflective waistcoat lent to us in Barton-on-Humber, our little party of four managed to thus avoid the very worst of the traffic on this unavoidable and treacherous road into the great Italian capital.

FOUR? I hear you ponder. Well, yes, the last fortnight we had a German companion, who on her pilgrimage full of trials had fallen in with us, and finding her fortunes turn for the better, stayed with us all the way to the arrival in Rome. The fourth came by way of a York friend and fellow musician needing a break from troubled times on the home front and forging a rapid plan to throw himself into the legendary Italian heat to be very splendid company for the last leg.

We shared the inescapable discussions over which turn to take, as well as every crumb of stale bread, hunk of sweaty cheese, every biscuit and every gorgeous honeydew melon. We also shared experiences of downright 'off days', like the day when our German friend thought for hours that she had lost all her papers, cards, etc. and we spent the morning walking to every place we had been to the evening before in order to search, as well as being taken by the sweetest, and also miniscule, nun from the convent hosting us, to inform the police of the loss. Another eternal impression of this extraordinary country was the picture of Sister Stefania, all of four foot nine with her wimple (Nick's word for it) in instructive conversation with the tall dark and exceedingly hairy police chief of Bolsena. I'm sure physical necessity prescribes that she was looking up to him, but I swear it looked the other way round! Anyway the lost identity kit returned many tearful hours later by detaching themselves from the packet of soft cheese they had adhered to in their plastic envelope! This was the same day a travel knife I was using to cut a delicious but tough Italian delicacy with, decided to snap out of its casing and twist at the same time to bite back, as it were, right into the side of my finger. Consensus seemed to demand stitches, but there were none to be had in this town. After walking the length of Bolsena three times clutching the gash I decided to hand the process of healing over to my protecting forces, my immune system, and trust The same saintly sister disinfected my finger to within an inch of its life, and so now, nearly a fortnight hence, all is well.

Thus we left this convent a day later than anticipated, filling our drinking bottles with deliciously cold water at 6 in the morning under the dense trellis of trailing kiwi plants hung with clusters of fruit, frustratingly close, yet not ready, and hugged the dear sister goodbye, who was already bustling around with garden care duties. Many and varied stretches of beautiful landscape followed, all without exception marked by the relentless and exceptional heat which has now reigned in mid and southern Italy for many weeks.

Three times we came into contact with outbreaks of fire. As we walked into the outskirts of Rome we stopped for a drink of Lemon Soda (our great favourite!) and found two violins hanging on the wall rather randomly, only to find our way barred at the edge of the great city itself by a fire in the park on our route, and the very place from which we were to have a singular overview of the whole city. Fiddles and fire in Rome do have strange connotations...

Well, the first couple of days we were rather dazed, puzzled by our shifting identities from 'pilgrim' status – welcome, respected, supported by individuals and societies – to ordinary, slightly shabby-looking tourists in a pecuniary metropolis with its fair share of officious officials, a place which has drawn up fences around its boundless riches and antiquities, which demand greater wealth to penetrate than we feel in command of at this point in time. No matter, we have found our equilibrium again, with the help of Lemon Soda and gelati, enjoying the wandering around, peering through the fences, and paying our dues in a very selective fashion (We went to see the Sistine Chapel today, an experience worthy of its own essay!), our companions having gone off on their own onward journeys.

Thanks to the tireless efforts of my darling mother to organize fireworks for our welcome here she brought us to the attention of the British Ambassador in Rome, a most charming gentleman who asked to meet us. His press secretary was the real mover and shaker who hosted us in the embassy after taking copious photographs of us in our walking outfits. I will attach the link to the Embassy's news pages, in the hope that you will enjoy looking at it, and maybe one or the other of you can somehow save it for us in a format that does not disappear with time? We cannot get to see any of the pictures on the tablet!

It is time to sign off, dear friends. As we turn from accountable charity walkers into normal old holidaying

Angela and Nick again, we cannot disappear without once again expressing our heartfelt thanks to you all for all your support, your good wishes, your lovely emails, your gift to us, but especially also to Medecins Sans Frontieres.

We will now begin the return slowly, via calls on children and parents along the way home to York, where we hope to arrive at the beginning of September).

With much love to you all from

Angela

Nick

THE END ?

OUTRODUCTION

Facts and figures

1 kilo = 2.2 pounds (10 kg = 22 lb)
1 kilometre = 0.62 miles (50 km = 31¼ miles)
1 mile = 1.6 km (50 miles = 80 km)
£1 = €1.25
€10 = £8
1 Swiss franc = €1.50
€10 = 6.66 Swiss francs
(at time of travelling)

Miles /km. walked in number of days walked + days off

338.5/541.6 England 18 + 2
83.2/133.2 Holland 5 + 3
128/205 Belgium 8 + 2
566/906 Germany 39 + 10
168/268 Switzerland 11 + 2
637/1019 Italy 43 + 11
1920.7/3072 TOTAL 124 + 30

Places stayed

Number of nights	Where
33	With friends /friends of friends
23	Pilgrims' hostels

22	B&Bs
21	Pubs/Gasthäuse/Osterie
15	Youth Hostels
10	Hotels
7	Hospitality Club hosts
7	Hikers' hotels/bunkhouses
5	Servas hosts
3	Couchsurfing hosts
3	Caravans
2	Abbeys
1	Ferry
1	Random stranger;

OR

53 hotels, B&Bs, pubs etc.; 45 pilgrims' hostels, Youth Hostels, bunkhouses; 36 friends and family; 15 hospitality clubs; 4 others.

Boots worn: 3 pairs

Socks worn through: 4 pairs

Plasters used: about 16

Beers drunk: about 250

Larks heard: about 250

Boars seen: 7

Snakes 3; storks 3; red kites 17; newts 2

Unknown creatures: 1 herd

Result of football: Spain 4 : Italy 0.

Money raised for Medecins Sans Frontieres: £12,740.

PS There have inevitably been great changes in us both as a result of making this journey – a journey which became at times a hike, at times a wander and finally a pilgrimage. Although we had not set out with the express intention of making a pilgrimage there was always an element of thanksgiving involved in the venture, and this was clarified during the time we spent on the Via Francigena. Then we were indeed stepping into the world of the pilgrim. This brought about many questions in itself, but the whole trip elicited many challenges, not least that of holding to the trust that we would be protected and sheltered along the way. Overcoming the physical challenge could best be summed up as "Keep on keeping on!", while since our return to 'normal society' we have been called upon to make many adjustments, which has not always been easy. Fortunately perhaps the greatest boon we have been given in return for making the effort required to complete our commitment has been a greater confidence in our capabilities, and we hope this has borne fruit in making this account readable.